GREAT BRITISH MOTORCYCLES

of the 1950s & 1960s

GREAT
BRITISH
MOTORCYCLES
of the 1950s & 1960s

Bounty
BOOKS

This edition published in 2015 by Bounty Books,
a division of Octopus Publishing Group Ltd
Carmelite House
50 Victoria Embankment
London EC4Y 0DZ
www.octopusbooks.co.uk

An Hachette UK Company
www.hachette.co.uk

First published in 2014 by Bounty Books
Material previously published in *Great British Motorcycles of the Fifties* and *Great British Motorcycles of the Sixties* (Hamlyn, 1980)

Copyright © 2015 Octopus Publishing Group Ltd

ISBN: 978-0-753727-62-1

A CIP catalogue record for this book is available from the British Library

Printed and bound in China

INTRODUCTION

GREAT BRITISH MOTOCYCLES OF THE 1950s

'Bikes of today are all very well,' complain the traditionalists, 'but they have no character – Yamahas and Suzukis, and shaft drive, and self-starters, and winkers; they cannot be called *real* motor cycles. Now, take an old B31 Beesa . . .'

Each enthusiast has his own reasons for looking back to the 1950s with a particular kind of affection. Japanese competition was then no more than a speck on the horizon, Germany and Italy were turning out some attractive machines, but above all it was the traditional British single and vertical twin which dominated the motor cycle scene, both at home and abroad.

However, during the early 1950s, buying a new machine was not so simple as all that. The demand was certainly there and, on the face of it, Britain's manufacturers should have been raking in fat profits. But those who are forever carping that British industry should have been investing more heavily in new equipment during this period, would be advised to take a closer look at the country's economic situation.

The struggles of the Second World War had left the nation in a sorry state, and the immediate need was to build up reserves of foreign currency. For that reason, factories both big and small were constantly being urged to export more and more of their production. Metals were in short supply, and stocks were only obtainable by flourishing a government permit – and, usually, such permits were granted only if the firm concerned could produce an order from an overseas customer.

Nor were export markets easy to find, because often other countries would either refuse entry to British products or (as in the case of the USA) place a heavy import duty on them. There were quotas and trade agreements to be negotiated and honoured, and it was not really surprising that our factories should find their major overseas markets in the countries of the Commonwealth. Indeed, in 1950, the first year of this decade, Britain's biggest customer for motor cycles was Australia.

However, the American market was just beginning to move, thanks in some measure to the efforts of Edward Turner and the Triumph company. Over a very long period, American riders had grown accustomed to the oversize, overweight vee-twins of their own industry, but wartime experience had shown them that bigness is not necessarily a virtue, and that there was a deal of enjoyment to be had from a relatively light, and vastly more manoeuvrable British machine.

Nevertheless, the vast distances of the United States permitted bikes to run at higher sustained speeds than was possible in Britain's crowded land, and it was this factor which led British factories to introduce such models as the 650 cc Triumph Thunderbird, and the BSA Golden Flash of the same capacity.

It might appear that every factory worthy of the name felt honour-bound to follow Triumph's lead and include a vertical twin in its post-war range, but that is not strictly true because there were some firms striking out along individual lines – Douglas, for instance, with a 350 cc transverse flat twin and torsion-bar springing, Sunbeam with an in-line, overhead-camshaft twin and shaft final drive, and Velocette, casting aside its pre-war traditions and staking everything on a little water-cooled, side-valve twin in a pressed-steel frame.

In the industry as a whole, there was a tendency towards grouping. Ariel and Triumph had long been linked under Jack Sangster's banner, and now the giant BSA firm joined in, taking Sunbeam with it. The London-based AMC group, already makers of AJS and Matchless, added Francis-Barnett, then James.

What with material shortages, international tariff problems, labour difficulties, and the continual demand for more bikes than they were able to produce, the factories just had not the resources available to cope. That is why, with the inevitable disruption a London Show would have caused, there was no major Earls Court Show in 1950.

A year later, the position had eased just slightly and, with a flourish of trumpets, Earls Court was again the major attraction of the 1951 autumn. It was not quite such a glittering affair as it had been in earlier times, though, because the year had brought a world shortage of nickel and, by government edict, austerity finishes were the order of the day.

Some trends were becoming evident, as the visitor wandered from one stand to another. More and more firms were adopting rear springing, albeit plunger type instead of the full pivoted rear fork (although Triumph managed to get extra mileage out of their old rigid frames, by adding a rear wheel which encompassed rudimentary springing within the hub). The traditional hearth-brazed lug frame was being ousted by the all-welded frame, due to advancements in steel-tube technology through wartime experience.

In trials and scrambles, the big four-stroke single was pre-eminent, but whereas in earlier days competing machines were mainly roadsters stripped of lighting and equipped with suitably knobbly tyres, purpose-built competition bikes were now emerging, exemplified by the 500T Norton, BSA Gold Star, or G80C Matchless.

The time-honoured Magdyno, a combined magneto and dynamo that had originated in the early 1920s, was on its way out and, instead, the alternator (the rotor of which could be mounted directly on the engine shaft, so avoiding the necessity of providing a separate drive) was making headway.

It was not all big stuff, of course. There had long existed a demand for a simple, ride-to-work lightweight, and in the course of any trip by (steam) train, nearly every signalbox along the way would be seen to have a small two-stroke, usually an Excelsior or a James, propped up against the outside stairway. Mostly these were much of a muchness, powered by reliable if none too exciting Villiers two-stroke units, but in 1948 the BSA Bantam had come upon the scene, initially for export only but later for general sale; the Bantam was a frank copy of the pre-war German DKW (as was the 125 cc Royal Enfield 'Flying Flea', used initially by the Airborne Forces but continued into civilian production as the Model RE), but was none the worse for that.

Enthusiasts had for so long regarded Triumph as wedded to

Heavy by present-day standards, but quite a lightweight in its own period, the Royal Enfield 346 cc Bullet is seen here in 1951 Trials guise (road-going, and scrambles versions were listed at the same price). The Bullet was the machine which overcame the trials rider's mistrust of rear springing

the vertical twin idea, that the introduction in 1952 of the 150 cc ohv Terrier single came as a distinct shock. But the wily Edward Turner, who was not only Triumph's chief designer but also the factory's overall boss, knew what he was about, because in the

An unusual shot of a Royal Enfield Bullet at speed in a Vintage MCC road race meeting. The rider is Steve Linsdell, of Bedfordshire, whose standard-looking but exquisitely tuned 1952 Bullet won most 350-cc class races in which it was entered from the 1977 season onwards

years to come the same basic layout was applied first to the 199 cc Triumph Tiger Cub, then to the 250 cc BSA C15 and eventually, by way of the 343 cc BSA B40, to the ultimate 498 cc Victor. It was scaled downward, too, to produce the 75 cc BSA Beagle and, smaller still, the 50 cc Ariel Pixie (these only proved that even as eminent a designer as Edward Turner can put a pencil wrong, just once in a while!)

At the start of 1950, the British motor cyclist was still bedevilled by fuel rationing, but in June of that year came the welcome news that restrictions on private motoring were being lifted at last. True, branded fuel had yet to return, and all that the pumps contained was the dreaded 75-octane 'Pool', but at least coupons were to be torn up and the enthusiast could make the most of the summer – always bearing in mind that at 3s (15p)

a gallon, it paid to check the carburettor for economy!

The familiar names did return, of course, and once more a rider could fill up with Shell, BP, or whatever his favourite brand might be; but then came the Suez Crisis in 1956, fuel was again in short supply and back came all the fuss and bother of ration books and coupons. Cost of administering the scheme, according to a parliamentary reply, was around £20,000 a week. Not until late May of 1957 did fuel rationing end, and by that time successive price increases had raised the price of 100-octane fuel to just over 5s (25p) a gallon.

By the mid-1950s pivoted-fork rear springing had become universal, mainly because proprietary rear-spring units by Girling or Woodhead-Monroe, were readily available to manufacturers. Villiers, who had hitherto built engine units of up-to-197 cc only, expanded their range to include a new 224 cc single of a more modern, rounded appearance than before. Then came a 250 cc single and, more interesting still, a 250 cc two-stroke vertical twin. At last, the small factories – Cotton, DMW, Panther, and that new firm with such unorthodox ideas as a cast-light-alloy frame beam, Greeves – could offer a wider range of models to the public.

The lowest powered transport in the first part of the 1950s had been provided by a wide selection of clip-on engines, designed to turn an existing pedal cycle into a moped of sorts. Of these, the BSA Winged Wheel, and the Cyclemaster, were complete powered rear wheels. Others (they even included the Firefly, a totally unexpected product of the illustrious Vincent company) were clamped above the front or rear wheel, or under the bottom bracket, there to drive direct on to the tyre by a friction roller.

The wartime 98 cc autocycle had all but disappeared, with the New Hudson as the last survivor, and in its place had come a lighter type of autocycle known as the moped. This, in turn, was to eclipse the clip-on, and it has to be admitted that British industry was late in foreseeing the trend. Oh, we tried, with Phillips and Norman both producing attractive-looking mopeds, but the Villiers 50 cc 3K engine was no match for the imported power units.

By the mid-1950s, a move towards enclosure and a general tidying-up was well in evidence with Vincent, of all people, leading the field. Their Black Prince and Black Knight models featured elaborate enclosure formed in a new wonder material, glass fibre (and the appearance of the machines was considered so futuristic that a squad of Vincents served to mount the Thought Police, in a film based on George Orwell's novel *1984*).

Soon, Triumph joined in, draping the rear of the new 350 cc 3TA Twenty-One twin in a pressed-steel cover, and announcing the bike as 'The Motor Cycle with a Wheel in Tomorrow'. However, it was left to Ariel to produce the biggest surprise of all. Designed by veteran Val Page, who had been responsible for

An exhibit from the 1952 Earls Court Show – a Vincent Black Shadow in touring trim, attached to a Garrard S90 single-seat sidecar. By rotating the front-fork auxiliary-damper upper mounting, the fork trail could be adjusted for solo or sidecar work

Cotswold farmer Ron Langston was a real all-rounder, equally at home as a road racer, scrambler, or solo or sidecar trials ace. High above the town of Kinlochrannoch, he balances his Ariel through the Scottish Six Days Trial of 1958

revitalising the Ariel programme as far back as 1926, the newcomer was the Leader, a two-stroke twin from a factory that had built its reputation upon four-strokes.

Unfortunately, the riding public tended to admire the Leader from a distance – and leave it at that. To help recover at least some of the tooling-up cost, the Ariel firm produced, for 1959, another version known as the Arrow. In essence, this was the Leader, but with simplified upper works, and shorn of the side enclosure and built-in legshields that, it had been hoped, would have endeared the original design to the city-gentleman type of customer.

Certainly the city-gent rider, the chap who commuted to work over shortish distances and did not want the bother of dressing-up in bulky motor cycle clothing, did exist. It was just that the Ariel Leader (and for that matter, the LE Velocette) was not quite what he wanted.

The Italians knew what he wanted, and were able to provide it with such untraditional confections as the Vespa and Lambretta. Ironically, Britain had foreseen the post-war scooter boom, and even in the mid-1940s BSA had been toying with a little side-valve model with semi-automatic transmission; that model, the BSA Dinghy, never did reach the production stage and neither did a later design, the very stylish 200 cc Beeza exhibited at Earls Court in 1955.

One scooter which did sell in small quantities was the Swallow Gadabout, a Villiers-engined two-stroke built by a famous sidecar company. But the Swallow was a shade too early, and it had gone by the time scooter mania got a hold on the country.

At long last, in 1958, the BSA group did indeed produce a pair of scooters, powered respectively by a verson of the 175 cc Bantam engine, and by a fan-cooled 250 cc overhead-valve vertical twin. Available to choice under a BSA-Sunbeam or Triumph Tigress name, the scooters were not at all bad, but they could have been better (the side panels, for example, should have been made quickly-detachable, as on the Lambretta, but instead were held in place by a dozen or so fiddly little screws).

They should have been introduced sooner, too, and once again Britain seemed to have climbed onto the bandwagon after the music had stopped.

Still, with the trading restrictions of the past largely overcome, British industry was in top gear and on full throttle as the 1950s drew to a close. Home registrations for January, 1959, were 90 per cent up on the same month of 1958, and 41 per cent higher than the average of the previous five years. And June's figures, aided by a glorious summer, were a fantastic 150 per cent better than those of the previous year.

As 1960 dawned, so the number of machines on British roads constituted an all-time record. A news item from Hong Kong mentioned that a new Japanese motor cycle had been seen in that city. Known as the Honda Dream, it was a 300 cc overhead-camshaft twin, with such exotic features as a pressed-steel, spine frame, electric starter motor, and built-in direction indicators. It would never catch on, of course . . .

However, about this book. The road tests are word-for-word reprints from contemporary issues of *Motor Cycle*, supplemented by potted histories of the model or type under test. To give as fair a picture as possible of the 1950s scene as a whole, I have not concentrated on the bigger-capacity models to the

exclusion of the lightweights – and if it might seem that there are a couple of surprising omissions; well, there are reasons.

To take the case of AJS and Matchless, Donald Heather, who ran the London part of the AMC group, refused for many years to provide road-test machines to the press. It was a policy which could not have done his firm much good, and yet it was not relaxed until the closing years of the 1950s. Then there was the BSA Gold Star. Again, this company never did supply an example for road-testing, and their reasoning was that the Goldie was not a true quantity-production model but, instead, was a rather specialised version of the standard 350 or 500 cc singles, built specifically for trials, scrambles, or clubman racing.

Those apart, however, I believe the models selected really were, in their special day and age, among the Best of British.

Bob Currie

INTRODUCTION

GREAT BRITISH MOTOCYCLES OF THE 1960s

That the 1960s saw the decline and virtual total eclipse of the once-proud British motor cycle industry is well enough known; what is really astonishing is that it should have taken place in such a short space of time. As the decade began, motor cycling was on the crest of a wave, with a total of 1,853,000 machines in use on the roads of Britain. Admittedly, that total included a proportion of Italian-made scooters, and German and French mopeds, but the bulk were certainly home-manufactured. Moreover, it did not take into account the many BSAs, Greeves, Dots, Cottons and Matchlesses, which were not registered for road use but kept solely for competition purposes.

Yet as 1969 drew to a close the tale was one of stark tragedy. The giant AMC group, embracing Matchless, AJS, Norton, James and Francis-Barnett had already gone to the wall, and though it is true that Norton and AJS had been salvaged by Dennis Poore and his new Norton-Villiers firm, production was at a rather lower level than before. Velocette were in deep trouble and would cease operations by 1970. Acquired by financial speculators, Royal Enfield first closed its old-established Redditch plant (to be parcelled out as a trading estate, the site value of the factory being worth far more than the new owners had given for the company) then went underground, to produce its final model, the 736 cc Series II

Interceptor, in former quarry workings in wildest Wiltshire.

The second-oldest firm in the industry (the oldest, Excelsior, had already ceased motor cycle manufacture in 1963 to produce, under Britax management, car seat belts and other accessories), Ariel closed the venerable Selly Oak works, moved in with BSA, then disappeared—save for an impossibly comic three-wheeled moped, to which BSA, the real perpetrators, had been too ashamed to apply their own trade mark. And although the crash of the BSA-Triumph group did not take place until a couple of years after the period covered by this book, the seeds of disaster had long been sown.

Now, it is all too easy to sit back and say that the Japanese swept into Britain with new and up-to-date designs, elbowed aside the obsolete British models, and helped themselves to the market. Except that it simply did not happen like that. In fact the British motor cycle market was already dead before the Japanese arrived, with many a long-established motor cycle dealer going out of business, or switching over to selling cars, the

Robin Good, on the Ariel Arrow he shared with Peter Inchley, gives Brian Setchell (650 Norton) a run for his money in the 1962 Silverstone 1000. After leading the 250 cc class for much of the distance, the Arrow finished second following a bout of electrical trouble

The ES400 was the only small-capacity Norton twin to feature electric starting

casualties even including Stan Hailwood's powerful Kings of Oxford chain.

If we must hunt for the true villain of the piece, let's call it the Affluent Society of those 'never had it so good' early 1960s. For many years following the Second World War the motor cycle was still regarded principally as working-class transport, a cheaper to run alternative to the unaffordable car. There were a few more exotic models of the type we would today term status symbols (the big Vincent vee-twins, for example, and the Ariel Square Four), but by and large the British industry earned its bread and butter with such utility jobs as the BSA C15, Triumph Tiger Cub, Royal Enfield Crusader, and James and Francis-Barnett two-strokes.

But as industry in general entered a boom period, the working man found himself with more money in his pocket, and suddenly the Austin Mini or Ford Popular were not so unaffordable, after all. This was roughly the same situation that had faced the German motor cycle industry a few years previously, when Horex, Adler, TWN and many another factory either closed, or changed to some other field (typewriters and office equipment, in the case of Adler and TWN).

In Britain, too, there were other factors affecting motor cycle sales, and not the least of these was the down-market image of the Leather Boys who haunted the caffs on city outskirts and, between playing rock n'roll on the gaudy juke-box, went off down the local by-pass for a ton-up tear-up. So maybe they

weren't true, US-style Hell's Angels. So maybe, in their own eyes, they were doing no harm to anyone. But what the ton-up crowd with their dropped-handlebar Road Rockets and T-One-Tens did to motor cycling as a whole was nobody's business.

Of course, there were always 'knockers' in certain newspapers and in TV who blew up everything larger-than-life and made a 'Shock! Horror!' spectacular of it all. Spurred on by such stories, the government of the day brought in the Hughes-Hallett Bill, effective from July, 1961, which restricted the holder of a motor cycle provisional driving licence to a machine of no more than 250 cc.

It has to be said that inexperienced youngsters, weaving in and out of the traffic on the Watford By-pass on clapped-out BSA A10s adorned with chequered go-faster tape, had brought it on themselves. But let it not be forgotten that the Hughes-Hallett Bill intended also that the age at which a lad could ride a moped should be lowered to 15 years; *that* bit has never been put into effect.

One more factor has to be considered, for successive Chancellors of the Exchequer treated the application of hire purchase restrictions, and of purchase tax itself, in yo-yo fashion, so the dealers never knew where they stood. In addition, Britain withdrew the General Agreement on Trade and Tariffs (GATT), which left the home market vulnerable to foreign markets.

If 1960 had been the high tide of motor cycle new-machine registrations, that tide was to go into the ebb with dramatic suddenness, as the monthly figures through 1961 indicated drops of up to 35 per cent below the equivalent period of 1960. It was the old Excelsior company which, early in 1962, found a loophole in the purchase tax regulations and began offering first a 150 cc roadster, and then a 98 cc lightweight, in part-assembled, finish-it-yourself kit form. The 150 cc Excelsior Universal, powered by Excelsior's own two-stroke engine, was priced at £103 19s, so saving the customer a whacking £40-worth of purchase tax.

But the firms who really latched on to the kit-form, no-purchase-tax idea were those supplying trials and scrambles machinery, headed by Sprite, a bouncy little Black Country factory headed by cheery Frank Hipkin. In turn, the importers of Bultaco and Montesa competitions machinery from Spain took up the scheme, and soon no trials or scrambles rider bothered to buy a complete, ready-built-up bike.

The close of 1961 found Associated Motor Cycles foundering in deep water, for their £219,000 profit of the previous year had turned into a thumping great £350,000 loss. Unhappily, it was true that AMC, in particular, had always been slow in perceiving market trends and responding to them. The scooter was a case in point, and Vespa and Lambretta had been allowed to gain too big a bridgehead in Britain before the home-base factories made any kind of challenge.

The attitude of AMC's top brass was that scooters would never catch on, being just a flash in the pan. Yet even AMC were at last forced into building a scooter (the 150 cc James); it embodied one or two good ideas, such as using the main frame tubes as crash bars, but it was too clumsy . . . and too late.

The two last criticisms could be levelled also at Velocette's majestic flat-twin two-stroke 250 cc Velocette Viceroy scooter, which featured car-type electric starting. Technically excellent though the specification may have been, its sheer size was enough to deter those attuned to the dainty Italian models. On the other hand, the true-born motor cyclist would not have looked at a scooter, no matter how honoured a name it bore. So at whom was the Viceroy aimed?

To the end, Velocettes were a company run by the Goodman family. Tooling up for Viceroy production had cost them far more than subsequent sales warranted, and the failure of this model was the direct cause of the collapse of the firm.

The wounds of the BSA-Triumph group were, to some degree, self-inflicted. Part of the trouble was that a number of key executives who had been with the combine for many years all reached retirement age at more or less the same time. They included home sales manager George Savage, development chief Bert Perrigo, group chairman Jack Sangster, and even Edward Turner, that very shrewd character who was a brilliant designer and an administrator of remarkable ability.

Turner's retirement took effect in 1962, but acting in a freelance capacity he was to produce one last design—a 350 cc double-overhead camshaft twin of which the prototype, ridden at

One of the less glamorous members of the 248 cc Royal Enfield family, the Wallaby was intended for sheep-herding on outback ranches in Australia

MIRA by Percy Tait, clocked 112 mph. As Turner designed it, the machine featured a train of gears to the overhead camshafts, but the model was subsequently re-engineered to incorporate an awkward right-angle chain driven camshaft. Launched with a panoply of trumpets in the dying days of BSA-Triumph it was, of course, the BSA Fury—or, if you prefer, Triumph Bandit—and it never did get into production.

Under the guidance of Harry Sturgeon, BSA-Triumph continued to flourish in the mid-1960s. The home market had all but disappeared, but overseas sales, especially to the USA, were such that the company collected the Queen's Award to Industry for their export performance, for two years in succession. Sadly, Harry Sturgeon died in 1967 after all too short a reign, and in his place the board appointed one Lionel Jofeh, late of the Sperry Gyroscope Company. From then on, the skids were under Small Heath, helped by the establishment of a wildly expensive research department based at a country mansion known as Umberslade Hall.

If we can now look across to the other side of the world, Japan ended the war with a huge home market crying out for personal powered transport. Well over forty factories came into being to plug the gap, one of them started by Mr. Soichiro Honda, who had bought a job lot of ex-Japanese Army small-capacity engines, and was soon engaged in fitting these into bicycle frames.

Competition was fierce, and by 1960 Japan was down to about ten major manufacturers, each with enormous production capacity. As their own home market became saturated, so the Japanese makers began an export drive, at first into nearby Far East markets, and later into the USA. For a while, this acted in the British industry's favour. Japanese motor cycles were small-capacity machines, and when the American purchaser of one such returned to the dealer, bitten by the bug and demanding something more powerful, the same dealer sold him a Triumph, or a BSA.

Headed by the appearance of Honda, Suzuki, Yamaha and Tohatsu models in European road racing, the Japanese machines began to infiltrate Europe and, eventually, Britain. Their marketing, however, was very different to that which had been employed by the now largely defunct British industry—mainly restricted to the weekly motor cycle press. Instead, Honda, the market leaders, took large spaces in the national newspapers, on poster hoardings, and even—an unheard-of-thing—on commercial television channels. The message was always the same: 'You Meet the Nicest People on a Honda!'

And indeed you did, because the appeal was to a new type of rider, who would never have crossed the threshold of the typical back-street motor cycle dealer's premises in a month of Sundays. But he would have no hesitation in walking into the bright High Street outlet of the Japanese franchise holder.

It may be asked why the British industry did not forsee the trend, and start building elegant little electric-start 125 cc twins, and automatic-transmission step-through scooterettes, since that was what the new public wanted. The answer is that nobody in this country ever had got fat on motor cycle manufacture, even in the boom years, and the banks were certainly not going to risk capital on the re-equipment of our factories to meet the new threat.

The British motor cycle world was ever a Cinderella industry, hammered by successive governments and clobbered by economic conditions. It was destined never to get to the Great Ball, but along the way it made some really great bikes. You'll meet many of them in this book.

BLACK SHADOW

The Series A 998 cc (84×90 mm) Vincent-HRD Rapide vee-twin which made headline news on its introduction in 1936 was, in essence, a double-up of the same factory's 500 cc high-camshaft single. The Rapide was designed jointly by Phil Vincent and Phil Irving and was – or so the legend goes – the outcome of a happy accident in which two tracings of a Comet engine had been placed on top of each other in narrow vee formation.

With much external oil piping, the Series A became known as the 'plumber's nightmare', but when the first post-war Vincent-HRDs were launched early in 1946, it was seen that the company had lived up to the promise it had made in its wartime advertising. It was far more than just a general tidying-up of the earlier design, for the two Phils had evolved something new in motor cycles. Advertised as 'The little big twin', the new Series B Rapide was indeed a lightweight thousand.

Motor Cycle tried out the prototype in May, 1946, and commented: 'It has the wheelbase of a five-hundred, and the weight of a five-hundred, and it handles like a TT five-hundred.' The short wheelbase was the whole key to the model's behaviour, and it was mainly achieved by discarding the conventional tubular frame of pre-war years and, instead, suspending the engine from a fabricated beam which served, also, as the oil tank.

Highlight of the Vincent stand at the 1952 Earls Court Show was this 998 cc Series C Black Shadow with various parts sectioned to show the internal workings and construction. The Series C had only another 18 months of life, before being superseded by the Series D range

Of course, the engine had to be redesigned to accept the stresses of acting as part of the frame, and to suit the new layout the cylinder angle was widened from 47 to 50 degrees. As before, the rear sub-frame pivoted under the control of springs beneath the saddle, but now the wheelbase had been reduced from 58.5 in of the Series A, to 56 in.

Two brake drums were used on each wheel, the rear wheel could be reversed in the fork ends to give a choice of final-drive sprockets, and a completely new servo clutch was intended to eliminate the pre-war problems of the standard Burman component.

Now, it so happened that one of the employees of Vincent-HRD's factory at Stevenage (which, incidentally, had been a horse-drawn carriage works in Georgian days) was a certain George Brown, who was a road-racing man of considerable ability. George approached Phil Irving with a plot, whereby a Series B Rapide would be given extra-special tuning, to permit it to compete with honour in sprints and such-like where a 1,000 cc class was operative. Phil agreed, and a bike was duly equipped with oversize carburettors, high-lift cams and other goodies, and polished internally to reduce oil drag.

This, then, was the machine which in due course came to be revered on tracks all over Britain as Gunga Din, first of a line of George Brown specials that was to continue with Nero and, eventually, Super Nero.

But Gunga Din was more than just a formidable sprinter. It was a mobile test bed, and from it Vincent-HRD evolved a road-going super-sportster aimed at retaining the low-speed sweetness of the Rapide, but adding somewhere around 15 mph to the Rapide's speed of 110 mph. Cylinders, cylinder heads and crankcases of the newcomer (announced in February, 1948) were given a special baked-on black finish, and the model was given the appropriate name of Black Shadow.

The incredible mixture of high speed and docility was obtained by a specification which included a compression ratio of only 6·45 to 1, and a 3·5 to 1 top gear ratio which meant that, at the bike's designed top speed of 125 mph, the engine shaft was turning over at a lazy 5,800 rpm. As on the Rapide, the clutch was a servo type, brought into action by a conventional single-plate clutch, but to cope with the additional power output there were six springs, as compared with the three employed in the Rapide.

Next move of the Stevenage team was to produce an out-and-out speed version of the Black Shadow twin. This was the Black Lightning, at first reserved for export only, and claimed to produce a maximum speed of 140 to 150 mph. Certainly the Black Lightning was given a great send-off, with one of the first to reach the USA being used by Rollie Free to gain the American national maximum speed record at 150·313 mph. In Belgium, the same week, Rene Milhoux broke the Belgian flying kilometer record at 143·2 mph, and the world sidecar standing mile at 94·0 mph.

The Series B Black Shadow, meanwhile, was soon succeeded by the Series C, introduced for 1949, the main feature of which was the patented Girdraulic front fork, a parallel-ruler design with additional hydraulic damper units; the upper mountings of the damper units could be rotated, to afford solo or sidecar trail, as required.

Another Series C refinement was the fitting of a small and fat hydraulic damper unit between the two springs controlling the cantilever rear suspension. This, then, was the Black Shadow as tested by *Motor Cycle* in their 11 August, 1949, issue. In effect it was the 1950 version, except in one very important respect.

For some time, Vincent-HRD dealers in the USA had been bombarding Phil Vincent with requests for him to drop the 'HRD' part of the machine's name. This he was very reluctant to do because, after all, he had entered the motor cycle manufacturing world, back in 1928, by purchasing the redundant 'HRD' trade-mark originally made famous by Howard R. Davies. But, argued the Yanks, folks that side of the Atlantic had the weird idea that 'HRD' meant that, somehow, the company was related to Harley-Davidson.

There being no room (or at any rate, very little room) in business for sentiment, Phil at last gave way, and from 1950 onwards the machines were known as plain Vincent. That meant not only a new tank transfer but, also, new timing chest and rocker-cap castings bearing the Vincent name. The opportunity was taken to switch from sand-cast to die-cast covers, giving an improved finish and, also, a slight saving in weight.

The next year's Shadow adopted a forged steel instead of bronze idler pinion in the timing train, in an effort to quieten the mechanical noise. There was, too, a metering device in the oil feed to the rocker gear, but the characteristic 'tap-tap-tap' was shushed but slightly.

It must be said that the Vincent was an acquired taste, a hand-built machine that was the post-war equivalent of the Brough Superior, and a glance at the 1951 Buyer's Guide shows why the Black Shadow was by no means a big-volume seller. The cost, all in, was a daunting £402 10s, which may not sound very much in these inflationary times, but must be compared with the contemporary 1,000 cc Ariel Square Four at £281, or the sporty 499 cc BSA Gold Star Clubman at £253.

By the mid-1950s, the number of potential customers with that kind of money to spare had fallen considerably, and the Vincent firm tried to keep going by producing a number of less-costly items, such as (of all things) a 50 cc bicycle auxiliary

known as the Firefly, a water-scooter with a disastrously-designed glass-fibre hull, and a range of lightweights which were mainly of NSU origin.

There was to be one startling last fling in the big-machine field, with the announcement late in 1954 of the Series D range, almost wholly shrouded in futuristic glass-fibrework, including inbuilt legshields, handlebar windscreen, and facia panel. There was a whole family of new names, too – Black Prince (instead of Black Shadow), Black Knight (instead of Rapide), and Victor (instead of the single-cylinder Comet). It was a bold move, but it met with little success, and in September, 1955, came the announcement that the factory was closing down. 'The product', said Philip Vincent, in explanation 'will not stand a higher retail price. Continuing escalating production costs have brought the company to the position where there is no financial return from the manufacture and sale of motor cycles.' It was understandable, but a pity, for all that.

Above: *in 1950, Manchester dealer Reg Dearden constructed a Shorrock-supercharged 998 cc Black Lightning. The intention was that road-racer Les Graham would make an attempt on the world motor cycle land speed record with it but, tragically, Graham was killed in the 1953 Senior TT, and the record-breaking project was abandoned*

Below: *most potent of the production Vincent models, the 998 cc Black Lightning was sold in racing trim only. This is the 1953 version*

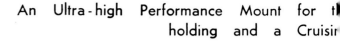

ROAD TESTS OF NEW MODELS	# 998 c.c. Vincent-H.R.D

**An Ultra-high Performance Mount for t\
holding and a Cruisir**

MERE mention of the name "Black Shadow" is enough to speed the pulse. Since the machine's introduction last year as a super-sports brother to the already famous Rapide, the sombrely finished "Shadow" has achieved wide distinction. It is a connoisseur's machine: one with speed and acceleration far greater than those of any other standard motor cycle; and it is a motor cycle with unique and ingenious features which make it one of the outstanding designs of all time.

So far as the standards of engine performance, handling and braking are concerned—the chief features which can make or mar an otherwise perfect mount—the mighty Black Shadow must

Every line of the 998 c.c. vee-twin Black Shadow is suggestive of powerful urge. Cruising speed is anything up to 100 m.p.h.!

be awarded 99 out of 100 marks; 99 because nothing, it is said, is perfect.

The machine has all the performance at the top end of the scale of a Senior T.T. mount. At the opposite end of the range, notwithstanding the combination of a 3.5 to 1 gear ratio, 7.3 to 1 compression ratio and pool quality fuel, it will "chuff" happily in top at 29-30 m.p.h. Indeed, in top gear without fuss, and with the throttle turned the merest fraction off its closed stop, it will surmount average gradients at 30 m.p.h.

In Britain the machine's cruising speed is not only limited by road conditions. It is severely restricted. It is difficult for the average rider in this country to visualize a route on which the

Black Shadow could be driven for any length of time at its limit or near limit. During the test runs speeds of 85-90 m.p.h were commonplace; 100 m.p.h. was held on brief stretches and, occasionally, the needle of the special 150 m.p.h. Smith's speedometer would indicate 110. No airfield or stretch of road could be found which would allow absolute maximum speed to be obtained in two directions, against the watch. Flash readings in two directions of 118 and 114 were obtained, and in neither case had the machine attained its maximum. Acceleration from 100 m.p.h., though not vivid, was markedly good.

The compression ratio of the test model, as has been remarked, was 7.3 to 1. This is the standard ratio but models for the home market and low-octane fuel are generally fitted with compression plates which reduce the ratio to 6.5 to 1. The greater part of the test was carried out on "pool," though petrol-benzole was used when the attempts were made to obtain the maximum speed figures.

Steering and road-holding were fully in keeping with the exceptionally high engine performance. A soft yet positive movement is provided by the massively proportioned Girdraulic fork. There is a "taut-ness" and solid feeling about the steering which engenders confidence no matter what the speed and almost irrespective of the condition of the road surface. Corners and bends can be taken stylishly and safely at ultra-high speeds. There was no chopping, no "sawing"; not one of the faults which are sometimes apparent on high-speed machines. Bottoming and consequent clashing of the front fork were, however, experienced once or twice. Low-speed steering was reather heavy.

Any grumble the critics may have had with regard to the Vincent rear suspension has been met by the fitting of the hydraulic damper between the spring plunger units. So efficient is the rear springing now, that never once was the rider bumped off the Dualseat or forced to poise on the rests. Even at speeds around the 100 m.p.h. mark, only the absence of road shocks gave indication that there was any form of rear-springing, such was the smoothness and lateral rigidity.

Straight-ahead steering was in a class by itself. The model could be steered hands off at 15 m.p.h. with engine barely pulling or just as easily at 95 to 100 m.p.h. The steering damper was required only at speeds over 115 m.p.h.

Used in unison, the four brakes (two per wheel) provided immense stopping power. Light pressure of two fingers on the front-brake lever was sufficient to provide all the braking the front wheel would permit. One of the front brakes, incidentally, squealed when in use. The leverage provided at the rear brake is small, and the brake operation was heavy.

The compact engine-gear unit remained exceptionally clean throughout the 700-mile test. Only a faint smear of oil and slight discoloration of the front exhaust pipe close to the port indicated that the model had been ridden at all

Black Shadow

Engine starting from cold was found difficult at first. Cold starting was certain, however, provided that only the front carburettor was flooded and the throttle control was closed. When the engine was hot, there was no difficulty.

After a cold or warm start the engine would immediately settle down to a true chuff-chuff tickover. Throughout the course of the test the tickover remained slow, certain and one-hundred per cent reliable. No matter how hard the previous miles had been, the twistgrip could always be rolled back against its closed stop with a positive assurance that a consistent tickover would result.

The engine was only tolerably quiet mechanically. At idling speeds, there was a fair amount of clatter, particularly from the valve gear. But so far as the rider was concerned all mechanical noise disappeared at anything over 40 m.p.h. All that remained audible was the pleasant low-toned burble of the exhaust and the sound of the wind in the rider's ears.

Bottom gear on the Black Shadow is 7.25 to 1. Starting away from rest can seem at first to require a certain amount of skill in handling the throttle and clutch. The servo-assisted clutch had a tendency to bite quickly as it began to engage.

Extreme lateral rigidity is a feature of the massively - proportioned Girdraulic fork. The trail can be altered for sidecar work in a few minutes

The Riding Position

The riding position for the 5ft 7in rider who carried out the greater part of the test proved to be first-class. The saddle height is 31in which is comfortable for the majority of riders. The footrests are sufficiently high to allow the rider complete peace of mind when the machine is heeled over to the limit, and were sufficiently low to provide a comfortable position for the 5ft 7in rider's legs.

Now famous, the 25½in from tip to tip, almost straight, Vincent-H.R.D. handlebar provides a most comfortable wrist angle and a straight-arm posture. All controls are widely adjustable—the gear pedal and brake pedal for both height and length. Both these controls, incidentally, move with the footrests when the latter are adjusted.

The gear change was instantaneous but slightly heavy in operation. Snap gear changes could be made as rapidly as the controls could be operated. The clutch freed perfectly throughout the test and bottom gear could be noiselessly selected when the machine was at standstill with the engine idling. However, because of the pressure required to raise the pedal it was sometimes necessary to select neutral by means of the hand lever on the side of the gear box, and also to engage bottom gear by hand.

In the 700 miles of the road test the tools were never required. In spite of the high speeds there was no apparent sign of stress. Primary and rear chains remained properly adjusted. There was very slight discolouring of the front exhaust pipe close to the port and a smear of oil from the base of one of the push rod tubes on the rear cylinder. The ammeter showed a charge at 30 m.p.h. in top gear when all the lights were switched on and the road illumination was better than average. An excellent tool-kit is provided and carried in a special tray under the Feridax Dualseat.

There are many ingenious features of the Vincent-H.R.D. which brand it as a luxury mount built by highly skilled engineers who at the same time are knowledgeable motor cycle enthusiasts. The Black Shadow finish is distinctive, obviously durable and very smart; and only a minor reason why the "Shadow" attracts a crowd of interested passers-by wherever it is seen!

Information Panel

SPECIFICATION

ENGINE : 998 c.c. (84 x 90 mm) vee-twin high camshaft o.h.v. with gear box in unit. Fully enclosed valve gear. Dry-sump lubrication : tank capacity, 6 pints. Four main bearings. Roller-bearing big-ends. Specialloid pistons. Cast-iron liners shrunk into aluminium-alloy cylinder barrels. Aluminium-alloy cylinder heads.

CARBURETTORS : Amal : twistgrip throttle control and twin handlebar-mounted air levers.

TRANSMISSION : Vincent-H.R.D. 4-speed gear box with positive-stop foot control. Gear ratios ; Top, 3.5 to 1. Third, 4.2 to 1. Second, 5.5 to 1. Bottom, 7.25 to 1. Servo-assisted clutch. Primary chain, ⅜in pitch triplex, enclosed in aluminium-alloy case. Secondary chain, ⅝ x ⅜in with guard over top run, R.p.m. at 30 m.p.h. in top gear ; 1,392 approx.

IGNITION AND LIGHTING : Lucas magneto with auto-advance. Miller dynamo : 7in head lamp : stoplight. Dynamo output, 50 watts.

FUEL CAPACITY : 3¼ gallons.

TYRES : Front, 3.00 x 20in. Avon ribbed : rear, 3.50 x 19 Avon studded.

BRAKES : Twin on each wheel : drums 7in diameter x ⅞in wide.

SUSPENSION : Girdraulic front fork with twin helical compression springs and hydraulic damping ; link action ; pivot-action rear springing hydraulically damped.

WHEELBASE : 56in. Ground-clearance, 5in unladen.

SADDLE : Feridax Dualseat. Unladen height, 31in.

WEIGHT : 476 lb fully equipped and with approximately ¾ gallon of fuel.

PRICE : £315 plus purchase tax (in Britain only) £85 1s. Price includes Smith's speedometer.

ROAD TAX : £3 15s a year (£1 0s 8d a quarter). Half rate if used only on standard ration.

DESCRIPTION : The Motor Cycle dated February 19th, 1948.

PERFORMANCE DATA

MEAN MAXIMUM SPEED : Bottom : 68 m.p.h.
Second : 87 m.p.h.
Third : 110 m.p.h.
Top : Not obtained.

ACCELERATION :	10-30 m.p.h.	20-40 m.p.h.	30-50 m.p.h.
Bottom	2.4 secs	2.8 secs	3 secs
Second	3.6 secs	4.2 secs	3.4 secs
Third	—	5.8 secs	4.8 secs
Top	—	—	7.6 secs

Speed at end of quarter-mile from rest : 96 m.p.h.
Time to cover standing quarter-mile : 14.2 secs.

PETROL CONSUMPTION : At 30 m.p.h., 96 m.p.g. At 40 m.p.h., 91.2 m.p.g. At 50 m.p.h., 86.4 m.p.g. At 60 m.p.h., 70 m.p.g.

BRAKING : From 30 m.p.h. to rest, 26ft 6in (surface, coarse, dry chipping).

TURNING CIRCLE : 14 ft.

MINIMUM NON-SNATCH SPEED : 21 m.p.h. in top gear.

WEIGHT PER C.C. : 0.48 lb.

SUNBEAM
S8

Despite the black-out restrictions, the ever-present shortages, and the inevitable queueing for the necessities of life, there was a definite lightening of the skies over Britain in November, 1944, a general feeling that the Second World War could not last much longer. And if anything could lift the spirits of motor cyclists, it was the advertisement which appeared in the November 2 issue of *Motor Cycle*.

'The Sunbeam post-war programme is settled!' it declared, 'Everything is ready! Planned. Agreed. Finalised. And now the Masterpiece is under lock and key. Behind closed doors. Replete with a crop of big surprises. Waiting for the "Cease fire" to sound and production to begin!'

The first of the promised surprises, though, came with the name at the foot of the advertisement, for it was issued by Sunbeam Cycles Ltd, Birmingham 11 – an indication that the Sunbeam name, acquired by AMC in the late 1930s, had changed hands yet again and was now in the BSA fold.

Erling Poppe, who was at one time in partnership with Gilmour Packman as co-manufacturer of P & P motor cycles, had long left the motor cycle field to become a designer of diesel vehicles. But during the war period he had been recruited on to the BSA design team.

One Erling Poppe project, which reached prototype stage but was never produced, was an ingenious scooter known as the BSA Dinghy. For the second project, the new Sunbeam, he was given the freedom to design whatever he liked – always provided that it was clean to ride, comfortable, smooth, and reliable.

BSA had already been experimenting with an in-line vertical twin, and the prototype engine, installed in Erling Poppe's office, was undoubtedly the inspiration for what followed. Nevertheless, Poppe brought a totally new approach to the scheme, and the Sunbeam as announced in March, 1946, was very definitely from the drawing board of an automobile engineer, rather than a motor cycle engineer.

No fewer than 30 patents had either been granted, or were pending. Shaft final drive, overhead camshaft engine, rear springing – all the 'dream' features mentioned in the correspondence columns of the wartime motor cycling press had been incorporated, and in theory it should have had the customers queueing up to offer their hard-earned cash. And yet . . .

Echoing car practice, the cylinder barrels of the Sunbeam were cast integrally with the crankcase. Drive to the overhead camshaft was by chain at the rear of the block. A pancake-type direct current generator (dynamo) was located at the front end of the assembly

Yes; and yet . . . Right through the ages, there have been plenty of examples of a maker striving to provide everything for which the public had been clamouring; except that, when it came to the crunch, the same public was apt to hang back and see what the other man thought of it, before going off to buy something humdrum but familiar.

The 487 cc (70 × 63·5 mm) Sunbeam engine followed car practice in combining the cylinder and crankcase in one light-alloy casting (cylinder liners were of austenitic iron, pressed into the block). A ribbed sump plate was bolted to the underside of the crankcase, and the high-tensile cast-iron crankshaft was inserted from the rear. Transmission was by way of a car-type single-plate clutch to an integral four-speed gearbox, and then by shaft to an underslung-worm rear wheel drive. On the first prototype, a rigid frame was employed, but before production began this was replaced by a frame with plunger rear springing.

The front fork was a telescopic type, with hydraulic damping of each leg, but it departed from normal practice by enclosing the springs in a separate, central housing. Rider comfort was aided by a cantilever-sprung saddle, the spring of which was concealed in the frame top tube. Still more comfort was promised by the use of 4·75 × 16 in tyres (massive, in the eyes of the 1946 public, who refused to be convinced that a bike with boots that big could handle properly).

The overhead camshaft was driven from the rear of the unit and operated the valves (which were set at an angle of 22·5 degrees, and worked in wedge-shape combustion chambers) through the medium of rocker arms. Power output was a very modest 24 bhp at 6,000 rpm and, on road test, the first S7 clocked a none too inspiring 72 mph.

Well, fair enough. The S7 was intended to be a luxury tourer, and for those who wanted a brisker performance a sports engine with 90-degree valves was under development. Indeed, a prototype sportster was built and, with larger carburettor than the S7, a lighter flywheel, and an 8 to 1 compression ratio, it returned an impressive 94 mph.

That was much more like it! Or it would have been, but the

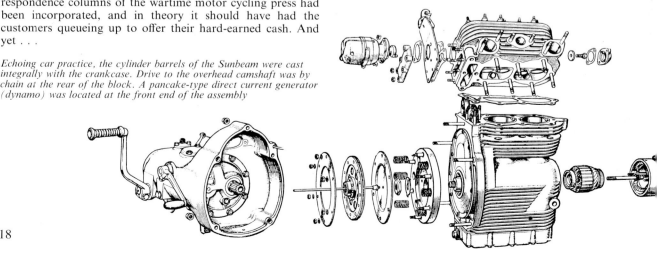

Sunbeam had an inbuilt disaster area. That underslung-worm drive to the rear wheel was incapable of transmitting very much power. Even in day-to-day use it became uncomfortably warm, and on the sports model it used to wear out completely within a few hundred miles.

The Wilkinson Sword Company had experienced similar problems with their four-in-line TAC motor cycle of 1910, and in the later TMC models they switched over to a crownwheel and bevel drive. Sunbeam, on the other hand, just shrugged their shoulders and dropped the idea of building a sports version.

Delayed by the late arrival of bits and pieces from outside suppliers, production did not begin until December, 1946, and the first 25 machines off the assembly line were hurriedly shipped out to South Africa, where Pretoria Police were to provide a sovereign's escort for King George VI's tour.

Clang, again! The engines were bolted directly into the frames, and while this had worked well enough on the toolroom-built prototypes, the production models vibrated like nobody's business. The South African batch had to be shipped straight back to the BSA branch works at Redditch (where the Sunbeams were to be built) for rapid modification.

The modification took the form of mounting the engine on rubber, and to permit it to wobble within the frame a short length of flexible piping had to be inserted into the exhaust system. That makeshift solution was to remain to the end of the Sunbeam's production life.

To help spread the appeal of the Sunbeam to a wider public, the S8 was added from 1949 onward. Rather less of a lumbering elephant than the S7, it achieved a saving of 30 lb in weight, by adopting the front fork and wheels of the BSA A10 twin; it was also £30 cheaper than the S7.

Expert renovator Colin Wall, of Birmingham, rebuilt the Maudes Trophy BSA Star Twin featured elsewhere. An earlier exercise by Colin was this Americanised Sunbeam S7, a concours d'elegance winner at many rallies in the 1960s

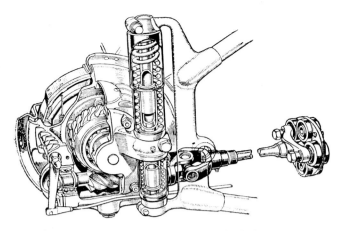

Use of an underslung worm drive to the rear wheel of the in-line Sunbeam twin was dictated by the low positioning of the gearbox output shaft. Unhappily, the worm drive was barely adequate for the power transmitted, and ruled out development of a sports version

Back at the factory, various Sunbeam experiments were put in hand, including a 250 cc single, and a 650 cc water-cooled four, but these never came to anything and, over the years, the amount of development devoted to the in-line twin was negligible. For 1950, Sunbeam dropped the antiquated inverted handlebar levers on the S7, and transferred the front fork springs to within the stanchions; a change in cam form was intended to lengthen the life of the rocker-arm pads.

Small changes in 1952 improved the camshaft-drive chain tensioner, and the oil-pressure switch, but one could sense that the BSA people had no real heart for the Sunbeam, and when it ceased production in 1956, nobody was really surprised. The tragedy was that the Sunbeam was intended for the gentleman tourist, and he just did not exist in sufficient numbers to make the exercise worthwhile.

487 c.c. Sunbeam

Luxury Tourer with Excellent Ste

WHEN the first thrilling post-war Sunbeam was announced it was acclaimed as a mount embodying most of the features demanded by the cognocenti. With its in-line parallel twin-cylinder engine and gear box in unit, shaft drive, coil ignition, unique appearance and many ingenious features it represented a complete breakaway from current motor cycle design.

The Model S8, of course, is the lightened version of the original design. It is a machine which has so many praise-

Numerous detail features of the S8 Sunbeam make it easy to clean and maintain

worthy attributes that it is hardly possible to single out any one of them and say of it that therein lies the model's attraction. But if there is one feature that leaves an outstanding impression after experience with the S8 it is the smoothness of the engine and transmission, especially when the engine is revving in the higher ranges. The end of every run during the test, irrespective of length, and under all but the very worst of weather conditions, was reached with regret.

There was no pace above 30 m.p.h. which could be said with certainty to be the machine's happiest cruising speed. The engine gave the impression that it was working as well within its limits at 75-80 m.p.h. as it was at 45-50 m.p.h. It thrived on hard work and was a glutton for high revs.

A pronounced tendency to pinking on pool fuel was noted when the machine was being accelerated hard in top or in third gears. Therefore, on the occasions when it was wanted to reach B from A just as quickly as the machine could be urged, the engine had to be revved very hard in the indirect ratios. Peak r.p.m. in bottom and second gears, and almost as high r.p.m. as were available in third were frequently used—with the most pleasing results. Steering and road-holding were so good that the rider was encouraged to swing the bends with joie de vivre.

No oil leaks became apparent in the 600-odd miles of the test. The exhaust pipes did not even slightly discolour. Nothing vibrated loose. The toolkit was only removed from its box on one occasion—and that was out of sheer curiosity. Mechanical noise was no more apparent at the end of a hard ride than it was at the beginning. Except on the odd occasions when grit found its way into the jet block, engine idling was slow and certain. When the engine was running at idling speed or only slightly faster it rocked perceptibly on its rubber mounting. This rocking was transmitted to the handlebars in the form of slight vibration and was apparent up to speeds of just over 30 m.p.h. in top gear.

Above, say, 33 m.p.h., there was complete smoothness. Even when the engine was peaking in the indirect ratios the machine was smooth to a degree never hitherto experienced with motor cycles. The harder the engine was revved the smoother and more dynamo-like the machine apparently became. Only the inordinate exhaust noise tended to restrict the use of really high r.p.m.; the exhaust noise, it should perhaps be added, was never obtrusive to the rider.

Starting the engine from cold during the recent icy spell, or when it was already hot, was so easy that a child could do it. When the engine was cold it was necessary to close the carburettor air-slide by depressing the easily accessible spring-loaded plunger on top of the carburettor and lightly flood the carburettor; then, with the ignition switched off, to depress the kick-starter twice; switch on the ignition, and the engine would tick-tock quietly into life at the first kick. The air-slide could be opened almost immediately after a cold start.

Because of the combination of well-chosen kick-start gearing and relatively low compression ratio, so little physical effort is required to operate the kick-starter that it can be depressed easily by hand pressure. If there was ever such a thing as tickle-starting, the Sunbeam most certainly has it.

An outstandingly high standard of mechanical quietness was yet another of the Sunbeam's qualities. Only the pistons were audible after a cold start. As near as could be ascertained, the valve-gear was noiseless. Low-speed torque was very good, and the engine would pull away quite happily in top gear from 19-20 m.p.h.

From idling to full throttle the carburation was clean and the pick-up without any trace of hesitation. Acceleration was all that could be expected from a machine which falls into a "luxury fast-touring" rather

Notable features to be seen in this view include the unit-construction, pancake-type dynamo, streamlined air-cleaner, and rear-springing

than a "sports" classification. When the mood was there, however, and the full engine performance was used in the indirect ratios, acceleration was markedly brisk.

Pressure required to operate the gear change was so light that the pedal could barely be felt under a bewadered foot. The range of movement of the pedal was delightfully short and allowed upward or downward gear changes to be made merely by pivoting the right foot on the footrest. Clean, delightful gear changing could be effortlessly achieved. Between bottom and second and second and third gears the pedal required a slow, deliberate movement. Between third and top gears the change was all that could be wished for—light and instantaneous. The clutch, too, was light in operation and smooth and positive in its take-up of the drive. It freed perfectly and continued to do so even after six standing-start "quarters." It required no adjustment during the course of the test.

Riding Position

For riders of all but unusually tall or short statures, a better riding position than that provided by the S8 could not be imagined. Saddle height is 30in. The footrests can be ideally situated (they are adjustable through 360 deg.) so that they provide a comfortable knee angle. Even at their lowest position of adjustment they are sufficiently high not to foul the road when the model is banked well over on sharp corners or fast bends, or when it is being turned round in the width of narrow lanes. The wrist angle provided by the handlebars was extremely comfortable.

Handling was at all times beyond criticism. There was no trace of whip from the duplex frame or of lack of lateral rigidity from the plunger-type rear suspension. With plunger-type suspension spring characteristics normally have to be rather "hard." Total movement was approximately 1¼in. The degree of cushioning is therefore not large. The hydraulically damped, telescopic front fork was very light round static load and behaved perfectly under all conditions.

Both brakes provided first-class stopping power. They were light to operate and smooth and progressive in action. They did not fade under conditions of abuse, never required adjustment

During the test, the unit remained free from oil leaks. Exceptional smoothness of running was a feature of the power unit

during the test, and were not adversely affected when the machine was driven hard through heavy rain and snow. The standard of mudguarding was very good. A long, road-width beam was provided by the 8in head lamp. Full lamp load was balanced by the 60-watt pancake generator at 30 m.p.h. in top gear.

Numerous detail features of the machine make it easy to clean and maintain. The ignition coil, voltage control regulator, ammeter and combined ignition and lighting switch are housed in a metal container below the saddle. Opposite to it the battery is housed in a lead-lined box of similar proportions and design. Both front and rear wheels are quickly detachable, the rear especially so. Ignition and oil warning lights are located in the head lamp, one on each side of the speedometer. The speedometer in this position was easily read when the rider was in a normally seated position. The instrument registered approximately seven per cent fast and ceased to function at 589 miles.

Finish of the test machine was black and chromium and the quality fully in keeping with the high engineering standards used on the machine.

Information Panel

SPECIFICATION

ENGINE : 487 c.c. (70 x 63.5 mm) in-line vertical-twin with chain-driven overhead camshaft. Valves set in single row at 22½ deg to vertical. Squish-type combustion chambers. One-piece aluminium-alloy cylinder head. Crankcase and cylinder block in one-piece aluminium-alloy casting with austenitic cylinder liners. Light-alloy connecting rods with lead-bronze big-ends. Wet sump lubrication ; sump capacity, 4 pints.

CARBURETTOR : Amal ; twistgrip throttle control ; air control on carburettor.

TRANSMISSION : Sunbeam four-speed gear box in unit with engine : positive-stop foot control. Bottom, 14.5 to 1. Second, 9 to 1. Third, 6.5 to 1. Fourth, 5.3 to 1. Sidecar ratios : Top, 6.13 to 1. Third, 7.4 to 1. Second, 10.3 to 1. Bottom, 16.6 to 1. Single-plate clutch. Final drive by shaft and underslung worm. R.p.m. in top gear at 30 m.p.h. (solo gearing), 2,034.

IGNITION AND LIGHTING : Lucas 60-watt "pancake" dynamo at front end of crankshaft. Coil ignition with auto-advance. 8in diameter head lamp.

FUEL CAPACITY : 3¼ gallons.

TYRES : Dunlop 4.00 x 18in rear ; 3.25 x 19in front.

BRAKES : 8in x ⅞in rear. 8in x 1⅛in front.

SUSPENSION : Sunbeam telescopic fork with hydraulic damping. Plunger-type rear suspension.

WHEELBASE : 57in. Ground clearance, 5¼in unladen.

SADDLE : Terry. Unladen height 30in.

WEIGHT : 423 lb with empty tanks and fully equipped.

PRICE : £179, plus Purchase Tax (in Britain only) £48 6s 8d. Price includes speedometer.

ROAD TAX : £3 15s a year ; £1 0s 8d a quarter. Half-duty if only standard ration is used.

MAKERS : Sunbeam Cycles, Ltd., Birmingham, 11.

DESCRIPTION : *The Motor Cycle, September 29, 1949.*

PERFORMANCE DATA

MEAN MAXIMUM SPEEDS : First : *35 m.p.h.
Second : *58 m.p.h.
Third : 80 m.p.h.
Top : 83 m.p.h.
*Valve float just beginning.

MEAN ACCELERATION :	10-30 m.p.h.	20-40 m.p.h.	30-50 m.p.h.
Bottom	3 secs	—	—
Second	5.2 secs.	4.2 secs.	4 secs.
Third	7.6 secs.	6.8 secs.	5.6 secs.
Top		9 secs.	7.2 secs.

Mean speed at end of quarter-mile from rest : 77 m.p.h.
Mean time to cover standing quarter-mile : 18.2 secs.

PETROL CONSUMPTION : At 30 m.p.h., 102 m.p.g. At 40 m.p.h., 92 m.p.g. At 50 m.p.h., 71 m.p.g. At 60 m.p.h., 62 m.p.g.

BRAKING : From 30 m.p.h. to rest, 25ft 6in (surface, coarse-textured tar-macadam).

TURNING CIRCLE : 15ft 9in.

MINIMUM NON-SNATCH SPEED : 12 m.p.h. in top gear.

WEIGHT PER C.C. : 0.91 lb.

Douglas
MARK III

Douglas flat-twins of pre-war days, with the solitary exception of the 1935 500 cc Endeavour, had always employed an engine with the cylinders disposed fore-and-aft in the frame. And anyway, the Endeavour scarcely counted; it was so much of a rush job that the engine unit was simply the Blue Chief turned around at right-angles, while the shaft final drive made use of a Morris 8 crownwheel and bevel (not even genuine Morris at that, but cheap 'pattern spares'). Reputedly, only about 50 Endeavours were ever sold.

But the machine announced in the motor cycle press of September, 1945, was a very different matter indeed. The engine was a transverse 348 cc overhead-valve flat-twin, direct coupled to a four-speed gearbox with final drive by chain. Full pivoted-fork rear suspension was incorporated, controlled by a longitudinal torsion-bar spring at each side, enclosed within the frame cradle tubes.

Each torsion bar was secured at the front end, but at the rear end was a short lever (mounted on splines, so that the springing could be adjusted to suit the load carried), with a linkage to the rear fork arm. Originally, the front springing, too, was to have been by torsion bar, with the spring rod housed in the fork stanchions and connected at the base to the short leading links carrying the wheel spindle. Before production began, however, this system was superseded by the Douglas Radiadraulic fork – similar in outward appearance, but embodying helical springs formed from square-section wire, and hydraulic damping.

To the public, the Douglas appeared to be a totally new design, one of the first such to appear on the post-war market. In fact, the engine was basically one that had been designed in wartime, to power portable generator plants. The designer was George Halliday (who, also, was the patentee of the torsion-bar springing system), but when the new Model T35 began to reach the showrooms (from July, 1946, onward) it was evident that all was far from well.

Not only was there considerable side-to-side shake at low engine speed, but quite often (especially in rain) one plug would cut out without warning – and cut in again, with interesting consequences, while the bike was being banked into a bend. Workmanship was poor, and in the first six months my own Model T35 suffered a split fuel tank, a stuck clutch mechanism (due to the case-hardening of the ramps wearing through), a collapsed front-wheel bearing and, finally, a frame break just above the gearbox on the left.

'Trouble is,' explained a Douglas service department foreman, 'no sooner do we train a lad up to a decent standard of workmanship, than off he goes to Bristol Aeroplane, for a much higher salary than we could ever afford!'

Obviously, something had to be done. Erling Poppe, the designer of the post-war in-line Sunbeam twin, had joined Douglas by this time as Technical Director, Walter Moore (designer of the CS1 Norton) was Works Superintendent, and for good measure the immortal Freddy Dixon, a Douglas designer and racer of the mid-1920s, was brought in as a consultant.

Dixon was mainly concerned with combustion chamber improvements, and the result of his work was the Mark III engine, with a new type of flat-top piston, a redesigned cylinder head and a kidney-shape rocker cover which no longer had the Douglas name cast into it. Cosmetic improvements included a restyled fuel tank (chromium plated, with blue side panels outlined in black and white).

Introduced for 1949, the standard Mark III retained the cast light-alloy woffle box silencer carried beneath the crankcase, and deeply valanced mudguards at front and rear. There was also a Mark III Sports, with exhaust pipes which swept up then straight back at each side, and this was possibly the prettiest of all the post-war Douglas machines.

The same season saw the introduction of yet another version, intended for trials work and with the transverse flat-twin engine mounted high in a frame which dispensed with rear springing entirely (for several years in the early 1950s the myth was prevalent that no rear-sprung model would ever make good in trials, because the springing did not permit the punch of the engine to be delivered, by way of the rear tyre, direct to the rockery).

The 1950 range included two very interesting newcomers, the 80 Plus and 90 Plus, the names being indicative of their maximum speeds. Based on the Mark III unit, their engines were specially tuned, had higher compression ratios than standard, and were capable of producing 25 bhp and 28 bhp, respectively, on the test bench. In practice, it was said that all the 'plus' engines were built to 90 Plus standard. If one reached 28 bhp on the brake (dynamometer), the bike was painted gold and called a 90 Plus; if it failed to reach this figure, the bike was painted maroon and termed an 80 Plus!

This pair, together with the rigid-frame trials model, the

The post-war transverse-flat-twin 348 cc Douglas was derived from a portable generator unit, and the first (Model T35) examples were disappointing in many ways. The legendary Freddy Dixon was brought in as a consultant and the engine, with redesigned cylinder head and piston, became the much more satisfactory Mark III

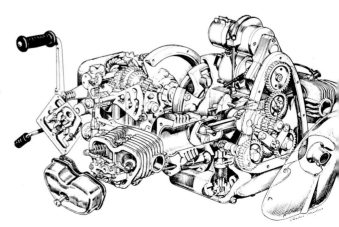

A flat-twin may seem totally unsuited for trials use. Nevertheless the Douglas factory made a serious attempt at producing a trials mount, and this 1951 example displays the special high-ground-clearance, unsprung frame devised for the model. Note the tremendous height of the saddle!

Mark III Sports, and the Mark III de Luxe of the road test which follows, made a total of five machines for the 1950 season. In addition, however, Douglas had come to an arrangement with Piaggio, of Italy, under which the standard 125 cc version of the Vespa scooter would be Bristol-built, also.

The 1950 Mark III de luxe was finished in new polychromatic light blue paintwork, and had discarded its woffle-box silencer in favour of long and rather tortuous exhaust pipes, on the ends of which sat tilted-up silencers. A new rear subframe structure of small-diameter tubing carried triangular tool boxes of cast light alloy. Finally, the big fixed front mudguard had been replaced by a guard which rose and fell with wheel movement.

For its day the Mark III was quite a potent job, and *Motor Cycle* must have been landed with a duff example, if all that they could obtain on road test was a mean maximum of 70 mph. Certainly the enthusiast-in-the-street regarded it as one of the quickest three-fifties around – even if it had been beaten out of sight in the Junior Clubman's TT Races by the BSA Gold Star.

It is one of the mysteries of Douglas production that there never was a Mark II, and the Mark IV had but a fleeting existence. Final development, therefore was the Mark V of 1951 to 1954. This was virtually the Mark III de luxe, but with straight, low-level exhaust pipes and a more sporty type of front mudguard; at first an optional extra, a dual seat was standard equipment on the later models.

During this period, the design and development departments had been at work on a new 348cc transverse twin. This was the Dragonfly, revealed at the 1954 Earls Court Show, and featuring Earles pivoted front fork, rear suspension controlled for the first time by conventional Girling damper units, and a much sleeker-looking engine unit fed by a single carburettor and with an alternator to supply the electrics. Most notable feature,

Very much a one-off was this experimental 500 cc transverse-twin Douglas, a suprise exhibit at the 1951 Earls Court Show. Although the machine was never produced, the cylinder-head design was used in the later 348 cc Dragonfly

however, was a headlamp nacelle springing from the front of the fuel tank, much after the style of the old Wooler.

The Dragonfly was to be the Douglas factory's final fling. Already in the hands of the Official Receiver, the works were bought by Westinghouse Brake and Signal Company in 1956, and all two-wheeler production had ceased by the following spring.

ROAD TESTS OF
NEW MODELS

348 c.c. Mark III

A Very Comfortable Touring Machine for Solo or Pillic

POST-WAR Douglas models have been available for about three years, and during that time have gained a following among those who prefer a machine with advanced features. These features are noteworthy, and include a horizontally opposed overhead-valve engine set transversely across the frame, a four-speed gear box in unit with the engine, and, specially interesting, pivoting-fork rear suspension controlled by torsion bars housed in the longitudinal cradle tubes of the frame.

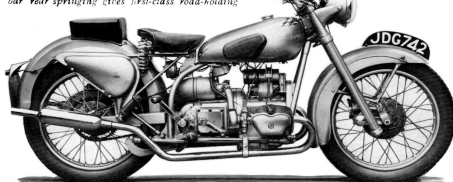

Douglas Mark III de luxe model. The torsion-bar rear springing gives first-class road-holding

The Mark III de luxe machine tested is the basic model of the range of five available for 1950 and is intended for touring purposes; riders interested in high-speed road-work, racing, trials, and scrambles are amply catered for by the four other models. The appeal of the Mark III de luxe lies in the fact that, while the absolute maximum speed available is not especially high, speeds of around 60 m.p.h. can be maintained indefinitely with a degree of mechanical and exhaust quietness, and of comfort, bettered by no other three-fifty on the market.

True to Douglas tradition, the machine under test started readily Though the crankshaft is longitudinal, the kick-

starter crank operates in the normal fashion and is geared to spin the crankshaft adequately. Almost without exception the engine would respond to one depression of the pedal, on which no special effort had to be exerted; indeed, sometimes a negligent half-swing of the crank was all that was needed.

These observations apply to starting with the engine hot or cold; the only difference in technique was that for cold starting the two carburettors needed to be flooded. Each carburettor is fitted with a hand-operated plunger for the air slide, but in practice it was found that flooding alone gave a sufficiently rich cold-starting mixture. Carburettor intakes are connected to a large Vokes air-filter (an extra) mounted above the gear box, and intake hiss is eliminated.

Engine idling was satisfactory, provided the ignition control was not in the fully advanced position. Failure to retard the ignition meant that there was a chance that the engine would stall unless the throttle was opened slightly and, therefore, the running speed increased.

With the machine stationary and the engine idling, the clutch freed perfectly and bottom gear could be engaged noiselessly. Clutch control operation was slightly heavy and the take-up of the drive inclined to be quick. The take-up was, however, perfectly smooth and progressive. Gear changing was positive and clean provided the pedal was moved slowly; very rapid changes could be made with no loss of positiveness, but, in such cases, clashing of the gear pinions—which could be felt rather than heard—was unavoidable. Slight whine emanated from the indirect gears. Timing pinions, also, could be heard as a mild whine when the machine was delivered, but were, unquestionably, less audible after 1,000 miles had been covered.

The riding position is such that the footrests are farther to the rear in relation to the saddle than the average British machine. Slightly unorthodox, also, is the handlebar, which is almost straight, mounted above the steering column, and clamped fractionally behind its axis. The rider has a sensation of being "over" the machine, well in command, and comfortable. In short, the riding position was adjudged first-class by a rider of average stature, and the only shortcoming was that the toe of a bewadered foot occasionally fouled a carburettor intake elbow casting.

With the machine's Radiadraulic bottom-link front fork and torsion-bar rear suspension, the road-holding and steering of the Douglas are far and away in advance of the majority of comparable machines. At all speeds, the road-holding is first-rate; this means that the suspensions absorb road shocks of the pot-hole variety encountered in built-up areas and on country lanes, and are equally effective on corrugations and other irregularities of fast main roads.

High-speed cornering could be indulged in with the comforting certainty that the front wheel would hold a precise line and that the

Efficient cylinder cooling is provided by the transverse engine mounting. The Radiadraulic fork features bottom links and hydraulic damping.

Douglas Twin

rear wheel would follow without any tendency to chop out. No traces of lateral whip in the frame were apparent and on no occasion did the rear springing or front fork bottom on maximum deflection. A steering damper is not fitted; if a damper were included in the specification, it would be completely superfluous.

As mentioned earlier, the Douglas is happy when cruising at speeds around a mile a minute and, of course, at lower speeds, though the engine is smoother from 40 m.p.h. up than at lower speeds in top gear. Below 40 m.p.h. a distinct hardness in power delivery can be felt. There is no vibration of the high-frequency type at any period of the engine-speed range, and torque reaction cannot be identified except when the engine is idling.

The engine responds to intelligent use of the ignition control. A quarter-retard setting was found the best for traffic work, with full retard for good idling at traffic stops. Pinking never occurs; there is, indeed, difficulty in provoking pinking by abuse.

Front and rear brakes, without being outstanding in efficiency, proved to be adequate for the performance of the machine. The rear-brake pedal is well placed for operation with a minimum of foot movement, and the front-brake lever can be grasped by an easy span of the fingers; front-brake operation was, however, inclined to be heavy.

Exhaust silencing was adequate at all engine speeds and mechanical noise did not obtrude. In over 1,000 miles of use, during which there were periods of high-speed open-road riding, the engine and gear box kept free from oil leaks. Valanced mudguards are fitted and give better-than-average protection. Instead of being attached to the fork legs, the latest design of front mudguard is retained on linkage connected to the wheel spindle. On the machine tested, play developed in the attachment bracket and could not be eliminated by tightening the pivot bolts. Eventually the brackets fractured.

A central stand with semi-circular feet is fitted. The machine could be rolled back on the stand with commendable ease, and rigid support for the machine is provided. The feet are spaced widely enough to be "safe" on cambered roads.

Each carburettor has a cast air intake elbow and an induction pipe leading to a large Vokes air-cleaner. The rear-brake pedal is adjustable for vertical position

Cast, light-alloy tool-boxes are fitted, one each side of the rear mudguard. These boxes are capacious and pleasing to the eye. The Lucas lighting set gave a good, properly focused driving beam; during the course of the test one tail lamp bulb distintegrated.

The speedometer was accurate at lowish speeds and not more than 2 per cent fast at 60 m.p.h. Finish of the machine tested was polychromatic light blue, with chromium plate for the exhaust system, handlebars, wheel rims, tank (except panels in blue), and incidental components. This blue finish is an alternative to black enamel at no extra charge.

The Douglas Mark III de luxe model is, as mentioned earlier, a touring mount which offers the tourist a reasonably high cruising speed in quietness and comfort. It is also a machine which will carry a passenger as well as the rider with consummate ease; during the test the pillion equipment was used and only a slight reduction in performance was apparent. It goes without saying, that the passenger spoke highly of the comfort given by the rear suspension.

Information Panel

SPECIFICATION

ENGINE : Douglas 348 c.c. (60.8 mm x 60 mm) horizontally opposed twin-cylinder o.h.v., mounted transversely in frame. Double-row ball bearing at crankshaft driving end, plain bearing at timing end ; gear-driven magneto. Dry-sump lubrication by vane-type pump ; 4 pt oil reservoir integral with crankcase.

CARBURETTORS : Twin Amal 27/4 ; twistgrip throttle control and independently operated air slides.

TRANSMISSION : Douglas gear box, four-speed, positive foot control ; in unit with engine. Bottom, 16.3 to 1. Second, 10.1 to 1. Third 7.24 to 1. Top, 5.86 to 1. Single-plate clutch ; secondary chain, ⅜in x ¼in with guard over top run. R.p.m. at 30 m.p.h. in top gear, 2,300.

IGNITION AND LIGHTING : Lucas Magdyno with manual ignition control on handlebar. Lucas 7in head lamp with domed glass.

FUEL CAPACITY : 3¾ gallons.

TYRES : Firestone—3.25 x 19in front and rear.

BRAKES : 7in diameter front and rear.

SUSPENSION : Douglas Radiadraulic bottom link front fork with hydraulic rebound damping. Torsion-bar controlled pivoting-fork rear springing.

WHEELBASE : 54¼in. Ground clearance, 5½in unladen.

SADDLE : Terry. Unladen height, 29¼in.

WEIGHT : 408 lb with approximately ¼ gallon fuel, oil container full, and full equipment, including pillion seat and footrests.

PRICE : £135, plus Purchase Tax (in Great Britain only), £36 9s. Pillion equipment and air cleaner extra.

DESCRIPTION : October 14, 1948, and October 27, 1949.

MAKERS : Douglas (Sales and Service) Ltd., Kingswood, Bristol.

PERFORMANCE DATA

MEAN MAXIMUM SPEED : Bottom* : 31 m.p.h.
Second* : 50 m.p.h.
Third* : 64 m.p.h.
Top : 70 m.p.h.
* Valve float occurring.

MEAN ACCELERATION :

	10-30 m.p.h.	20-40 m.p.h.	30-50 m.p.h.
Bottom	3.2 secs	—	—
Second	4.6 secs	5.2 secs	6.8 secs
Third	—	7.4 secs	7.5 secs
Top	—	10.2 secs	9.4 secs

Speed at end of quarter-mile from rest : 58 m.p.h.
Time taken to cover standing quarter-mile : 20.4 secs.

PETROL CONSUMPTION : At 30 m.p.h., 86 m.p.g. At 40 m.p.h., 82 m.p.g. At 50 m.p.h., 74 m.p.g. At 60 m.p.h., 61 m.p.g.

BRAKING : From 30 m.p.h. to rest, 31 feet. (Surface: bitumen-bonded, rolled granite chippings, wet.)

TURNING CIRCLE : 16ft 6in.

MINIMUM NON-SNATCH SPEED : 18 m.p.h. in top gear.

WEIGHT PER C.C. : 1.17 lb.

BSA BANTAM DE LUXE

Although it may seem a trifle odd to include a cheap and cheerful little two-stroke in a collection of classic bikes of the 1950s, when that model is the BSA Bantam the choice can be justified. Used by everyone from Post Office telegram boys to gas-meter readers, and from missionaries in New Guinea to sheep-herders in the Australian outback, no bike had ever before gained such universal affection – unless, maybe, you count the BSA 'round tank' of the mid-1920s. Come to think of it, that one, too, was a product of the BSA branch works at Redditch, rather than of Small Heath itself.

It is no secret that the Bantam was only British by adoption, and its origin was the DKW RT125, built at the Zschopauer Motorradwerk, in Saxony. Plans of the DKW were acquired by the Allied forces as war reparations, and copies were passed to several factories, including Harley-Davidson. Also DKW-based, the 125cc Royal Enfield 'Flying Flea' had been in production at Redditch since 1939, but the BSA technicians, unlike Royal Enfield, decided to make a 'mirror image' power unit, in which the various parts were not only converted from metric to inch dimensions but were 'opposite hand' to the German originals.

The first the British public knew of the scheme was a press announcement in March, 1948, that 'to meet a specific contract obtained from an overseas market' (actually, it was Sweden) BSA had evolved a new 123cc (52 × 58 mm) two-stroke engine-gear unit. Details embraced concentric kick-starter and gear-lever shafts, a Wico-Pacy flywheel magneto, and a small Amal carburettor.

Two months later, it was announced that a complete lightweight motor cycle was on the stocks, the first BSA two-

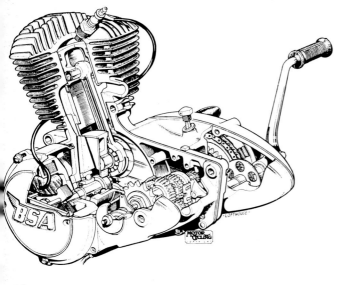

Simple but effective, that was the BSA Bantam. It originally had a 123 cc engine, but was complemented in 1954 by the Bantam Super with a 148 cc power unit, seen here in a sectioned drawing

stroke since the abyssmal 175 cc two-speeder of 1928-29. This, too, was reserved for export only, and it featured an all-welded tubular frame, undamped telescopic spring forks, valanced mudguards (the front being fixed to the fork stanchions), direct lighting, and – nice touch, this – a bulb horn mounted through the steering head. Apart from cream tank panels the colour, like that of the Sunbeam S7 from the same Redditch works, was mist green.

Quantity production of the Model D1, which had yet to gain its Bantam name, began in July, 1948, and by the October had progressed well enough for some to be diverted at last to the home market. Now it was indeed the Bantam (a model name used also by Douglas in 1934), selling at a tax-inclusive price of £76 4s, plus a further £4 if a customer fancied a D-shaped Smiths speedometer.

Ironically, back in East Germany a small group of former DKW employees at about this time were struggling to get the Zschopauer Motorradwerk back into production. Their first product, too, was the RT125, initially under an IFA label. Later, they simply reversed the factory name so that it was Motorradwerk Zschopau or, in short, MZ.

Shortly after the first batch of Bantams reached Australia, the local racing lads began carving and hacking, welding lumps to the underside of the combustion chamber, and filing pieces out of the piston. Running at compression ratios of up to 15 to 1, they got 125 cc-class racing under way at minimal cost.

In Britain, too, enthusiasts such as John Hogan and Fron Purslow started to pit their modified Bantams against the sleeved-down pre-war Royal Enfield and New Imperial four-strokes in short-circuit racing. And Bantam owners were quick to take advantage of the newly-announced 125 cc Isle of Man TT of 1951.

By that time George Pickering, Reg Jackson and others were regularly picking up awards in trials, while Jackie Bodenham and Jimmy Bray kept the BSA flag flying in scrambles (where, it must be admitted, the Dot-Villiers had yet to make its formidable presence felt).

In fact, BSA had added a 'competitions' Bantam to the standard catalogue, although the description was warranted only by the fact that it had lowered gear ratios, a bigger rear tyre, and a tilted-up 'flat-fish' silencer.

The original D1 Bantam was augmented by the 148 cc (57 × 58 mm) D3 Bantam Major in 1954, with plunger-type rear springing (available also on the D1 de Luxe) and a more generous allowance of cylinder barrel and head finning. The 'flat-fish' silencer was replaced by a torpedo type with detachable baffle unit.

Mainly for institutional sales (Post Office, Forestry Commission, etc), the rigid-frame D1 123 cc model remained in production until 1956, when the plunger-sprung model only was marketed. In the same year, the Bantam Major fitted a pivoted rear fork, and a dual seat, and the competitions versions of the 123 and 148 cc models were dropped from the catalogue.

The last move was a bit surprising, because Brian Stonebridge

By 1960, when this 173 cc D7 Bantam Super was on offer, the little BSA had become slightly more sophisticated. The unusual lubrication system allowed the drive-side main bearing to be oiled by the primary chain, while the ignition-side main bearing was oiled from the gearbox

had joined the Small Heath competitions department in 1955 and, virtually for sheer devilment, had started to make Bantams fly a lot quicker than before. Brian himself scored a sensation at Shrubland Park, while John Draper with a Stonebridge-tuned 148 cc engine, won the lightweight class of the Experts Grand National scramble. Even more enterprising, Draper kept his Bantam Major on the 1956 Scottish Six Days Trial leader board all week, eventually tieing for sixth place with Sammy Miller (497 cc Ariel).

But it seemed that the BSA bosses just did not want to know, and the efforts of the competitions department received little encouragement from above.

The 173 cc (61·5 × 58 mm) D5 Bantam Super came upon the scene in 1958, evolving into the D7 of the same capacity from 1960 onwards. It was to gain still more power, becoming the

The Bantam in its almost final guise, as the 173 cc three-speed Bantam de Luxe of 1966, selling at £135. Last of the line was the four-speed D14/4 announced in 1968

D10 in 1967, the four-speed D13 a year later and, finally, the 14 bhp D14/4.

Even by May, 1951, 50,000 Bantams had been built, and the eventual tally must have been well over half a million. True, there were occasional mistakes – such as the time when the engineering department, without consulting the drawing office, put in hand a method of holding disc plates to the flywheel sides by light centre-punch peening; *that* caused a few wrecked engines before the trouble was rectified. But by and large, the Bantam did just what was expected of it. It was not glamorous, nor did the general public want it to be, but as the 1960s were coming to a close, so the whizz-kid brigade staffing the new BSA research establishment at Umberslade Hall tried to take it up-market.

But for all the extra potency of the D14/4, it was a harsher and less forgiving machine than its forbears.

It was during the winter of 1966-67 that the lads of the BSA competitions shop hatched another plot. By then, an off-road version of the Bantam was in production under the name of the Bushman, and while making a promotional film for Australia, world moto-cross champion Jeff Smith, and competitions manager Brian Martin, were struck by the Bushman's trials potential. They went into consultation with Michael Martin, who was involved with Bantam engine development, and with Mick Bowers.

Using a BSA C15 Trials front fork, a Triumph Tiger Cub rear fork, Victor Enduro air cleaner, and other bits from standard models, they built a small batch of experimental trials models, and on one of these Dave Rowland created a sensation by finishing second in the Scottish Six Days Trial (Sammy Miller was the winner).

'Not interested', said the BSA hierarchy. 'The trials market is too small to bother about.' And with indecent haste they killed off the Bantam, even putting a sledge-hammer through the jigs so that it could never be resurrected. But its ghost, at least, lives on – as the MZ TS150 Eagle.

ROAD TESTS OF NEW MODELS

B.S.A. 123 c.c. Bantan

High-performance Two-stroke with Excellent Front

SINCE the B.S.A. 123 c.c. Bantam was introduced three years ago, it has earned for itself a wide following among two-stroke enthusiasts. Now, with the A.C. generator available and probably more especially the addition of neat, plunger-type rear suspension, the model's appeal has been further enhanced.

The degree of comfort provided by the combination of the telescopic front fork and rear suspension is quite exceptional for a machine in the 125 c.c. class. Badly surfaced, cobbled roads and tram tracks can be traversed at speed without the wheel-

Rear springing gives the 123 c.c. B.S.A. Bantam de Luxe a high degree of comfort

hop sometimes experienced with lightweights. The rear suspension is commendably light round the static load position so that small road shocks—as well as severe ones—are satisfactorily absorbed.

More than this, however; because of the excellent build-up provided, bottoming on full-shock loading was never experienced with a 10½-stone rider in the saddle. Both front and rear suspensions occasionally could be made to bottom on rebound, but never seriously.

Steering and road holding were of the true confidence-instilling variety no matter what the speed and irrespective of

the conditions. The angle to which the model could be heeled over was limited only by the height of the footrests, but even that was sufficient not to cause concern except when heeling the model over rather farther than is strictly necessary under normal conditions.

Holding a chosen line on a corner or bend called for no effort and appeared to be all but automatic. On greasy cobbles and wood blocks the handling earned full marks. It was possible to ride the Bantam feet-up at the slowest crawl. Straight-ahead steering was very, very good.

Ignition on the A.C. generator model is, of course, by battery and coil, and the ignition switch is in the head lamp. To make a cold start the drill was to switch on the ignition, flood the carburettor and close the strangler and, with the throttle held rather more than one-third open, operate the kick-starter. Starting from cold generally needed two or perhaps three digs on the pedal. When started from cold the engine required only about a quarter of a mile to warm up. After the first few seconds the strangler could be opened the merest fraction; then, later, it could be fully opened. It was, incidentally, required for each cold start.

When the engine was hot, starting could be accomplished by making only a negligent half- or quarter-swing on the kickstarter. Operating the kickstarter required little muscular effort, but it was necessary to finish the swing early so as not to come up against the footrest with one's foot.

Mechanical quietness of the engine was excellent and at no time at all were traces of two-stroke rattle identified. The standard of exhaust silencing, however, was not all it might have been both for the rider's and pedestrians' comfort.

Best fast cruising speed of the test machine was in the region of 40 m.p.h., though a maximum cruising speed of 45 m.p.h. could be held for hour after hour apparently without detriment to the engine. In fact, the engine just could not be made to tire. It was driven on full throttle, or nearly so, during 300-odd miles of the test and no ill-effects manifested themselves. At the bottom end of the r.p.m. scale the engine pulled very well indeed. It two-stroked smoothly and evenly at speeds down to 23 m.p.h. in top gear on a flat road where there was no appreciable head wind. The engine did not idle reliably at very low tick-over speeds.

Engine balance was very good and unimpaired at all normally used revs. Vibration was only apparent when the engine was screamed mercilessly in bottom and second gears. The transmission, too, was beautifully smooth and "taut," giving the impression, almost, that there was no rear chain there at all.

Acceleration and power on hills were probably rather better than those associated normally with small two-stroke machines. Similar praise might well be used in connection with the brakes. Both were smooth and

Concentric shafts for kick-start and foot gear-change levers are employed. The crankcase has a commendably neat exterior

e Luxe

Suspension

powerful in operation and required only light pressure at the hand, or foot, control, as the case may be. During the course of the test the front brake cable required adjustment on one occasion.

The gear change operates on the up-for-upward changes and down-for-downward changes principle. Except for the fact that it was not possible to position the gear-change lever so that it could be operated without moving the right foot from its footrest, no criticism could be applied to the gear change; even this is a small criticism, since the pedal provides a short, light movement. Noiseless upward changes could be easily effected between any pair of gears, provided that the pedal was moved with a slow deliberate movement. If desired, upward changes could be made just as quickly as the controls could be operated and, though the gears with this treatment emitted a slight "click" as they engaged, there was no danger of missing a gear or, apparently, of causing harm.

Downward changes could always be executed quickly, lightly, easily. The clutch freed perfectly; it was smooth in its take-up of the drive and light in operation. Bottom gear could always be selected noiselessly from neutral notwithstanding a rather high idling speed. Neutral was easily located from either first or second gears.

A high standard of comfort was provided by the combination of a good riding position and controls that were smooth and light in operation and well placed. The handlebars are of the rather wide and flat variety and have the grips comfortably positioned in relation to the saddle. Probably an even greater standard of comfort would be provided if the footrests were mounted slightly farther forward.

Apart from the fact that the rear chain appeared to be receiving too much oil and, in delivery tune, the exhaust pipe joints became messy, the only oil which appeared outside the engine-gear unit was that resulting from flooding the carburettor. The petroil filler cap also had a tendency to leak slightly.

A Lucas A.C. generator, with battery and coil ignition, was fitted to the machine tested

A driving beam that allowed full-throttle riding after dark was provided by the 6in head lamp. The dipswitch was conveniently placed on the left handlebar, and the head-lamp switch itself had a sweet, positive action. The ammeter is illuminated when the lights are switched on. The lamp and coil load was balanced at 30 m.p.h. in top gear. An "emergency" position is provided in the combined light and ignition switch. This causes the battery and rectifier to be by-passed, the coil in this case being fed directly from the A.C. generator (so that the machine can be started even if the battery is flat). With the emergency position of the switch in use, sufficient current was available to provide easy starting on the kickstarter.

The tool-box provided is fitted on the seat pillar. It is large enough to accommodate comfortably the tool-kit, but not, in addition, a repair outfit. The colour scheme is green, cream and chromium and the general appearance very smart.

Information Panel

SPECIFICATION

ENGINE : B.S.A. 123 c.c. (52 x 58 mm) single-cylinder two-stroke with three-speed gear in unit. Roller-bearing big-end ; ball bearings supporting mainshafts. Domed crown, Lo-Ex, aluminium-alloy piston. Detachable aluminium-alloy cylinder head. Petroil lubrication.

CARBURETTOR : Amal needle-jet type with twistgrip throttle control. Air filter, with external lever for cold-starting strangler.

TRANSMISSION : B.S.A. three-speed gearbox in unit with engine. Positive-stop, fully enclosed, foot-change. Top, 7.0 to 1. Second, 11.7 to 1. Bottom, 22.0 to 1. Cork insert clutch running in oil. Primary chain ⅜ x 0.225in in oil-bath chain case. Secondary chain ½ x 0.305in with guard over top run.

IGNITION and LIGHTING : Coil. Lucas 45-watt A.C. generator, Westinghouse rectifier and Lucas 5-amp. battery. Twin filament, 24 w. main bulb.

PETROIL CAPACITY : 1¾ gallons.

TYRES : Dunlop, 2.75 x 19in front and rear.

BRAKES : 5in diameter internal expanding front and rear.

SUSPENSION : Telescopic front fork with a single helical spring in each leg. Plunger-type rear-springing.

WHEELBASE : 50¼in. Ground clearance, 5in.

SADDLE : Mansfield. Height, 28in unladen.

WEIGHT : 171lb with dry tank and fully equipped.

PRICE : £74 3s. 6d., plus purchase tax (in Britain only), £20 0s. 7d.

ROAD TAX : £1 17s. 6d. a year ; 10s. 4d. a quarter. Half-rate if standard ration only.

MAKERS : B.S.A. Cycles, Ltd., Small Heath, Birmingham, 11.

DESCRIPTION : *The Motor Cycle*, October 6, 1949.

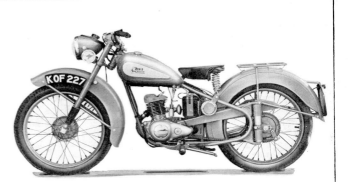

PERFORMANCE DATA

MEAN MAXIMUM SPEED : Bottom : 22 m.p.h.
Second : 40 m.p.h.
Top : 46 m.p.h.

MEAN ACCELERATION :

	10-20 m.p.h.	15-25 m.p.h.	20-30 m.p.h.
Bottom	3.2 secs	—	—
Second	4.2 secs	4.4 secs	4.2 secs
Top	—	8.4 secs	8.0 secs

Mean speed at end of quarter-mile from rest : maximum.
Mean time taken from rest to 30 m.p.h. : 7.8 secs.

PETROIL CONSUMPTION : At 20 m.p.h., 160 m.p.g. At 30 m.p.h., 144 m.p.g. At 40 m.p.h., 112 m.p.g.

BRAKING : From 30 m.p.h. to rest, 32 feet. (Surface, dry tar-macadam.)

TURNING CIRCLE : 11 feet.

MINIMUM NON-SNATCH SPEED : 13 m.p.h. in top gear.

WEIGHT PER C.C. : 1.4 lb.

ROYAL ENFIELD
BULLET

'It seems to me there has been more rubbish talked, and criticism made, about Enfields than about any other marque. I'm glad I have managed to turn a few heads by showing just what a Bullet can do!' So says Bedfordshire nurseryman Steve Linsdell, whose performances with a home-tuned 346 cc Royal Enfield Bullet in Vintage MCC meetings of the late 1970s have been little short of astounding. Steve's Bullet, a village hack purchased for just £10, began life as a 1950 model exactly as road-tested here.

Subsequent modifications included regrinding the cams (basically to BSA Gold Star profiles), opening up the inlet port and fitting a bigger inlet valve and, perhaps the major significant change, substituting a caged-roller big-end bearing for the admittedly archaic white-metalled free-floating big-end bush first adopted by Royal Enfield in the 1930s and used throughout the Second World War in the thousands of 346 cc Model WD/CO ohv singles supplied to the British Army.

The origin of the Bullet name is older still, and dates from September, 1932, when three new sports models (respectively of 248, 346, and 499 cc) were added to the Royal Enfield range.

The depth to which the cylinder barrel of the Bullet engine was spigoted into the crankcase mouth is seen clearly in this exploded view of a 1952 power unit. The semi-unit-construction, four-speed Albion gearbox was bolted directly to a facing at the rear of the crankcase

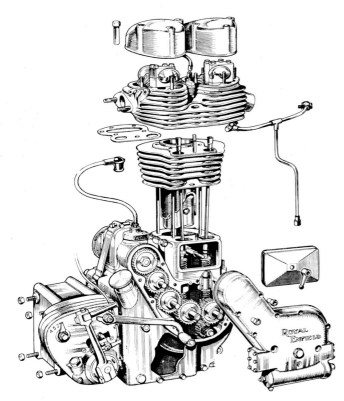

Common to all three, even at that remote period, were foot-change four-speed gearboxes which embodied an external gear-position indicator, an oil compartment integral with the crankcase, dry-sump lubrication and, naturally, the rubber-block cush-drive rear hub pioneered by Royal Enfield in the mists of history. Chilled-iron valve guides, and nitrided valve stems, were features very much in advance of contemporary motor cycle engineering.

That 1932 Bullet, however, had an inclined engine, exposed valve gear, Pilgrim oil pump, and chain-driven magneto, and for the true ancestor of the post-war model we turn to the 346 cc (70 × 90 mm) Model G, first revealed to the public in August, 1935.

Features of the new Model G included vertical cylinder, cast-in pushrod tunnel, totally-enclosed valve gear, magneto driven by train of gears, and a unique double-ended eccentric oil pump. This was the unit which was eventually to form the basis of the military machine and, indeed, the Model G was to continue into peacetime production – little changed except for the now almost obligatory telescopic front fork.

But in February, 1948, the Royal Enfield works trials team of Charlie Rogers, George Holdsworth, and Jack Plowright made a surprise appearance at the Colmore Cup Trial on three brand-new models equipped with oil-damped, pivoted fork rear suspension. These were the first prototypes of what was to be the new 346 cc Bullet, and although their Colmore Cup Trial debut was only modestly successful (Rogers and Plowright each won first-class awards, Holdsworth a second-class), the machine was to cover itself with glory in the International Six Days Trial that same autumn, when Charlie Rogers and Vic Brittain, both on Bullets, were members of the victorious British Trophy squad.

Although the layout of the Bullet engine was, obviously, inspired by the Model G unit, and the famous floating big-end bush was retained, in many other respects it was a complete redesign. Notably, the barrel was spigoted into the somewhat higher crankcase mouth by almost half its length, and the cylinder head was of light-alloy instead of cast-iron. Internals included a light-alloy connecting rod in RR56 material, and an oval-turned piston in low-expansion alloy. Power output was 18 bhp at 5,750 rpm.

The four-speed gearbox was bolted directly to a facing on the rear of the crankcase in semi-unit-construction style, and this permitted the use of a duplex primary chain tensioned by a slipper. The model joined the range for the 1949 season, priced at £171, as against the £146 asked for the standard (and still rigid-framed) Model G.

Not unexpectedly, the Bullet was tried in the Isle of Man Clubman's TT, where five models were entered for the Junior race, two of them ridden by Bill Lomas, and Sam Seston (who was later to become better known as a trials sidecar ace). Sad to say, only one of the five machines finished, although for the first two laps Bill Lomas had kept his Bullet up among the leading dozen.

Indeed, it was in the trials field, rather than as a speedster, that

the Bullet was to make its mark. At first, though, it had considerable prejudice to overcome. Trials machines, said the pundits, had to have rigid rear ends, otherwise they would be unable to find grip. With Royal Enfield's own rear spring units, the Bullet offered no more than 2 in rear wheel movement, but at least it was a start, and with teenager Johnny Brittain demonstrating just how well a springer could perform, the machine gained acceptance.

Gradually, a whole family of 346 cc Bullets came into being: trials, scrambles, and roadster. By the mid-1950s, Armstrong rear damper units had supplanted Enfield's own (and incidentally, now offered 3 in of wheel travel), and the coming of branded, higher-octane fuels had allowed the manufacturers to raise compression ratio to 7·25 to 1; this, in conjunction with new cam profiles, brought a welcome increase in performance.

For 1956, a completely new all-welded frame was introduced, as also was a crankshaft-mounted alternator, but the latter was reserved for lighting and battery-charging purposes, and an independent ignition supply was provided by a Lucas rotating-magnet magneto. By this time the 692 cc Super Meteor vertical twin (which was just a double-up of the 346 cc single) had had the benefit of a year's development, and in turn the Bullet was able to enjoy the development feedback of a modified combustion chamber and larger-diameter inlet valve.

The older-type frame was still fitted to the 346 cc cast-iron engined Clipper (in effect, the old Model G), but eventually the new frame was standardised and the old frame jigs were shipped out to the Enfield India subsidiary – where, ironically, they are still in use, although the Redditch works where they had originated has long disappeared.

On the competitions side, the trials Bullet evolved into the 346 cc Trials Works Replica, before being superseded by a 248 cc unit-construction trials mount derived from the Crusader. Meanwhile the roadster version soldiered on, with no more major changes, until the end of 1963 when a new 346 cc Bullet found its way into the Royal Enfield catalogue. But this, too, was a Crusader derivative owing nothing to the earlier Bullet and so, at last, the floating big-end bush had been laid to rest.

Above: *best-known exponent of the 346 cc Trials Bullet was Wolverhampton's Johnny Brittain. He is seen making a feet-up climb of Foyers, on the shores of Loch Ness, during the 1960 Scottish Six Days Trial, in which he was destined to finish fifth with 30 marks lost*

Above, left: *close-up of a classic trials unit of the 1950s, the 346 cc Bullet in 1951 form. Use of the crankcase castings to incorporate an oil tank was typical Royal Enfield practice. Unusually, the big-end bearing was a floating bronze bush, white-metal coated inside and out, operating in a forged light-alloy connecting rod*

ROAD TESTS OF
NEW MODELS

346 c.c. Royal Enfield

Overhead-valve Three-fifty With Sporting Performance

BEFORE the war there were several sports three-fifties on the market. Their engines thrived on revs and could withstand full-throttle driving all day long; they had manual ignition control, full-blooded exhausts, and slick gear changes. The performance approached that available from a 500 c.c. machine. In short, they were "enthusiasts mounts," which paid dividends when handled by an expert rider.

The Royal Enfield 346 c.c. Bullet revives the spirit of the type and has the advantage over its predecessors of

Front and rear suspension systems of the Bullet provided a high standard of riding comfort

ten years' research. With its excellent telescopic front fork and pivot-action rear suspension, the machine is endowed with handling qualities that are second to none. At the bottom end of the scale, the engine will pull uncommonly well, with a degree of smoothness surpassing that of many a modern parallel twin.

Minimum non-snatch speed of the Royal Enfield was a genuine 15-16 m.p.h. in top gear. From this speed the machine would accelerate quite happily, assuming intelli-

gent, co-ordinated handling of ignition lever and throttle. Above 20 m.p.h. in top gear, the ignition lever was required only if very hard acceleration was wanted. Above 25 m.p.h. in top, the ignition control was not called for at all. It was next to impossible to make the engine pink.

In restricted areas, on gradients that are sufficient of a drag to demand third gear from several five-hundred twins, the Bullet would climb effortlessly and smoothly in top gear, and it was even possible to shut off and open up again without the need to change down. Outstandingly good flexibility was one of the machine's most endearing characteristics. At the opposite end of the range, there was no limit that need be imposed to save the engine from being overdriven. Fifty m.p.h. averages were obtained without fuss or bother. If desired, the model would cruise in the upper sixties, and it was apparently as happy and effortless at that gait as it was at 45 m.p.h.

Engine characteristics were of the most pleasing kind. Use of small throttle openings and changing up at comparatively low revs gave a performance of the most gentlemanly character; the machine was then as docile as the most genteel tourer. In traffic, top gear was generally engaged at between 22 and 25 m.p.h. Out of restricted areas, with the machine given its head, the engine came into its own. Affection for the machine built up into high admiration.

The power comes in with a surge when the engine is revving in the higher ranges. Full performance in the gears results in remarkably good acceleration. During fast road work on the test machine, upward gear changes from second and third respectively were best made at about 48 m.p.h. and 65 m.p.h. The exhaust was loud with this type of riding and, though having a note that was stirring to the enthusiast, was probably objectionable to non-motor cyclists.

An aid to brisk acceleration was the excellent gear change. Upward or downward changes could be achieved by making an easy, short, light movement of the right foot. The change was entirely positive and it appeared to be impossible to "scrunch" a change or to miss a gear.

Starting from cold was generally accomplished at the third or fourth dig on the kick-starter, assuming a fairly accurate control setting and no flooding. It was necessary to close the air lever, set the ignition at three-quarters advance, and open the throttle fractionally. The correct throttle setting was very important

A neutral selector operated by a separate pedal on the end of the gear box is a feature of the machine

Bullet

if an easy start was to be achieved with certainty. The Bullet is fitted with a special compression-release valve in place of the more usual exhaust-valve lifter. The valve has the same effect as an exhaust-lifter; the control was well placed for ease of operation.

The same cannot be said of the front brake and clutch controls, which required considerably too great a hand reach. The clutch was rather heavy in operation. It freed perfectly at all times and did not appear to be adversely affected by abuse. It was sweet and smooth in its take-up of the drive. Bottom gear could be effortlessly selected from neutral when the engine was running and the machine stationary. The Royal Enfield is, of course, fitted with a neutral selector. This is operated by a separate pedal on the end of the gear box. To select neutral from any gear except bottom it is only necessary to lift the clutch and depress the pedal to the limit of its travel.

The engine was moderately quiet mechanically. There was a fair amount of noise from the valve gear. The piston was audible just after a cold start. Towards the end of the 600-mile test, a slight oil-leak appeared at the cylinder-head joint and there was oil seepage, too, from the oil-filler cap. Apart from this, the engine—and, indeed, the whole machine—remained remarkably clean.

No praise is too high for the steering and road-holding. The telescopic fork has a long, easy movement that suits the characteristics of the pivot-action rear-springing—which itself provides a higher standard of comfort than the majority of spring-frames available today. Whether the machine was being ridden slowly or at high speeds, the suspension absorbed road shocks most satisfactorily.

This excellent suspension has great advantages during bend-swinging or cornering at speed. Wavy- or bumpy-surfaced bends could be taken fast with the knowledge that the rear wheel would follow the front one with un-

A sturdy centre stand as well as a prop stand is fitted. The tool-box is of ample size

erring accuracy. Excellent comfort was provided over cobbled, city streets. Low-speed steering was first-class, allowing the rider to raise his feet to the rests the instant the clutch began to bite and to keep them there at the slowest crawl without resort to body lean or other balancing tricks.

Fitted as standard is a neat air cleaner. There are sturdy centre and prop stands, both of which are easy to use and both of which, when in use, ensure that the machine is absolutely safe from falling. The tool-box is of sensible proportions. The speedometer in its light-alloy forged housing is neatly mounted and easily read. Pillion footrests are fitted as standard.

Probably most outstanding of all is the machine's smart appearance coupled with its complete "functionality." Finish of the frame and mudguards is battleship grey; the tank is chrome and silver, and the usual parts are chromium-plated.

Information Panel

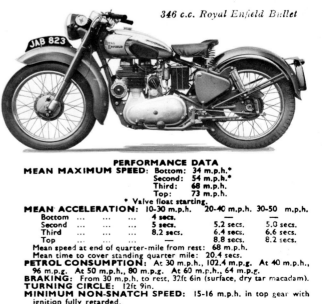

346 c.c. Royal Enfield Bullet

ENGINE: 346 c.c. (70 x 90 mm) single-cylinder o.h.v. Fully enclosed valve-gear operated by push-rods. Plain big-end bearing. Double-ball bearing on drive-side of mainshaft. Large-diameter plain bearing on timing side. Compression ratio, 6.5 to 1. Dry-sump lubrication. Oil-tank cast integral with crankcase; capacity, 4 pints.

CARBURETTOR: Amal: twistgrip throttle control; air slide operated by handlebar control.

IGNITION AND LIGHTING: Lucas Magdyno with manual ignition control. 7in head lamp with pre-focus light unit.

TRANSMISSION: Royal Enfield four-speed gear box with positive-stop foot-change incorporating patented neutral finder. Bottom, 15.8 to 1. Second, 10.2 to 1. Third, 7.37 to 1. Top, 5.67 to 1. Multi-plate clutch with bonded and cork inserts. Primary chain, ⅜in duplex, with hard-chromed slipper-type adjuster. Secondary chain, ⅝ x ¼in, with guard over top run. R.p.m. at 30 m.p.h. in top gear, 2,250.

FUEL CAPACITY: 3¼ gallons.

TYRES: Dunlop, 3.25 x 19in. Ribbed front, Universal rear.

BRAKES: 6in diameter front and rear.

SUSPENSION: Royal Enfield hydraulically damped front fork. Swinging-fork rear suspension with hydraulic damping.

WHEELBASE: 54in. Ground clearance, 6¼in unladen.

SADDLE: Terry. Unladen height, 29½in.

WEIGHT: 351 lb, with empty fuel tank (oil-tank full) and fully equipped.

PRICE: £140, plus Purchase Tax (in Britain only), £37 16s 0d.

ROAD TAX: £3 15s a year. £1 0s 8d a quarter. Half-duty only if standard ration is used.

MAKERS: Enfield Cycle Co., Ltd., Redditch, Worcs.

DESCRIPTION: *The Motor Cycle*, 11 March, 1943.

PERFORMANCE DATA

MEAN MAXIMUM SPEED:			
Bottom:	34 m.p.h.*		
Second:	54 m.p.h.*		
Third:	68 m.p.h.		
Top:	73 m.p.h.		

* Valve float starting.

MEAN ACCELERATION:	10-30 m.p.h.	20-40 m.p.h.	30-50 m.p.h.
Bottom	4 secs.	—	—
Second	5 secs.	5.2 secs.	5.0 secs.
Third	8.2 secs.	6.4 secs.	6.6 secs.
Top	—	8.8 secs.	8.2 secs.

Mean speed at end of quarter-mile from rest: 68 m.p.h.
Mean time to cover standing quarter mile: 20.4 secs.

PETROL CONSUMPTION: At 30 m.p.h., 102.4 m.p.g. At 40 m.p.h., 96 m.p.g. At 50 m.p.h., 80 m.p.g. At 60 m.p.h., 64 m.p.g.

BRAKING: From 30 m.p.h. to rest, 32ft 6in (surface, dry tar macadam).

TURNING CIRCLE: 12ft 9in.

MINIMUM NON-SNATCH SPEED: 15-16 m.p.h. in top gear with ignition fully retarded.

WEIGHT PER C.C.: 1.01 lb.

Of all the 500 cc vertical twins on the British market in the 1950s, the Royal Enfield must surely rank among the most ruggedly handsome. It had, too, an internationally proved sporting character (although, surprisingly, as an off-roadster rather than as a roadburner). And yet, with all that was going for it, the model never did achieve a very large following.

Based in Redditch, Worcestershire, the old-established Enfield Cycle Company rarely brought out a new design without incorporating as many existing parts as practicable. This policy applied to the 496 cc twin (first introduced in November, 1948) as much as to any other model in the range, and with bore and stroke dimensions of 64 × 77 mm it was, to some extent, a double-up of the 248 cc Model S single.

Designed and developed by Ted Pardoe and Tony Wilson-Jones, the machine made use of the familiar double-ended plunger oil pump employed on Enfield four-strokes since the early 1930s. Familiar, too, was the practice of embodying a half-gallon oil reservoir with the crankcase castings. And by housing the new engine in the pivoted-rear-fork frame already proved successful on the 346 cc Bullet single, production was certainly facilitated.

However, in other respects the twin broke new ground, for in conception and construction it was unlike its competitors from other British factories. Mounted on a common crankcase were two independent cast-iron cylinder barrels, each carrying its own light-alloy head with integral rocker box. The exhaust camshaft was carried along the front of the engine, the inlet camshaft at the rear, but the short pushrods were located at the outer ends of each camshaft (so that there would be an uninterrupted flow of cooling air between the cylinders, claimed the manufacturers).

Unlike most other British vertical twins, Ted Pardoe's 496 cc Royal Enfield employed two independent cylinder barrels, each with its own cylinder head. The camshaft drive chain was tensioned by means of a jockey sprocket carried on a moveable quadrant

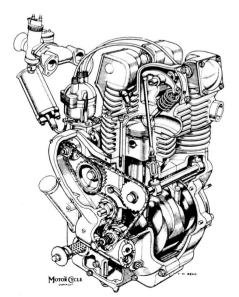

The camshafts were driven by chain, which was tensioned by a jockey pulley mounted on an adjustable quadrant. The crankshaft, carried on one timing-side ball bearing and one drive-side roller bearing, was a hollow, one-piece casting in alloy iron, with integral central flywheel, and was both statically and dynamically balanced before assembly (a practice carried out on Royal Enfield twin crankshafts right to the end of Interceptor production in the early 1970s).

Catalogued as a gentle tourer, the 496 cc Twin had a compression ratio of 6·5 to 1 in 1948 (which permitted it to run on the equivalent of present-day two-star fuel) and a leisurely power output of only 25 bhp at 5,500 rpm. No tearaway was this, but a top-gear slogger of immense charm and almost totally devoid of vibration.

Prototype testing had been carried out in the Swiss Alps, yet in a way that was an omen, because in the not too far distant future the model was to carry the British flag proudly in similarly mountainous terrain.

Throughout its production run, the Twin was to be dressed in various shades of grey with, for its first season, a most attractive battleship grey causing it to stand out from the pack. A change to silver grey came in 1950, for which season, also, a new cast-light-alloy front fork yoke incorporating the speedometer mounting was fitted.

It was in 1951, though, that the 496 cc Twin (it never did carry any other model designation) came into the headlines. That year, the strenuous International Six Days Trial was to be held in the mountains of Northern Italy, and greatly to the surprise of enthusiasts everywhere, the British team selectors invited the Royal Enfield works to prepare three twins for the tests to be held in mid-Wales.

The tests were successful, and when the teams were announced it was seen that 'Jolly Jack' Stocker, on one of the twins, was included in Britain's Trophy squad (which, in fact, was entirely vertical-twin mounted). In the trial itself, not only did Britain gain the International Trophy, but the Enfield works team which, in addition to Stocker, comprised Johnny Brittain and Stan Holmes on two more twins, collected a maker's team award with no marks lost.

True, there had been an anxious moment during the final day's speed test when Stan Holmes' model blew a cylinder head gasket, but because the design made use of separate heads, he was able to continue and retain his gold medal.

The ISDT twins had featured new die-cast crankcases, forged front-fork ends, and front mudguards which rose and fell with the wheel. These improvements were transferred to the production models for 1952, and it may be noted that the new crankcases brought the dry weight down to a very commendable 390 lb.

Again, Enfield twins were included in the British ISDT effort for the 1952 trial, located in the Bad Aussee district of Austria, but by then a 692 cc twin – a virtual double-up of the 346 cc Bullet – had joined the range, and two of the bigger twins were prepared for Trophy teamster Jack Stocker, and for one-legged sidecar driver Harold Taylor. The 496 cc version was not forgotten, and while Don Evans had one for the Vase 'A' team, Johnny Brittain used another as a Vase 'B' team member.

Alas, the event was tough, wet, and muddy. Don Evans came off heavily on the third day, suffering concussion which led to his retirement a day later, and Johnny Brittain dropped out of the fifth day with engine failure.

Nevertheless, the trial did bring a benefit to the standard twin which, thereafter, blossomed out with die-cast cylinder heads, a redesigned crankcase breather, and new low-expansion pistons. Less happily, due to a world shortage of chromium the handsome plated fuel tank was now painted all over and adorned with an embossed flash as still exhibited on Enfield India three-fifties.

To this point, the standard road going twins had employed a direct current dynamo and coil ignition, but a surprise change for 1954 was to a Lucas Magdyno system – at first as an optional extra, but later as original equipment.

Gradually, the 496 cc Royal Enfield twin slipped into the background. It still remained in the programme, but the factory gave more prominence to the 692 cc twin, which developed from the mildly-tuned Meteor into the Super Meteor, and then into the quite potent Constellation. With other models in the range, the small twin was given a cast-light-alloy fork-top headlamp mounting known as a Casquette, and for 1957 there was a considerable rejig whereby it gained, at last, a crankshaft-mounted alternator, and a new all-welded frame similar to that designed for the latest singles.

For all that, the good old 496 cc Twin was on its way out, and after just one more year of production it was supplanted by a newcomer of the same 496 cc capacity, but of rather different aspect. This was the Meteor Minor, in essence a double-up of the 248 cc Crusader and employing the Crusader's 70 × 64·5 mm dimensions, 8 to 1 compression ratio, pistons, and so on. Very much more livelier in performance than the older twin, the Meteor Minor was, perhaps, more in tune with the times. The general public no longer wanted a soft, chuffy stroller of a machine. But that, surely, was their loss.

Above: Motor Cycle's *Midland editor in 1951 was George Wilson, who made good use of a 500 cc Royal Enfield twin in reporting that September's International Six Days Trial, held at Varese in Northern Italy*

Below: *in addition to supplying a 500 cc Twin to British ISDT teamster Jack Stocker, the Royal Enfield factory also prepared three models for Sweden's 1951 Silver Vase squad. They are here seen preparing for the weigh-in at the start of the trial*

ROAD TESTS OF NEW MODELS

496 c.c. Royal

High Performance Allied to Excellent Handlin

WHEN deciding as to whether this machine or that meets one's requirements it is usual to assess good and bad features and make comparisons. In the main—where five-hundreds are considered—the features mostly concerned in the check-up are: handling, braking, gear change, highest comfortable cruising speed, acceleration and smoothness. In all of these, with possibly one exception, the 496 c.c. Royal Enfield Twin gains full marks; which makes it all the more disappointing that, because of problems of supply

The Royal Enfield Twin is a good-looker. Finish is in light grey

and export demands, delivery to the home market is still severely restricted.

So good are the majority of the Royal Enfield's features that it is difficult to select one and say of it that herein lies the model's most magnetic attribute. The engine started easily from hot or cold, requiring no particularly meticulous setting of the controls. To start from cold it was merely necessary to flood lightly, close the air lever, switch on the ignition and give a gentle prod on the kickstarter. The

air lever could be opened almost immediately the engine had started. The engine would idle as slowly and reliably after a cold start as it would after its normal working temperature had been reached. Mechanical noises were not marked and were inaudible to the rider when he was astride the machine.

From idling right up the throttle scale the pick-up was clean-cut and lively. Bottom gear could be selected effortlessly and noiselessly when the machine was stationary with the engine idling. At all times the clutch freed perfectly and it was silky smooth throughout the engagement period. The gear change proved to be perfect. No delay in pedal-movement was necessary when making upward or downward changes between any pair of gears. All that was required was a quick, light flick of the right toe. Neutral could be selected easily from bottom or second gears by means of the gear lever. The neutral selector could not be readily operated by a bewildered foot, because of its height and proximity to the kickstarter.

At traffic speeds the Royal Enfield proved to be tractable to an extent not hitherto experienced with a modern parallel twin. It would trickle happily at 15 m.p.h. in top gear—and indeed at an even lower speed if care was used in the manipulation of the twistgrip. From 20 m.p.h. in top gear, acceleration was all that was required under normal driving conditions. At such low speeds the combination of the engine's smooth power delivery and the famous Enfield cush-hub in the rear wheel eliminated any suggestion of roughness. Vibration was negligible throughout the speed range.

Acceleration through the gears was such as to give a favourable impression of the engine's capabilities. Cruising speeds of 60, 70 and 75 m.p.h. were commonplace throughout the test. There was at no time the slightest indication of excessive heat. The engine remained free from oil leaks until the performance data were being obtained; then cylinder-head seepage occurred. When the maximum-speed figures were being recorded there was a hindering diagonal wind.

Another factor contributing to the high average speeds obtainable was the good standard of the exhaust silencing. Only when the engine was revving at high r.p.m., such as when the road speed was in the region of 55-60 m.p.h. in third gear, was it felt that the exhaust noise might prove objectionable to pedestrians. Be-

Power unit is up-to-the-minute in design. Cylinder heads and cylinders are separate castings

Enfield Twin

Machine With Numerous Attractive Features

Coil ignition is employed. The high-output dynamo is chain driven

cause of the engine's excellent low-speed torque, acceleration in the higher gears is particularly good.

It is widely held in these days that the best rear suspension is achieved with the oil-damped, pivot-fork design. The excellence of the Royal Enfield suspension bears this out in every respect; a high standard of comfort is provided and high speeds are possible on the worst of surfaces. The test machine was driven over the time-section used in the British Experts' Trial and the time taken was within minutes only of that of the faster five-hundreds competing in the event. Corners and bends could be taken stylishly at speed, the wheels hugging the chosen line in the highest, confidence-instilling manner. The machine cornered with the effortless ease of a lightweight. Low-speed steering was equally good; the model could be ridden feet-up, slowly, and to a standstill. Handling on greasy surfaces was markedly good. The worst of road shocks were well cushioned from the rider—to such an extent, indeed, that there was a deliberate tendency between to ride over broken road edges, and seek out sunken man-hole covers.

Both brakes proved to be rather spongy. The front brake lacked real power, no matter how hard it was applied.

A comfortable riding position, as well as one which provided excellent control of the machine at high or low speeds, was furnished by the relationship between saddle, footrests and handlebar. The handlebar is mounted to the rear of the facia and has an orthodox bend, providing a sensible wrist angle. The reach was such that the rider naturally adopted a straight-arm posture. Relationship between the saddle and footrest was such that an angle of more than 90 deg was formed at the knee; but a disadvantage was that, in their optimum position, the footrests were not sufficiently high from the road and were often grounded during fast cornering or when the machine was being turned in narrow lanes. Riding comfort, it was felt, would have been enhanced had the tank width been less across the kneegrips.

The controls were reasonably well positioned for ease of operation. More hand reach than is desirable for easy and rapid manipulation was required to operate the clutch and front-brake controls. Throttle, rear-brake and gear controls were all light in operation; both rear-brake and gear pedals are readily adjustable relative to the footrests.

Two stands are fitted, a prop and a centre stand. The propstand leg was too long for easy manipulation and general machine safety. Moreover, it was weak at the hinge, the welding fracturing during the test. Operation of the centre stand required knack plus considerable effort.

Finish of the machine is a smart battleship grey and chromium. The combination of an attractive colour scheme and trim lines make the machine æsthetically right. More important, however, is that with its good all-round performance and excellent handling the Royal Enfield Twin takes its place proudly among the foremost machines in its capacity class.

Information Panel

SPECIFICATION

ENGINE : 496 c.c. (64 x 76 mm) parallel twin o.h.v. with separate cylinders and heads. Fully enclosed valve-gear. Ball and roller bearings supporting one-piece alloy-iron cast crankshaft. Plain, split big-end bearings. Light-alloy connecting rods. Slightly-domed aluminium-alloy pistons. Standard compression ratio, 6.5 to 1. Dry-sump lubrication with the oil compartment cast integral with, and at rear of crankcase : capacity, 4 pints.

CARBURETTOR : Amal, twistgrip throttle control and handlebar-mounted air lever.

IGNITION AND LIGHTING : Coil through vertical distributor incorporating auto-advance and retard. Lucas 3½in dia. dynamo. Switch, ammeter, voltage control and ignition warning light carried in box alongside seat tube. Lucas 7in headlamp.

TRANSMISSION : Royal Enfield four-speed gear box with positive-stop foot-change incorporating neutral-finder. Bottom, 13.9 to 1 Second 9.0 to 1. Third, 6.5 to 1. Top, 5.0 to 1 Multi-plate clutch with bonded and cork inserts. Primary chain, ⅜in duplex with hard-chromed, slipper-type adjuster Secondary chain, ½ x ⅜in with guard over top run. R.p.m. at 30 m.p.h. in top gear. 1,950.

FUEL CAPACITY : 3¼ gallons.

TYRES : Both Dunlop. Front, 3.25 x 19in ribbed. Rear, 3.50 x 19in Universal.

BRAKES 6in diameter front and rear.

SUSPENSION : Royal Enfield hydraulically damped front fork. Swinging-arm rear suspension with hydraulic damping.

WHEELBASE 54in.

SADDLE : Terry. Unladen height, 29½in.

WEIGHT : 410lb fully equipped and with full fuel and oil tanks.

PRICE : £167 10s plus Purchase Tax (in Great Britain only), £45 4s 6d.

ROAD TAX : £3 15s a year ; £1 0s 8d a quarter.

MAKERS : Enfield Cycle Company Ltd., Redditch, Worcs.

DESCRIPTION : *The Motor Cycle*, 4 November, 1948.

496 c.c. Royal Enfield Twin

PERFORMANCE DATA

MEAN MAXIMUM SPEED : Bottom : *35 m.p.h
Second : *56 m.p.h.
Third : *75 m.p.h
Top : *85 m.p.h
*Valve float starting

MEAN ACCELERATION	10-30 m.p.h.	20-40 m.p.h.	30-50 m.p.h.
Bottom	2·4 secs	—	—
Second	4 secs	3·2 secs	3·8 secs
Third	6·2 secs	5 secs	4·8 secs
Top	—	6·8 secs	6·4 secs

Mean speed at end of quarter-mile from rest : 75 m.p.h.
Mean time to cover standing quarter-mile : 16·2 secs.

PETROL CONSUMPTION : At 30 m.p.h., 81 m.p.g. At 40 m.p.h. 74 m.p.g. At 50 m.p.h., 65 m.p.g. At 60 m.p.h., 57 m.p.g.

BRAKING From 30 m.p.h. to rest, 38ft (surface, damp tar macadam).

TURNING CIRCLE : 13ft.

MINIMUM NON-SNATCH SPEED : 12 m.p.h. in top gear.

WEIGHT PER C.C. : 0.83 lb.

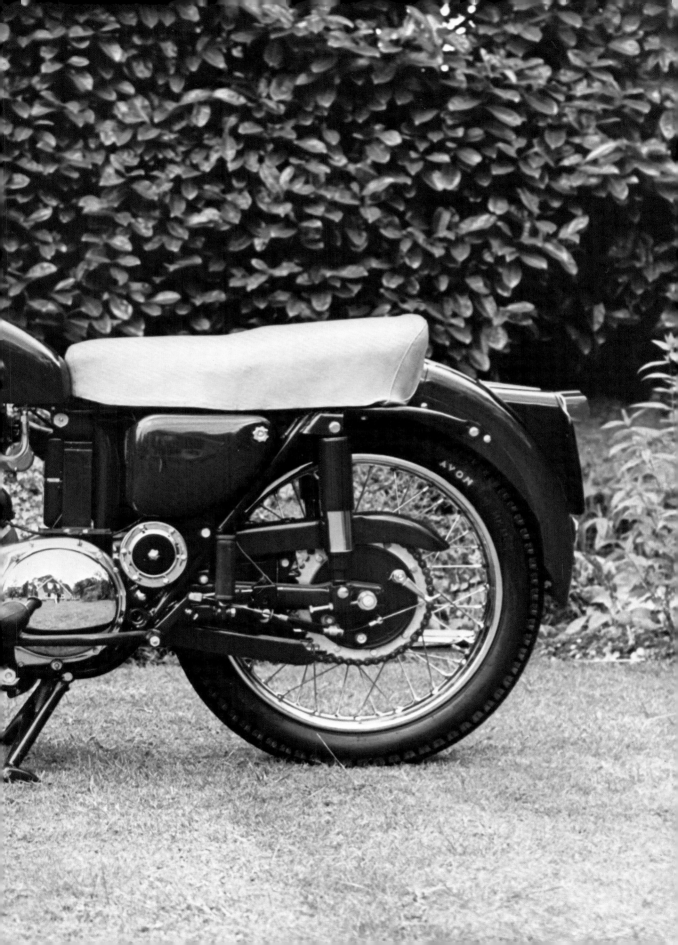

ARIEL
RED HUNTER

Credit for that much-loved single from Selly Oak, the 497 cc Ariel Red Hunter, lies at the door of two famous designers. Certainly it was Edward Turner who, for 1933, evolved the first red-and-chrome-tank beauties to carry the Red Hunter name; but the engine on which he based the exercise was a Val Page product – in much the same way that, three years later, Turner was to take Page's Triumph range of Mark V singles and, with the touch of the expert cosmetician, transform them into the handsome Tiger series.

As a preliminary to the story, however, let us start with the 1931 Ariels. This was the last year of Page's upright-engined 497 cc single, because the main emphasis had switched to a pair of duplex-frame 497 cc machines respectively two-valve and four-valve ohv, in which the engines sloped so much as to be near horizontal.

For 1932, the two-valver was dropped, in favour of a new short-stroke 499 cc four-valve unit, mounted upright in a single-down-tube frame. The new engine looked most impressive, but big trouble was looming on the horizon. Britain was entering a deep financial depression, and before 1932 was out, the Ariel company was bankrupt.

Jack Sangster, the managing director, threw in his personal fortune, and managed to save enough from the wreckage to keep the Ariel name alive, although operations were on a more restricted scale, carried out in one small part of the former Ariel premises. To emphasise Jack Sangster's faith, the new firm took the title of Ariel Works (JS) Ltd.

Obviously, there was no hope now of continuing the full eight-model range as had been listed for 1932, with its multiplicity of types and frame designs. Economy of production was the watchword and, accordingly, Edward Turner proposed a 1933 range, still of eight models but all employing the same frame, even though they extended from a 350 cc single to the 600 cc Square Four.

In truth the range was slightly less extensive than it seemed, because there were three 348 cc singles (three-speed standard, four-speed standard, and Red Hunter), two versions of the 557 cc side-valve, and *four* 497 cc models comprising three-speed standard, four-speed standard, four-speed de luxe, and Red Hunter.

Essentially, the three-fifties were smaller-bore versions of the five-hundred, and so it all boiled down to just *one* basic two-valve ohv engine. For that, Turner took the 1931 Val Page design, but gave it the crankcase and timing-chest assembly of the 1932 four-valve.

Top-of-the-range singles were the 348 (72 × 85 mm) and 497 (86·4 × 85 mm) Red Hunters, a catchy name, but rather more than that because they each had a shapely new chromium-plated fuel tank with bright red top and side panels lined with gold paint, while a big triangular tank-top panel served to display the speedometer, ammeter, filler cap, and panel lamp.

For the larger-capacity mount (but not the smaller), each customer was provided with two pistons; the 7 to 1 compression ratio piston was for road use, and with it the engine developed a claimed 28 bhp. The alternative high-compression piston was for racing, and although no power output was quoted, it was reputed to give the Red Hunter a maximum in excess of 90 mph.

Probably it did, but although Hartley-tuned Ariels were to do very well in the less-important racing events, it has to be said that the only Senior TT Ariel victory was cinematic, when George Formby, riding a Red Hunter thinly disguised as a 'Rainbow', took the laurels in the 1935 film, *No Limit*.

Trials and scrambles, though, were something else, and in the off-road type of competition such riders as Len and Joe Heath, Monty Banks, Alfie West, Jack White, and many more were to take the Red Hunter right to the top of the tree. Indeed, an October, 1936, Ariel advertisement could trumpet the fact that Red Hunter models had won no fewer than 32 important trials during the 1936 season, and that did not take into account the lesser events, class cups, and first-class awards.

Possibly the most elegant British single of all, the 497 cc Ariel Red Hunter is seen here in 1955 form. Colour was claret, with a light tan dual seat

Gradually, the trials versions of the Red Hunters evolved into models in their own right, with lighter, higher-ground-clearance frames, and it is an interesting fact that the 350 cc W/NG ohv machines built for the British Army during the Second World War were really detuned Red Hunter engines, fitted into Ariel trials frames. The point was certainly appreciated by the troops to which the machines were issued!

As intimated in the opening paragraph of our 1951 road test, actual changes in engine specification were remarkably few over the years, which speaks volumes for the 'rightness' of the original design. The type of cylinder head seen here, with separate light-alloy rocker boxes, had been introduced as far back as 1938, and the compensated-link plunger rear springing was an optional extra in the 1939 programme.

In post-war years the 497 cc engine was to gain still greater trials fame, because it formed the heart of GOV132, almost certainly the most illustrious trials machine of all time and the bike on which Sammy Miller made his reputation. Right up to the two-stroke invasion of the 1970s, too, the Ariel was an absolute must for sidecar trials work, as Ron Langston, Alan Morewood, Peter Wraith, Roger Martin, and Roy Bradley demonstrated, week after week throughout the muddy winter months.

Of course, these were competition variants on the original Red Hunter theme, but there were variants in the roadster range, also. By 1954 pivoted rear-fork suspension was in use, with the fork arms formed from box-section pressings, and a new cylinder barrel with integral pushrod tunnels had been adopted. For the following year, there was a light-alloy cylinder head on the 497 cc model (but not the 348 cc) and, eventually an all-alloy engine – as used in the trials and scrambles Ariels – could be specified for the roadster.

Possibly the most handsome Red Hunters of all, although this is a personal opinion, were those from 1956 onward. By that time a new duplex tubular frame was in use, and the headlamp

At one time, the 497 cc Ariel was used almost universally for sidecar trials work. The outfit used by Frank and Kay Wilkins was typical of the 1950s

was housed in a somewhat ecclesiastical cowl. There were full-width hubs, automatic rear chain lubrication, full rear chain enclosure if required, and a gorgeous finish of claret, set off by the lovely light tan of the dual seat.

On the competitions side, the award-gathering continued – led, of course, by Sammy Miller, but not forgetting the efforts of Gordon Blakeway, Ron Langston, Bob Ray (out of retirement to win the 1957 Beggars Roost Trial with only one mark lost) and, across in Ireland, Benny Crawford.

By the time Miller's HT5 trials mount reached the zenith of its development, it weighed under 250 lb. That was the good news. The bad news was that the road-going Red Hunter from which the HT5 had been derived was dead – mortally wounded in 1959 (or so it was said) by an Arrow.

No individual trials machine ever achieved such fame as GOV132, Sammy Miller's highly-special 497 cc Ariel, which won nearly 600 awards in events such as this 1959 national Bemrose Trial

ROAD TESTS OF NEW MODELS

497 c.c. Ariel Re

Famous Overhead-valve Sports Model T

FOR nearly twenty years Ariels have listed a 497 c.c. Red Hunter. Since the original two-valve model was introduced in 1933, very few changes in the engine design have taken place, though detail modifications such as total valve-gear enclosure and telescopic forks have become part of the general scheme of things to keep the model in step with current trends.

As all who study design practice well know, when few changes are made to any machine it means that (a) the manufacturer concerned is not suffering mechanical bothers, and (b) that

A straightforward and robust single – the Red Hunter Ariel

the model is proving popular with the public. And so far as the Ariel Red Hunter is concerned, the reasons behind these twin facts are simple ones: the design is straightforward and the construction robust; and, considered in its particular "type classification," the Red Hunter's all-round performance is most satisfying.

Cold or hot, engine starting was always easily accomplished: when cold on the second or third kick-starter depression, and when hot, invariably on the first. A certain cold start required only that the carburettor was flooded lightly, then, provided the

throttle was barely open, the engine would fire, as has been mentioned, on the second or third prod on the kick-starter. With the exhaust-valve lifter operated in the approved manner, kick-starting called for no physical effort of any consequence. The air lever was at no time required during the test.

For the remaining starts after the first of the day, very light flooding was again sufficient to provide the required mixture strength. As soon as the engine had started, the twistgrip could be rolled right back against its closed stop with the certain assurance that a reliable tickover would result. At idling speeds, valve-gear and piston were audible if the ignition was fully advanced. On full retard, however, at which ignition setting the slowest and most reliable idling resulted, the piston was all but silent.

On the road with the Red Hunter, engine noises—piston slap chiefly—were apparent only as an undertone, which was barely heard above the sounds of the wind, and, at high engine r.p.m., the exhaust. Exhaust noise was not obtrusive in open country, but it was too reverberant when the machine was being driven in average-width city streets.

From idling speeds right up through the speed range the pick-up was clean-cut and brisk. Though the tendency to pinking was not particularly marked—even when the sidecar was fitted—it was necessary to use the ignition control in close conjunction with the throttle if the best results were to be obtained. Low-speed torque is particularly good; good to a degree, indeed, that gives one the initial impression that the engine falls into the "woofly" big-single class. Minimum non-snatch speed in top (solo) gear was 17 m.p.h., and the transmission at speeds above that was entirely free from harshness. Transmission smoothness, in fact, proved to be one of the Red Hunter's superior features.

Acceleration from 20 m.p.h. could be satisfactorily brisk in either top or third gears without fuss, provided the ignition control was used judiciously. However, if the right grip was twisted in earnest, and the full performance used in the indirect gears, the Red Hunter was transformed from a single definitely possessing those characteristics which are called "gentlemanly" into one in the famous big-single tradition: a tradition that will assuredly never die so long as there are motor cyclists.

In this case, acceleration was all that the majority of avid sports riders are ever likely to require. Peak r.p.m. in the indirect gears is achieved remarkably quickly. The gear change is utterly positive, and the pedal may be operated by pivoting the right foot in a short arc about the footrest. Snap changes could be made if desired, there being no doubt about certain engagement, though the change would be accompanied by a scrunch from the pinions. Snap upward gear changes, however, are rarely, if ever, required outside

Excellent low-speed torque was a feature of the 497 c.c. overhead-valve engine

Hunter Single

Solo and Sidecar Forms

The Watsonian Albion coupé sidecar was found to be roomy and comfortable

the sphere of competitive events, and the Red Hunter gear change was clean and sweet provided one caused the pedal to pause in mid-travel, or moved the pedal with a leisurely, deliberate movement. Pedal movement was pleasantly short and light. All the indirect gears were silent on both drive and overrun.

The clutch freed perfectly, and it was light in operation and sweet in its take-up of the drive. It required no adjustment or other attention throughout the test. As with all other hand-operated controls, that for the clutch was well placed in relation to its respective grip. The grips, in turn, go to provide, in conjunction with the footrest and saddle position, what is probably one of the most comfortable riding postures of the present day. The handlebar is of the flat, nearly straight pattern with the grips turned slightly to the rear.

Supreme comfort, however, was not the only attribute of the Ariel's riding position. In addition, it proved to be one which automatically sets the rider in a posture which means much in terms of maximum control—whether the speed be a traffic-crawl or a 70 m.p.h. bat on a fast dual-carriageway. Speeds in the 70 m.p.h. category were commonplace during the test, and were in no way considered excessive so far as the engine's capabilities were concerned. At 40 m.p.h. to 50 m.p.h. the engine was at its best, developing sufficient power to deal with steep gradients without a slackening in speed, and turning over with delightful smoothness. Above 60 m.p.h. there was high-frequency vibration which was not apparent lower down the scale.

If the machine had proved an attractive solo, it was found to be even more likeable as a sidecar mount. When fully laden with a complement of three males (scaling *in toto* some 30-stone), it would cruise quite comfortably at speeds in the region of

50-55 m.p.h. The speedometer fitted, incidentally, proved to have an error of rather more than 10 per cent. Acceleration was apparently little impaired by full loading, and neither was handling affected. Although there was sometimes, at high speeds on irregular surfaces, an impression of more than desired lightness in the fork and rear-springing characteristics, neither suspension was found to bottom even on cross-country going.

The Watsonian Albion sidecar gave satisfaction in nearly every direction. Six-foot adults found it roomy, there being plenty of leg space whether the legs were stretched out or bent at the knees. A greater than average stature male—5ft 10in tall—could wear a hat inside and still have adequate clearance below the hood. But, in any case, the hood was seldom required—thanks to the adequate side panels, there are no draughts and all but the heaviest rain was deflected overhead.

Information Panel

The 497 c.c. Ariel Red Hunter single

SPECIFICATION

ENGINE : 497 c.c. (81.8 × 95 mm) single-cylinder o.h.v. Fully-enclosed valve gear operated by push-rods from a single cam. Double-row roller bearing big-end. Roller and ball main bearings supporting drive-side of mainshaft, ball bearing on timing side Compression ratio, 6.8 to 1. Dry-sump lubrication with double-plunger pump ; tank capacity, 6 pints.
CARBURETTOR : Amal ; twistgrip throttle control. Air slide operated by handlebar lever.
IGNITION and LIGHTING : Lucas Magdyno with manual ignition control. Long 3in 45w dynamo. 7¼in headlamp, with 30/30w main bulb controlled by handlebar switch.
TRANSMISSION : Burman four-speed gear box with positive foot control. Bottom, 12.6 to 1. Second, 8 to 1. Third, 6 to 1. Top 4.7 to 1. Sidecar ratios : Bottom, 15.3 to 1. Second, 9.7 to 1. Third, 7.2 to 1. Top, 5.7 to 1. Multi-plate clutch with cork inserts. Primary chain, ½ 0.305in in cast-aluminium oil-bath case. Secondary chain, ⅝ in with guard over both runs.
FUEL CAPACITY : 3¼ gallons.
TYRES : Dunlop. Front, 3.00 20in ribbed ; rear, 3.25 19in studded.
BRAKES : Both 7in diameter 1⅛in wide ; fulcrum adjusters
SUSPENSION : Ariel telescopic front fork. Ariel link-type rear-springing, with springs for compression and rebound.
WHEELBASE : 56in. Ground clearance, 5in unladen.
SADDLE : Lycett. Unladen height, 30in.
WEIGHT : 385lb, with one gallon of fuel and fully equipped.
PRICE : £146 ; with Purchase Tax (in Britain only), £185 8s 5d. Spring-frame extra, £16 ; with P.T., £20 6s 5d.
ROAD TAX : Solo £3 15s a year ; £1 0s 8d a quarter. Sidecar, £5 a year ; £1 7s 7d a quarter.
MAKERS : Ariel Motors; Selly Oak, Birmingham, 29.
DESCRIPTION : *The Motor Cycle, 28 November, 1950.*

SIDECAR

MODEL : Watsonian Albion single-seater coupé.
CHASSIS : Tubular construction with Silentbloc wheel mounting. Silco-manganese, 1¼in wide seven-leaf quarter-eliptic rear springs ; eyes and shackles fitted with grease nipples. Front suspension by four coil springs. Taper-roller bearing wheel hubs. Wheel fitted with 3.25 19in tyre. Four-point chassis attachment with adjustable rise lug to allow correct fitting to different makes of machine.
WEIGHT : 90lb approx.

BODY : Ash framework panelled in sheet steel. Dimensions : Overall length, 85in ; squab to nose, 54in ; width inside at shoulder level, 21½in ; height from cushion to roof, 34in ; squab, 23in high × 21½in wide ; seat, 20 20in ; luggage boot, 15in deep × 22in wide 29in long. Weight, approximately 110lb. Luggage grid and bumper bar standard.
PRICE : Complete, £57 10s 0d ; with P.T. (in Britain only), £72 16s 8d.
DESCRIPTION : *The Motor Cycle, 6 October, 1949 ; 9 November, 1950.*

PERFORMANCE DATA
(Sidecar figures in brackets)

MEAN MAXIMUM SPEED : Bottom :* 40 (30) m.p.h.
Second :* 62 (49) m.p.h.
Third : 77 (62) m.p.h.
Top : 85 (63) m.p.h.
* Valve float occurring.

MEAN ACCELERATION :

		10-30 m.p.h.	20-40 m.p.h.	30-50 m.p.h.
Bottom	...	3.2 (3.8) secs	3.4 (—) secs	— (—) secs
Second	...	5.2 (5.8) secs	4 (7.2) secs	4 (7.4) secs
Third	...	— (—) secs	5.4 (8.4) secs	5.8 (9.4) secs
Top	...	— (—) secs	6.8 (11.4) secs	6.8 (13.4) secs

Mean speed at end of quarter mile from rest : 71 (54) m.p.h.
Mean time to cover standing quarter-mile : 13 (22.2) secs.
PETROL CONSUMPTION : At 30 m.p.h. 112 (70) m.p.g. At 40 m.p.h 84 (53) m.p.g. At 50 m.p.h, 67 (40) m.p.g. At 60 m.p.h 53 (32) m.p.g.
BRAKING : From 30 m.p.h. to rest, 29ft 6in (52ft) (surface, dry tar macadam).
TURNING CIRCLE : 14ft 4in.
MINIMUM NON-SNATCH SPEED : 16 (13) m.p.h. in top gear with ignition fully retarded.
WEIGHT Per C.C. : 0.77 (1.18) lb.

BSA
STAR TWIN

One line in the road test of the 1952 497 cc BSA Star Twin says it all; '. . . the Star Twin has few equals as a machine for sustained, high-speed road work.' Just how incontrovertibly true was that observation, the events of September of the same year were to prove, because BSA embarked on what just has to be the most audacious test ever carried out in the full glare of the spotlight.

The idea was simple enough. An official observer from the ACU would be invited to visit the BSA factory at Small Heath, Birmingham, and there select at random from the batch currently under construction, three perfectly ordinary Star Twins. The three machines would then be put through a demonstration ride, every move being logged by the observer to ensure that there was no cheating.

But *what* a demonstration ride! It was to be no less than a 5,000-mile tour of Europe, taking in the International Six Days Trial on the way. Three riders were selected (Norman Vanhouse, Fred Rist, and Brian Martin), and in view of the stiff task ahead, the three chosen machines were each equipped with such ISDT necessities as competitions-style number plates, tank-top map case and toolbag, ex-RAF clock, and 49-tooth, instead of 45-tooth, rear sprockets.

In due course the trio reached Vienna, where the addition of more ISDT equipment (air bottle, extra tyre security bolts, sump undershield, etc) was permitted. It is a matter of historical record that all three completed the event with clean sheets, earning BSA a manufacturer's team award and also, for Birmingham MCC, a club team prize.

Then it was on with the tour, through Germany, Denmark, Sweden, and Norway, and so to a tumultuous welcome on their return to Birmingham. The ride earned for BSA the coveted Maudes Trophy, presented for the most meritorious demonstration ever carried out in a particular year, and never was the cup more justly earned.

The three Star Twins had been registered as MOL 301, MOL 302, and MOL 303, and nobody really knows what happened to them after they had been returned to the factory. Possibly, as was usual BSA practice, they were sold off cheaply to employees. Certainly MOL 301 and MOL 302 seem to have departed to that motorway in the sky, but many years later MOL 303 was to come to light again in curious circumstances.

There it was, partly cannibalised, and at some stage in its past life half-heartedly converted to a chopper, sitting forlornly on a scrapheap at the rear of a small Birmingham motor cycle shop, just about to close its doors for ever.

At that point it was rescued by Birmingham vintage enthusiast Colin Wall and, over a considerable period, gradually restored to the condition in which it had originally left Small Heath for its ISDT exploit, 26 years before. It was the model which Norman Vanhouse had ridden through the test, and man and machine were at last reunited when Norman rode the reborn MOL 303 in the Mallory Park 'Parade of the Greats', in the spring of 1978.

Resembling the Val Page 650 cc Triumph twin of the early

1930s in employing a single camshaft at the rear, and with the gearbox bolted to the crankcase in semi-unit-construction style, the original 495 cc (62 × 82 mm) Model A7 BSA was intended for introduction in 1940, but the Second World War put the mockers on that scheme, and it was not until 1946 that it was at last produced. First example off the post-war assembly track was flown straight to Paris for display at the first Motor Cycle Show held since the return of peace.

It is likely that Val Page, in his spell at BSA immediately before the war, had laid down the basic lines of the twin, but the actual detail design work was by Herbert Perkins. However, the Model A7, as first made, did have a number of built-in bothers. In particular, the combustion chamber shape did not cope very well with the 75-octane pool petrol of the day, the engine used to overheat in consequence, and would 'run on' for several seconds after the ignition was switched off.

Meanwhile Bert Hopwood had been recruited on to the design staff, and the 646 cc (70 × 84 mm) Model A10 Golden Flash which joined the range for 1950 was from his drawing board. Ostensibly, it was an enlarged version of the A7, but in fact the resemblance was only superficial. Major difference was

Big brother of the BSA Star Twin was the 650 cc BSA Golden Flash, designed by Bert Hopwood. Internal construction of both engines was similar, and each featured a rear-mounted camshaft and sloping pushrods.

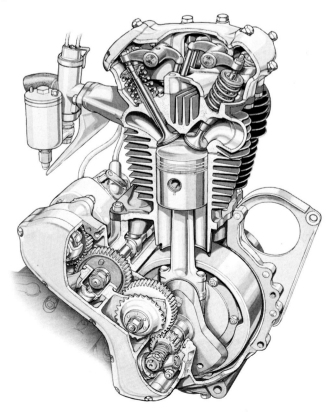

Above: *(left to right) Norman Vanhouse, Fred Rist and Brian Martin on their BSA A7 Star Twins, before setting out on their victorious 1952 Maudes Trophy test. As part of the test, all three machines won gold medals in that year's ISDT.*

Right: *Norman Vanhouse, Brian Martin, and former BSA competitions manager, Bert Perrigo are reunited with MOL303, one of the three Maudes Trophy machines, at Mallory Park's 1978 Vintage Race of the Year. On the left is Colin Wall, who restored the bike from scrap condition.*

in cylinder-head design, the bigger unit employing narrow angle valves, a shallower combustion chamber, and more generous head finning.

The first A7 Star Twin, with high-compression pistons, twin carburettors, and plunger-type rear suspension had been added to the range for 1949, but both this model and its more humdrum A7 forebear were given an entirely new engine from 1951 onward. Bert Hopwood had been at work, and the new unit was shorter in stroke but larger in bore and, as might be expected, had 95 per cent of its parts interchangeable with those of the 646 cc A10 Golden Flash. The latest cylinder head, too, was A10 pattern, and incorporated inlet and exhaust valves in austenitic steel. Capacity was now 497 cc. The sports version, the A7 Star Twin, reverted to a single Amal carburettor.

And so to 1952, the momentous year in which the trio of Star Twins captured the Maudes Trophy. But that was not the only remarkable Star Twin achievement of the year, because in the United States, the BSA distributor for the West Coast, Hap Alzina, got to work on a model with which Gene Thiessen was to make a bid for the American Class C (standard catalogue machine) speed record.

No major changes to the bike were permitted, but by careful workbench attention Hap Alzina got the unit to turn out 40 bhp, using 80 octane fuel and a compression ratio of 8 to 1. The result was an outstanding success, with Thiessen taking the record with a two-way flying-mile speed of 123·69 mph.

For the past season or so, the finish of the Star Twin had been uninspiring. The world nickel shortage had accounted for the dropping of the chromium plated tank and, instead, the tank finish had been all-silver enamel, with embossed metal badges. But the finish improved for 1953 when chromium-plated tank side panels returned, and the Star Twin adopted its most handsome livery yet, with a frame of dark green, tank and mudguards in polychromatic light green, and large three-dimensional name badges in Diakon clear plastic. Mechanical details were unchanged, except that the front brake drum diameter was increased to 8 in.

Nevertheless, the model was nearing the end of its run, and when the 1955 BSA programme was revealed, the Star Twin was missing. In its place came a slightly more sophisticated 497 cc sports twin, equipped for the first time with pivoted instead of plunger rear suspension, and with high-lift cams, high-compression pistons, and a one-piece light-alloy cylinder head. The two-tone green finish was retained, but the name had changed to the Shooting Star.

ROAD TESTS OF
NEW MODELS

The 497 c.c. B.S.A

A High-performance Model in the

ZESTFUL acceleration, excellent road holding, and the ability to devour the miles in unobtrusive fashion, are but a few of the attributes of the 497 c.c. B.S.A. Star Twin. Fitted with the compact, semi-unit construction B.S.A. engine and gear box, the machine is the sports version of the now celebrated A7. A redesigned engine was employed for 1951. Good as the pre-1951 Star Twin was, the present model is decidedly better. There is now only one carburettor instead

The Star Twin now has a single carburettor and an 8in-diameter front brake

of two; and carburation, once the engine is warm, is as clean as could be desired. With the present B.S.A. gear box, the gear-change is among the best encountered on present-day machines.

A sports machine in the true tradition, the Star Twin requires "knowing" if it is to give of its best on Pool-quality fuel. The throttle must be used intelligently in conjunction with the manual ignition control; engine revolutions must be maintained in the higher ranges; in short, there must be knowledgeable understanding of the engine's characteristics. These requirements fulfilled, the Star Twin has few equals as a machine for sustained, high-speed road work.

Used to the full in conjunction with the indirect gear ratios, the twin-cylinder engine provides acceleration of no mean order. In bottom and second gears the speed can be stepped up with exhilarating rapidity; and even in third or top gears the build-up from medium to peak r.p.m. is shatteringly quick. At 70 m.p.h. in top gear, the machine noticeably surged forward in response to a tweak of the twistgrip. Vibration was negligible. No matter how hard the engine was driven or for how long, there was at no time any indication that it was being over-driven.

During the test, cruising speeds in the seventies were used as often as road conditions permitted; 70 m.p.h., indeed, was felt to be the machine's happiest cruising speed. The engine turned over smoothly and sweetly, and with no more fuss than there was in the fifties. That it would cruise without being over-driven at higher speeds, say, 75-80 m.p.h., there is little doubt; but, at speeds of over 70 m.p.h., wind pressure became tiring to the rider's arms. At a true road speed of 65 m.p.h., the speedometer registered approximately 5 m.p.h. fast.

An idea of the Star Twin's performance may be gained from the fact that on several (admittedly favourable) occasions during the course of the 700-mile test, 20 miles were covered in as many minutes. Notwithstanding such usage, no engine oil leaks were apparent at the end of the test. A small seepage of oil appeared at the oil-tank filler-cap, and some messiness resulted through excessive oil issuing from the oil-tank breather if the tank was over-filled.

Engine performance is but one of the ultimate factors in the attainment of high road averages. Steering and road-holding are equally important; as far as the B.S.A. was concerned, these characteristics were fully up to desirable standards. The long, soft action of the B.S.A. telescopic front fork dealt adequately with every type of going encountered. Steering was of the hairline variety. A steering damper is fitted; during most of the test it was set just barely biting.

The action of the plunger-type rear springing was pleasantly soft around the static-load position and it proved to be equally effective whether the machine was ridden one- or two-up. A criticism is that the suspension clashed on the occasions when deep road irregularities (such as sunken manhole covers) were encountered. Steering was good whether the machine was on greasy city surfaces, or ridden at speed on the open road.

For a person of average height, the riding position could hardly be bettered. Seat height is 30in—a height which permitted a comfortable knee angle while allowing easy straddling of the machine for kick-starting. The position of the brake-pedal pad was such that the brake could be applied without the foot being taken off the rest; an adjustable brake-pedal stop—a new feature—allows the pedal to be set in the optimum position relative to the footrest. Some discomfort to the rider's knees resulted from contact with the angular edge of the tank knee-grips.

That the Star Twin is a sports machine has been amply illustrated, and it might be thought

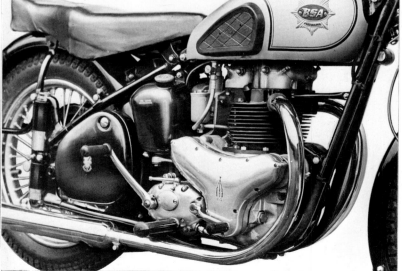

Though endowed with zestful performance characteristics, the 497 c.c. engine was found to be pleasantly flexible

from this that the engine would prove intractable under slow-running conditions. Yet the reverse is true. During town riding the machine proved to be pleasantly flexible. As intimated earlier, knowledgeable handling of the ignition control was called for; the long ignition lever fitted to the left handlebar is pleasant to use and, because of its length, greatly facilitates accurate settings.

Upward or downward gear changes could be effortlessly achieved by lightly pivoting the right foot on the footrest. Pedal movement was short and feather-light, and clean, precise upward or downward gear changes called for no special care. Racing-type upward gear changes were accompanied by a slight click from the gear box as the pinions engaged—a click which could be heard rather than felt. Clean, noiseless downward changes could be made as rapidly as the clutch and gear pedal could be operated.

Both front and rear brakes were smooth and progressive and, applied in unison, provided satisfactory stopping power, even for a machine in the Star Twin's performance class. The 8in front brake was very good, yet did not provide quite all the power of which this type of brake is known to be capable. During the course of several hundred miles of fast road work, both brakes came in for hard usage. In spite of this, no fade was experienced, and only slight adjustment was called for.

Little effort was required to operate the kick-starter. With the temperature below freezing point, the engine would start from cold at the second or third kick—this provided that the carburettor was lightly flooded and normal cold-starting procedure followed. The air lever could be fully opened after the engine had been running for about a minute.

The degree of exhaust and mechanical quietness was commendably high. With the machine stationary and the engine idling on full retard, no individual source of mechanical noise could be identified. Slight piston-slap could just be detected when the ignition was set at full advance. Induction hiss is eliminated by the built-in air-cleaner. Effective at all speeds,

A picture showing the compactness of the semi-unit construction of engine and gear box

the silencers produced a pleasant yet unobtrusive exhaust note.

Mudguarding on the Star Twin was only reasonably effective. Operation of the centre-stand called for a fair amount of muscular effort until the knack had been mastered. Its use is facilitated by the lifting handle on the left side and a curved, "roll-on" extension piece on the left leg of the stand. Adjustment of the primary chain is by moving the slipper-tensioner inside the chain case; the adjusting screw protrudes through the bottom of the case. Another commendable feature is that the guard for the rear chain has a deep back plate which effectively shields the chain from much of the road grit shed by the rear tyre. Other notable features are the B.S.A. really quickly detachable wheels; and the use of heavy-gauge clutch and front brake control cables. A comprehensive set of tools is provided.

The standard of finish on the Star Twin is extremely high. A general colour scheme of black and silver is employed; the tank is finished in matt-silver, lined in red, and it bears a handsome "Star Twin" insignia.

Information Panel

SPECIFICATION

ENGINE : 497 c.c. (66 x 72.6 mm) o.h.v. vertical twin. Fully enclosed valve gear operated by push-rods from a single camshaft. Plain-bearing big-ends. Mainshaft supported by roller and plain bearings. Compression ratio, 7.2 to 1. Dry-sump lubrication ; tank capacity, 4 pints.

CARBURETTOR : Amal ; twistgrip throttle control ; air-slide operated by handlebar lever. Built-in air cleaner.

IGNITION and LIGHTING : Lucas magneto with manual ignition control on left side of handlebar. Separate, 3in diameter Lucas dynamo ; 7in headlamp ; 30 24w headlamp bulb.

TRANSMISSION : B.S.A. four-speed gear box with positive-stop foot control. Bottom, 12.9 to 1. Second, 8.8 to 1. Third, 6.05 to 1. Top, 5.0 to 1. Multi-plate clutch with fabric inserts. Primary chain, ⅜in duplex running in cast-aluminium, oil-bath case. Rear chain, ⅝ x ⅜in, lubricated by breather from oil tank. R.p.m. at 30 m.p.h. in top gear, approximately 1,950.

FUEL CAPACITY : 3½ gallons.

TYRES : Dunlop ; front 3.25 x 19in ; rear, 3.50 x 19in ; both studded tread.

BRAKES : 8in diameter front, 7in diameter rear ; finger-operated adjusters.

SUSPENSION : B.S.A. telescopic front fork with hydraulic damping ; plunger-type rear springing.

WHEELBASE : 54½in. Ground clearance, 4½in. unladen.

SEAT : B.S.A. dual-seat. Unladen height, 30in.

WEIGHT : 423 lb fully equipped and with one gallon of fuel.

PRICE : £174, with Purchase Tax (in Great Britain only), £222 6s 8d. Extras : dual-seat in lieu of saddle, £3 (P.T., 16s 8d) ; prop-stand, 15s (P.T., 4s 2d).

ROAD TAX : £3 15s a year ; £1 0s 8d a quarter.

DESCRIPTION : *The Motor Cycle,* 19 October, 1950.

MAKERS : B.S.A. Cycles, Ltd., Small Heath, Birmingham, 11.

PERFORMANCE DATA

MEAN MAXIMUM SPEED : Bottom : 37 m.p.h.*
Second : 55 m.p.h.*
Third : 86 m.p.h.
Top : 92 m.p.h.
* Valve float just starting.

MEAN ACCELERATION :

	10-30 m.p.h.	20-40 m.p.h.	30-50 m.p.h.
Bottom	3 secs	2.4 secs	—
Second	4.2 secs	3.2 secs	3.2 secs
Third	6 secs	5.4 secs	4.8 secs
Top	—	7.2 secs	6.8 secs

Mean speed at end of quarter-mile from rest : 84 m.p.h.
Mean time to cover standing quarter-mile : 16.8 secs.

PETROL CONSUMPTION : At 30 m.p.h., 89 m.p.g. At 40 m.p.h., 75 m.p.g. At 50 m.p.h., 70 m.p.g. At 60 m.p.h., 64 m.p.g.

BRAKING : From 30 m.p.h. to rest, 30ft 6in (surface, dry tar macadam).

TURNING CIRCLE : 13ft 6in.

MINIMUM NON-SNATCH SPEED : 22 m.p.h. in top gear.

WEIGHT per C.C. : 0.73 lb.

Excelsior
TALISMAN

Excelsior, who were the first firm in Britain to take up motor cycle manufacture on a commercial scale ('Founded 1874' ran the legend on the tank transfer; but in fact their earliest powered machines dated from 1897), led something of a Jekyll-and-Hyde existence in pre-Second World War days. At the bottom end of the scale were the cheap Villiers-engined lightweights, starting with the fully-equipped 98 cc two-speed Universal at only 14 guineas (£14.70). But the same factory produced the very up-market overhead-camshaft Manxman models, in 250, 350 and 500 cc sizes and listed as super-sports roadsters or as outright road racers.

The Manxman was designed by H. J. Hatch and Eric Walker, and was an exclusive Excelsior product, although at the time the works in Kings Road, Tyseley, Birmingham had no engine-building facilities and so engine production had to be farmed out – initially to Blackburnes, but later to Beans Industries.

Expansion of the factory to meet War Department contracts meant that Excelsior could return to peacetime trading in 1945 with the benefit of a well-equipped machine shop and so, for the first time, Excelsior engines could actually be made on the premises. However, the prestige Manxman failed to return to the market, although it can now be disclosed that a post-war prototype was indeed built and tested on the road.

Instead, the new facilities were employed on two-stroke engine production, notably of the 98 cc Excelsior Spryt and Goblin engines used in Excelsior's own autocycles (forerunners of the moped) and in the Brockhouse Corgi mini-scooter derived from the wartime Excelsior Welbike paratrooper's machine.

A 149 cc two-stroke unit was added and then, in October, 1949, came a 244 cc (50 × 62 mm) two-stroke parallel twin

No fewer than five ball and roller races supported the built-up crankshaft of the 244 cc (50 × 62 mm) Excelsior Talisman two-stroke twin. Current for lighting and ignition was supplied by a Wico-Pacy flywheel alternator mounted on the left-hand end of the crankshaft

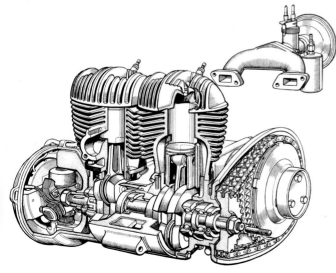

known as the Talisman. It was, apart from the water-cooled Scott, the only unit of this layout in British production, and its appearance on the company's stand at the London Show attracted a great deal of attention.

The specification included a five-bearing mainshaft, three-piece crankcase construction with vertical joints, and separate cast-iron cylinders and light-alloy heads. An Albion four-speed gearbox was bolted to the rear face of the crankcase in semi-unit-construction style, and ignition was by a Wico-Pacy 36-watt flywheel magneto-generator housed in a compartment on the right of the crankcase assembly.

Plunger-type rear springing of an unusual kind, in which the spring boxes themselves travelled up and down fixed rods, afforded 1·75 in rear wheel movement, and undamped front forks with two-rate internal springs looked after the front wheel.

Smartly finished in maroon, with cream panels to the fuel tank sides, the Talisman was a very fetching little machine. It weighed 220 lb, handled well (as one might expect from a factory with a racing background), and if the performance was a little less than world-shattering, at least the power delivery was smoother than anything the unsophisticated motor cyclist of the day had experienced hitherto. The rear springing, although offering the barest minimum of movement, was better than the rigid frames still very much in evidence, while the undamped spring front forks were an improvement over the old girder type.

The original Talisman, listed as Model TT1, was joined for the 1952 season by a twin-carburettor version known as the Sports Talisman, or STT1. This was distinguished by a rather pleasant all-over finish of beige, with red striping, by gaiters on the front fork, and by a distinctly ugly dual seat in place of the TT1's single saddle. Performance had gone up, too, and the 'Sports' was able to achieve a mean speed of 64 mph, not at all bad by the standards of the day.

Sales of the Talisman Twin did not break any records, though (which was a pity, because on the whole it was a nice little bike) and the firm began to look elsewhere for sales outlets for their engines. That is how they made contact with a very peculiar little three-wheeler, built at Seymour Wharf, Totnes, Devon, which carried the absolutely appalling name of The Worker's Playtime. Two prototypes, powered by 244 cc Talisman engines, were built but that was about all.

Excelsior had a shade better luck with some of the other three-wheeler projects which seemed to proliferate in the 1950s, notably the London-built Powerdrive and Coronet (which used a 328 cc Talisman twin). There was, too, the Wolverhampton-made Frisky, which managed to reach limited production – and, finally, the Berkeley, which had such an important part to play in the Excelsior story that a paragraph or two must be reserved for this alone.

Meanwhile, back to the bikes, and to the introduction for the 1953 season of a pair of Talisman twins (TT2 standard, and STT2 sports) with pivoted-fork rear suspension and a redesigned frame incorporating an engine cradle. Other features included a fork-top instrument facia, and a much more elegant

By 1955 the Excelsior Talisman Sports STT2 had progressed from plunger springing to a conventional pivoted rear fork. The new frame incorporated, also, a tubular cradle, but traditional brazed-lug construction was still being employed

dual seat. The plunger-sprung TT1, still with single saddle, and STT1 sports were continued (although these were just unsold stock).

The following year saw the introduction of full-width wheel hubs, and in subsequent seasons there was a revised cylinder head design with hemispherical combustion chamber and very much deeper finning, and a number of styling and colour-scheme changes.

The next major step was the production of a 328 cc twin for the Coronet three-wheeler and the new 1958 Super Talisman. The autumn of the same year saw Excelsior in production with yet another version, the 328 cc S9 Special Talisman, of which the power unit differed mainly in that it now had a 60-watt Miller alternator instead of the Wico-Pacy unit. At this particular

period several factories (among them Triumph and Francis-Barnett) had gone overboard for semi-enclosure of the rear wheel. Excelsior joined the craze, but with not very happy results. The sheet metal cover at the rear of the machine was just plain clumsy, as also was the attempt to emulate Triumph's fork-top headlamp nacelle.

One feature which may have seemed a good idea at the time was the inclusion of a tool cavity in the top face of the tank. The lid, secured by a pair of Oddie snap fasteners, was supposed also to serve as the fuel tank filler cap. It leaked.

But at this stage we must return to the Berkeley three-wheeler mentioned a few paragraphs ago. Designed by Laurie Bond (who was responsible also for the design of the Bond three-wheeler), this was a sporty little two-seater with a glass-fibre body, produced in Biggleswade, Bedfordshire, by a well known firm of caravan manufacturers.

To power the Berkeley, the Excelsior company evolved a 492 cc three-cylinder engine, which was really three of the cylinders of the 328 cc Talisman (58 × 62 mm) arranged on a seven-bearing crankshaft with the throws at 120 degrees. A Siba Dynastart unit served to provide electric current and, also, gave the little car electric starting.

Another version of the Berkeley used the 328 cc engine. It was a good little vehicle, but an unfortunate experience on the American market led to the collapse of Berkeley and, not having been paid for engines supplied, Excelsior folded, too. The company was bought by Britax, and still forms part of that group, but is now concerned solely with making car and motor cycle accessories.

244 c.c. Excelsior

A Vertical Twin Two-stroke Lightweight w

SINCE its introduction late in 1949, the 244 c.c. Excelsior parallel twin two-stroke, the Talisman, has achieved no small measure of popularity. The Talisman Sports, which made its bow at last year's London Show and which recently came into production, embodies modifications that are mainly

Luxury features include plunger-type rear springing, twin carburettors and a special twin-seat adjustable for height

in the nature of "gilding the lily"—except that the "gilding" process has included functional as well as ornamental features. Among the refinements are twin Amal carburettors. As a result, increased maximum speed has been obtained.

Salient characteristics of the twin two-stroke engine are its "four-cylinder" torque and well-nigh perfect balance. Almost throughout the entire speed range the engine delivers its power in a turbine-like flow, without fuss or vibration. Only at one small period (a period bracketed by a bare 2 m.p.h.) could the slightest of vibration tremors be detected; this was at 40-42 m.p.h. in top gear. No palpable vibration was apparent at the handlebars.

Like most two-strokes, the Excelsior would not fire evenly

Impressive twin power unit. Note also the pivoted crank of the kick-starter pedal and the rectifier mounted below the tank

with the engine on light load. For instance, at a steady 30 m.p.h. along a level road, with no headwind, the twistgrip had to be eased off fractionally, then opened again if a tendency to four-stroking was to be avoided. Under such conditions, the minimum speed in top gear (on a fixed throttle opening) required to avoid four-stroking was approximately 34 m.p.h. This does not mean, of course, that there was not good two-stroking at low speeds. On the contrary, due to the exceptionally good low-speed torque, the engine was so flexible that it would pull evenly away from speeds as low as 12 m.p.h. in top gear. At any speed between 15 and 50 m.p.h. in top gear, the throttle could be wound open without any protest from the engine, and immediate results were forthcoming.

Acceleration through the indirect ratios, as well as in top gear, was extremely lively for a 250 c.c. machine. A comfortable cruising speed for both engine and rider was adjudged to be 50 m.p.h., though even when the engine was held on full throttle for long periods, it gave the impression that it would hum on tirelessly for as long as the rider wished. Under these conditions there was not the slightest sign of overheating; the cylinder head and barrel fins remained relatively cool, and the exhaust pipes did not become even slightly discoloured. The power unit remained absolutely oil-tight, but burnt oil leaked from the joint between silencer and exhaust pipe.

When the maximum speed, acceleration and fuel consumption figures were taken, a stiffish breeze was blowing which had some adverse effect. It should be mentioned that the engine just failed to reach its ultimate peak revs in second gear, because of a period of four-stroking occurring high up in the r.p.m. range. When the engine was held on full throttle in bottom gear, the revs climbed slowly through, and clear of, this four-stroking period and attained absolute maximum.

It is an axiom that the smaller the engine, the greater should be the number of gears. In hilly country, four carefully chosen gear ratios enable a small-capacity engine to be kept turning over happily, as distinct from slogging hard or over-revving. However, such was the flexibility of the Excelsior that it tended to make the four-speed gear box appear something of a luxury rather than a necessity. There were occasions, of course, such as when overtaking slower traffic on hills, on which the four-speed gear box was a valuable asset.

Only slight effort was required to operate the gear-change pedal, which has a short arc of travel. Quick-action gear changes, both upward and downward, could be made without fear of "scrunching." Some deliberation had to be exercised when engaging neutral; otherwise there was a tendency to overshoot the neutral position.

It was felt that the gear pedal was a little too low, in relation to the most desirable footrest position, for maximum ease of operation when making downward gear changes, i.e., moving the pedal upward. Though the pedal is located on serrations, and is therefore adjustable, its adjustment for height is limited by the position of the magencrator case. The clutch was exceptionally light to operate; it was smooth and progressive in taking up the drive.

Starting the engine from cold, even after it had been standing all night, was invariably accomplished

alisman Sports

Attractive Performance

first kick provided the following simple preliminaries were observed : the float chamber tickler was depressed until the fuel just began to appear at the base of the mixing chambers; the air lever was fully closed and the twistgrip was set one-third open. After the engine had been running for a few minutes, the air control could be opened fully. Starting with the engine warm could usually be effected by a leisurely prod on the kick-starter, with the throttle set one-third open. The kick-starter crank is mounted concentrically with the gear pedal; if the ball of the foot was used when operating the kick-starter, the crank could be moved through its full arc of travel without the foot-rest obstructing it.

For its exhaust silencing and quiet running, the Excelsior gained full marks. Even under conditions of brisk acceleration, the exhaust note was little more than an unobtrusive buzz. At cruising speeds on the open road, especially when there was a slight breeze, the rider could not hear a sound from the machine unless his head was turned sideways—then the pleasant thrum of the exhaust could be heard, but no more. At maximum speed, very slight piston rattle (" two-stroke rattle ") was audible.

Both steering and road-holding are first class. The machine could be whistled round bends and corners without deviating a fraction from the desired line. Handling was equally good at high or low speeds. All road shocks were cushioned, and an appreciated degree of comfort was provided by the telescopic front fork and the plunger-type rear springing. It was felt that a softer action of the front fork would have further enhanced the riding comfort.

An excellent riding position is furnished by the relationship between dual-seat (adjustable for height), handlebar and footrests. The split handlebar is accommodated in sockets which lie one on each side of the top fork bridge. By swivelling the bars in their sockets, adjustment for both height and angle of the grips is obtainable. The handlebar control levers are of the clip-on type and are therefore adjustable; they fell easily to hand. The twin-rotor twistgrip throttle control for the two carburettors was inordinately stiff in operation, and no amount of lubrication of the cables resulted in much improvement.

Perfectly positioned in relation to the footrest, the brake pedal

Both exhaust pipes are led into one pipe which feeds into a silencer on the left side of the machine

pad could be depressed merely by swivelling the foot lightly on the rest. An adjustable stop for the brake pedal is provided. Though subjected to hard usage, both front and rear brakes retained their efficiency. Applied in unison, they provided commendable stopping power.

The driving light provided by the Lucas pre-focus lamp unit was considered adequate for the full performance of the machine to be used at night. The total lamp load was balanced on the ammeter at 38-40 m.p.h. in top gear. Mounted on top of the fork bridge, the speedometer was easily read by day or by night; it registered accurately at 30 m.p.h. and was 2½ m.p.h. fast at 50 m.p.h.

Parking equipment consists of a spring-up central stand; even after much practice this proved difficult to operate. Embodied in the gear box is a dip-stick; an excellent feature in itself, it nevertheless proved awkward to read as, during extraction, it fouled the right-hand carburettor. Two spacious tool boxes, provide good facilities for carrying tool-kit, repair outfit and spares. The Talisman Sports is finished in beige enamel, with the fuel tank lined red and bearing the Excelsior motif.

Information Panel

The 244 c.c. Excelsior Talisman Sports

SPECIFICATION

ENGINE : 244 c.c. (50 x 62 mm) two-stroke parallel twin. Separate cast-iron cylinder barrels and light-alloy heads : crank throws at 180 deg : crankshaft supported on four ball bearings and one roller bearing : roller-bearing big-ends : aluminium-alloy, flat-top pistons. Compression ratio 7.8 to 1. Petroil lubrication.

CARBURETTORS : Amal ; twistgrip throttle control ; air-slides operated by handlebar lever.

IGNITION AND LIGHTING : Wico-Pacy flywheel mag-generator, with rectifier and battery. 7in headlamp with pre-focus light unit. 24 24 w headlamp bulb.

TRANSMISSION : Four-speed gear box with positive-stop foot control. Bottom, 17.78 to 1. Second, 10.86 to 1. Third, 9.22 to 1. Top, 6.09 to 1. Two-plate cork-insert clutch running in oil. Shock absorber incorporated in clutch. Primary chain, ⅜ x ⅜ in in cast-aluminium case. Rear chain, ⅜ x ¼in with guard over top run. Engine r.p.m. at 30 m.p.h. in top gear, 2,380.

FUEL CAPACITY : 2¾ gallons.

TYRES : Dunlop, 3.00 x 19in front and rear.

BRAKES : 5in-diameter front, 6in rear.

SUSPENSION : Excelsior undamped telescopic front fork. Plunger-type rear springing.

WHEELBASE : 50½in. Ground clearance, 5in unladen.

SEAT : Excelsior twin seat. Unladen height, 30in.

WEIGHT : 250lb fully equipped and with one gallon of fuel.

PRICE : £136, plus Purchase Tax (in Britain only), £173 15s 7d.

ROAD TAX : £1 17s 6d a year ; 10s 4d a quarter.

MAKERS : Excelsior Motor Co., Ltd., King's Road, Tyseley, Birmingham, 11.

DESCRIPTION : The Motor Cycle, 15 November, 1951.

PERFORMANCE DATA

MEAN MAXIMUM SPEED : Bottom : 30 m.p.h.
Second : 45 m.p.h.
Third : 55 m.p.h.
Top : 64 m.p.h.

MEAN ACCELERATION :

	10-30 m.p.h.	20-40 m.p.h.	30-50 m.p.h.
Second	4.6 secs	5.4 secs	—
Third	5.6 secs	6.4 secs	9.0 secs
Top	8.2 secs	7.6 secs	10.0 secs

Mean Speed at end of quarter-mile from rest : 57 m.p.h.
Mean time to cover standing quarter-mile : 23 secs.

PETROIL CONSUMPTION : At 30 m.p.h., 96 m.p.g. At 40 m.p.h., 88 m.p.g. At 50 m.p.h., 67 m.p.g. At 55-60 m.p.h., 60 m.p.g.

BRAKING : From 30 m.p.h. to rest, 29ft 11in (surface, dry tar macadam).

TURNING CIRCLE : 13ft.

MINIMUM NON-SNATCH SPEED : 12 m.p.h. in top gear.

WEIGHT PER C.C. : 1.02 lb.

TIGER 100

Edward Turner was a crafty kind of character, but still, when a man is wearing two hats – that of chief designer, *and* that of managing director of Triumph Engineering Co Ltd – crafty is what he has to be. Good husbandry and the economic use of raw materials is the province of the managing director, and so no part had to be any heavier than necessary. Many minor lightnesses add up to a general major lightness, and such was Turner's skill as a designer, that the 498 cc Triumph Speed Twin which startled the motor cycle world of 1937, was in fact lighter than the 500 cc single it replaced.

And Edward Turner was crafty in another direction, because it was his policy never to introduce a sports model until its touring counterpart had been given at least a year's production run, during which any bugs could be eliminated. The early Speed Twin did have a few bugs. For example, the six-stud fixing of the cylinder block to the crankcase was a weakness, overcome by the mid-season introduction of a thicker base flange, and an eight-stud fixing.

The Tiger 100, unveiled in the weekly press in late August, 1938, created almost as much of a sensation as the Speed Twin had done, a year before. It was, of course, a hotted-up edition of the touring model with, from the start, the benefit of the beefier cylinder-base fixing. But there was, also, a whole lot more to whet the enthusiast's appetite.

Polished flywheels and con-rods, for instance; forged, flat-top pistons with valve cutaways in the crown; a compression ratio of 8 to 1; a gas-flowed cylinder head, and the ability to rev to 7,000 rpm.

One feature greatly appreciated by the sportier type of motor cyclist was a patented silencer of which the tail pipe, end cap and baffle could be detached, to leave a pukka racing megaphone. In fact, the Tiger 100 was intended primarily for clubman racing, while for those who wanted to tackle the more serious stuff, a bronze cylinder head was on offer at £5 extra.

As with the Tiger singles, the sports twin was finished in silver sheen, outlined in black and with die-cast name badges.

Triumph decided to have a go at collecting the Maudes Trophy and so, in February, 1939, two machines – a Speed Twin and a Tiger 100 – were selected from stock then, under ACU observation, were ridden up to John O'Groats, down to Land's End, and then to Brooklands, where they were subjected to a six-hour speed test. Freddie Clarke and Allan Jefferies shared the Speed Twin in 1½-hour spells, and Ivan Wicksteed and David Whitworth alternated as the Tiger 100 pilots.

The test was successful, with the Tiger 100 averaging 78·50 mph for six hours, and putting in a last lap at 88·46 mph. That year, several other factories were making determined efforts to win the Maudes Trophy (BSA were indulging in a Round Britain ride, and Panther were scorching up and down the Great North Road on a big sloper), but the ACU judged the Triumph test to be the more meritorious, and so the Maudes came to Coventry.

Clubman racers were not slow to put the Tiger 100 to the track test, and there were literally dozens of Tigers at the Brooklands

Clubmans Day in April, 1939, and at Donington Park a month later (where, incidentally, T100s finished first, second, third and fifth in the Clubmans 500 cc event).

Not many 1940 models were produced before the wartime halt to civilian production, but it is worth noting that the changes included a new full-skirt piston, check springs on the girder front fork, and a speedometer dial with concentric rpm scales for each gear.

Under the heading 'First of the New', the Triumph company, now located at Meriden, announced their post-war range on 1 March 1945, before the shooting had actually stopped. The T100 was there, much as before except that a telescopic front fork was fitted, and the crankcase had adopted a new and soon to be familiar appearance because, instead of the pre-war Magdyno electrics, there were now separate magneto and dynamo, respectively at rear and front. The megaphone silencer was dropped, but with each T100 a certified test card would be issued.

As peacetime motor cycling got under way, so the demand for rear springing grew. Even to add plunger suspension would have meant making new, or at least modified, frame jigs, but the canny Edward Turner had another solution. In the late 1930s he had patented a large-diameter rear hub which contained its own springing system; now he brought the drawings out of storage and put the Sprung Hub into production, at £20 extra to the standard rigid-frame models.

First major change was for 1949, when the tank-top instrument panel current since 1939 was dropped in favour of a fork-top headlamp nacelle. The chromium-plated fuel tank was discontinued a year later, and replaced by a painted-all-over silver tank with chrome-plated horizontal styling bands along the sides; another familiar Triumph feature to make its appearance that year was the tank-top parcel grid.

Next significant date was 1951, when the Tiger 100 blossomed out in a new die-cast light-alloy cylinder block with close-pitched finning. Nor was that all, because the rather disappointing Grand Prix racing model had been deleted from the range and, instead, a complete racing kit was listed for the T100 at £35. This embraced a racing camshaft, high-compression pistons, stronger valve springs, twin carburettor mixing chambers, a rev counter, etc, all of which boosted the 33 bhp output of the Tiger 100 to something over 40 bhp.

The racing kit remained available until 1954, when the T100, in common with other Triumphs, discarded the sprung hub and at last went over to a pivoted rear fork. The semi-racing T100C variant, equipped with twin carburettors, was discontinued but a twin-carburettor head was included in the list of optional extras for the standard model.

In listing the technical changes of the Tiger 100, we are slightly ahead of the competitions story, but in spite of a 1952 Clubmans Senior TT victory by Bernard Hargreaves, in this type of racing the Triumph usually came off second-best by comparison with the BSA Gold Star. Still, there was more cheerful news for Triumph owners from America, where Johnny Allen, in 1955,

To avoid expensive frame jigs, the Triumph company devised an intriguing suspension system in which the springs were concealed within the rear hub itself. This allowed the firm to provide rear springing for a rigid-framed machine. The photograph shows a 1948 Tiger 100 with spring wheel

broke the AMA national Class C stock-machine record with a two-way speed of 123·952 mph.

By 1957 the pre-unit-construction Triumph engine was nearing the end of its production life, but there was one last change for the Tiger 100; the fitting, for the 1957 season, of a new light-alloy cylinder head with splayed instead of parallel inlet tracts. Enthusiasts liked the new 8 in front brake, with cast-in air scoop, but they were much less happy about the new die-cast tank badge – a futuristic effort known derisively as the 'space rocket', or 'five-bar gate'.

The Triumph Engineering Company Ltd had taken over from the older company in 1936 and so, to mark the 21st anniversary of TEC, the name 'Twenty-One' was given to the 1957 350 cc Model 3TA, harbinger of a new policy of unit-construction. In the next year or two there would be a 490 cc version (the 5TA Speed Twin) plus a sports model carrying on the old Tiger 100 name, but these were complete redesigns, and their relationship to the original Tiger 100 had grown remote.

Announced in 1957 at an extra cost of almost £12 was this special cylinder head for the Tiger 100, with widely-splayed inlet tracts and a pair of Amal Monobloc carburettors

The small chromium-plated cover just forward of the kickstart spindle shows that this 1958 Triumph Tiger 100 has the patented 'Slikshift', introduced that year. Initial movement of the gear pedal operated the clutch. Customers disliked the idea, which was hastily dropped

ROAD TESTS OF NEW MODELS

498 c.c. Triump

Outstanding Sports Twin with a Scintillating Perforr

FOR a number of years the 498 c.c. Triumph Tiger 100 has enjoyed an enviable reputation as a super-sports mount with a Jekyll and Hyde personality, docile and gentle when the occasion demands, such as in heavy traffic, yet possessed of truly tigerish characteristics when given its head on the open road. In 1951 its appeal was widened by the introduction of a light-alloy cylinder block and head and, as an extra, a conversion kit for transforming the model into a pukka racing machine. The model's success in the competition sphere was

Finish of the Tiger 100 is silver, black and chromium

recently underlined by victory in the 1952 Senior Clubman's T.T.

It is on the open road, as "Mr. Hyde," that the Tiger 100 really comes into its own. Acceleration up to speeds in the seventies is vivid yet smooth. The engine seems to revel in the continued use of full throttle, and high average speeds are not difficult to maintain. The rapidity with which the speedometer needle could be sent round to the 80 m.p.h. mark in third gear, and held between 80 and 85 m.p.h. in top for as long as road and traffic conditions permitted, made averages of over 50 m.p.h. commonplace.

Twice in one day the 102-mile journey between the Midlands and a London suburb was covered in an hour and three-quarters, in spite of the usual volume of week-day traffic. On these trips the speedometer frequently read 87 m.p.h. for some miles, though the rider was normally seated and clad in a stormcoat and waders. Long main road hills pulled the needle back no farther than the 80 m.p.h. mark. Checked electrically, the speedometer was found to register $2\frac{1}{2}$ m.p.h. fast at 30 m.p.h. and approximately 5 m.p.h. fast at all speeds between 40 and 80 m.p.h.

In spite of the hardest of driving methods, there was never the slightest sign of engine tiredness, nor was there any tendency for the engine to "run on" when the ignition cut-out was operated after prolonged use of the maximum speed performance. At the conclusion of one particular day's riding, which comprised some 300 miles—many of them on full throttle—the only visible signs of hard riding were discoloration of the exhaust pipes for a few inches from the ports, an oil leak from the cylinder head joint, a faint smear at the base of the push-rod tubes and a slight oil deposit on the rear-wheel rim.

Except at high engine r.p.m. there was no vibration. At no speed, indeed, was vibration sufficient to warrant criticism. Provided normal use was made of the gear box and manual ignition control, there was no undue tendency for the engine to pink, even though the fuel employed throughout the test was the usual low-octane Pool petrol.

The exhaust note was pleasant and inoffensive whether the Tiger 100 was trickling through towns and villages or being driven hard. Mechanically, as is to be expected with light-alloy cylinders and heads, the engine was slightly noisy, though this ceased to be apparent to the rider when the road speed rose above 35 m.p.h. Most of the mechanical noise was from the pistons, and it was emphasized mainly by the complete absence of induction noise; responsible for this last condition is a large Vokes air filter incorporated as a standard fitting.

Top gear maximum speed figures were taken, on a 1,650-yard straight, both with and without the air filter. Downwind speeds were identical (97.06 m.p.h.) in each case; upwind, without the filter and using the same 170 main jet, there was a speed increase of 1.79 m.p.h. compared with that obtained with the filter in position.

Engine starting, whether the unit was hot or cold, was invariably accomplished at the first kick. The air control, which is situated beneath the left-hand side of the twinseat, was never required during the course of the test. When the engine was cold, the only pre-starting drill was flooding of the carburettor. Provided a small throttle opening was used, there was no need to retard the ignition. As would be expected, the tick-over was rather "lumpy" on full advance, but the idling was improved when the ignition was one-third retarded; however, for complete reliability, the tick-over had to be set faster than some consider desirable.

As to "Dr. Jekyll," though a certain amount of docility and low-speed flexibility is inevitably sacrificed in the interests of top-end performance the Tiger 100 is nevertheless very well-mannered

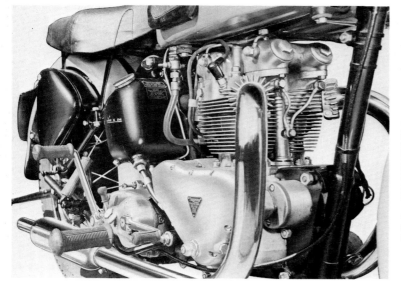

The high-efficiency power unit has impressive and pleasing lines

Tiger 100

Fast Road Work or Racing

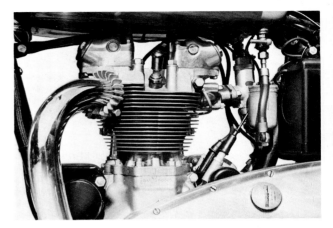

The light-alloy cylinders and heads are die-cast and are characterized by their close-pitch fins

It could be driven unobtrusively at speeds in the region of 30 m.p.h. in top gear. Fuel consumption under these conditions was markedly good. Oil consumption was negligible throughout the test.

The relationship between the handlebar, with its distinctive, rearward sweep, the footrests and the twinseat provided a comfortable riding position for all normal conditions. For prolonged, ultra high-speed work, a slightly more rearward footrest mounting or a raised support on the twinseat would have been appreciated —these solely to relieve the arms of tension caused by wind pressure. Much appreciated was the slenderness of that part of the tank which lies between the rider's knees; the width was just right for maximum comfort and controllability.

Located on a serrated shaft, the gear pedal was adjustable to a position which gave easy operation without removing the foot from its rest. The rear brake pedal came conveniently under the ball of the left foot. The reach from the handlebar to the clutch and front-brake levers was felt to be a trifle too great. Horn button and dipswitch were excellently positioned for left and right thumb operation respectively. The twistgrip, which incorporates a knurled, self-locking friction adjuster, was slightly heavy in operation. The pillion footrests were well positioned for passenger comfort and the twinseat provided comfortable accommodation for two. Riders of large build, dressed for long-distance travel, might desire slightly greater length in the seat.

Pleasantly close, top and third gear ratios are well-chosen in relation to engine characteristics; in fact, the gear change between them was so slick as to encourage more frequent changes than was necessary—just for the sheer pleasure of it. In order to achieve silent changes between bottom and second, and second and third gears, a leisurely movement of the pedal was called for. Owing to slight clutch drag on the machine tested, bottom gear could not be engaged silently when the machine was stationary with the engine idling. Neutral selection was easy from either bottom or second gears. The clutch was delightfully sweet in taking up the drive. It was light in operation and appeared to be impervious to abuse.

Both brakes were smooth, reasonably powerful, and progressive in action. The front brake by itself was good but required somewhat heavy pressure. Rear-brake pedal travel was rather too long to permit maximum braking effort.

The Triumph front fork has a soft action around the static-load position; it absorbed road shocks in an exemplary manner. Occasionally, with the added weight of a pillion passenger, it was made to bottom under conditions of heavy braking. The sprung rear hub provided reasonable comfort at touring speeds but rather more movement would have been preferred at high speeds.

On corners and bends the Tiger 100 could be heeled over confidently and stylishly. On very bumpy bends taken at speed there was a slight tendency to roll. Straight-ahead steering was first class. Bumpy surfaces and gusty winds produced an impression of lightness, which could be curbed by a turn of the steering-damper knob.

With its fine blending of silver, black and chromium, the finish of the machine is a credit to the manufacturers. To sum up, the Tiger 100 is a thoroughbred sporting five-hundred, calculated to inspire pride of ownership both on account of its magnificent all-round performance and its handsome appearance.

Information Panel

498 c.c. Triumph Tiger 100

SPECIFICATION

ENGINE : 498 c.c. (63 × 80 mm) vertical twin o.h.v.; fully enclosed valve gear. Die-cast aluminium-alloy cylinder block and head ; Hiduminium alloy connecting rods ; Duralumin push rods ; plain bearing big-ends ; mainshafts mounted on ball and roller bearings. Dry-sump lubrication ; oil tank capacity, 6 pints.

CARBURETTOR : Amal ; twistgrip throttle control ; air slide operated by Bowden cable with lever situated under seat. Large Vokes air filter included.

TRANSMISSION : Triumph four-speed gear box with positive-stop foot control. Bottom, 12.2 to 1. Second, 8.45 to 1. Third, 5.95 to 1. Top, 5. to 1. Multi-plate clutch with cork inserts operating in oil. Primary chain ½ × 0.305in, in oil-bath case. Rear chain, ⅝ × ¼in, lubricated by bleed from primary chain case. Guards over both runs of rear chain. R.p.m. at 30 m.p.h. in top gear, 1,938.

IGNITION AND LIGHTING : Lucas magneto with manual control. Separate Lucas 60-watt dynamo. 7in-diameter headlamp.

FUEL CAPACITY : 4 gallons.

TYRES : Dunlop. Front, 3.25 × 19in ribbed. Rear, 3.50 × 19in Universal.

BRAKES : Triumph 6⅞ × 1⅛in front ; 8 × 1⅛in rear ; hand adjusters.

SUSPENSION : Triumph telescopic front fork with hydraulic damping. Triumph spring hub in rear wheel.

WHEELBASE : 55in. Ground clearance, 6in unladen.

SADDLE : Triumph Twinseat ; unladen height, 31in.

WEIGHT : 383 lb with approximately one gallon of fuel, full oil tank, and fully equipped (including pillion footrests and prop stand).

PRICE : £175, plus Purchase Tax (in Britain), £48 12s 3d. Spring hub extra, £16, plus £4 8s 11d P.T. Pillion footrests and prop stand extra.

MAKERS : Triumph Engineering Co. Ltd., Meriden Works, Allesley, Coventry.

DESCRIPTION : The Motor Cycle, 9 November, 1950.

PERFORMANCE DATA

MEAN MAXIMUM SPEED : Bottom : *41 m.p.h.
Second : *60 m.p.h.
Third : 85 m.p.h.
Top : 92 m.p.h.
* Valve float occurring.

MEAN ACCELERATION :

	10-30 m.p.h.	20-40 m.p.h.	30-50 m.p.h.
Bottom	2.3 secs	2.2 secs	—
Second	3.0 secs	3.0 secs	2.6 secs
Third	—	4.6 secs	4.6 secs
Top	—	5.6 secs	5.8 secs

Mean speed at end of quarter-mile from rest : 79 m.p.h.
Mean time to cover standing quarter-mile : 16.6 secs.

PETROL CONSUMPTION : At 30 m.p.h., 101.6 m.p.g. At 40 m.p.h., 83.2 m.p.g.; At 50 m.p.h., 70.4 m.p.g. At 60 m.p.h., 59.2 m.p.g.

BRAKING : From 30 m.p.h. to rest 28ft 6in (surface, dry tar macadam).

TURNING CIRCLE : 16ft.

MINIMUM NON-SNATCH SPEED : 17 m.p.h. in top gear.

WEIGHT PER C.C. : 0.8 lb.

BSA
B31

If one motor cycle had to be chosen to represent the solidly reliable British overhead-valve medium-weight single of the 1950s, then high on the list of candidates for the honour must be the 348 cc BSA B31. The B31 was a workaday relative of the glamour-puss Gold Star, and did not hit many headlines during its long lifetime; but even today, in the industrial areas of the country, many a B31 can be seen giving the same sterling service it produced when new. And many another, relegated to the depths of the garage when family needs meant the purchase of a car, is now being brought back to life as second-string transport.

Entirely a post-war product, the B31 was a member of BSA's first civilian programme, announced in August, 1945. Most handsome it looked, too, with the silvered panels of its chromium-plated fuel tank set off by black striping. It had a rigid frame, of course, but front suspension was by BSA's recently-patented hydraulically-damped telescopic fork.

The BSA people described the new three-fifty as a sports unit with excellent slogging power (which, indeed, it was). On 73 octane pool petrol and a compression ratio of only 6.8 to 1, it could whip up to just over 70 mph.

But of course, new designs rarely come out of the blue, and for the true ancestry of the B31 we must go back to the 1940 Small Heath catalogue. Surprisingly, the 499 cc M24 Gold Star was an absentee from that year's range, but there was an interesting newcomer, the 348 cc B29 Silver Sports, which employed the early Goldie's robust bottom-end assembly, plus a cast-iron

This is how the 348 cc BSA B31 looked when first produced in 1945. The speedometer, mounted in the top of the fuel tank, is an echo of pre-war practice. Tank panels were silver, with black lining

cylinder head with integral rocker boxes housing hairpin valve springs.

Only a handful of B29 Silver Sports models were ever built, due to the war (and most of those were requisitioned by the Army). However, a military version of the B29 had been under evaluation for some time and, early in 1940, the factory received an urgent order for a thousand, to replace machines lost in the Dunkirk evacuation. The order was never put in hand, because the British Army had hasty second thoughts and, instead, settled for yet another batch of side-valve M20s.

Nevertheless, the B29 Silver Sports had not been forgotten, and in the immediate post-war period it was to sire an entire brood of three-fifties. First of these was the B31, still with the hairpin-valve-spring type of integral rocker box, but employing coil-spring valve operation. By January, 1946, the first B32 had come upon the scene – in effect a trials job, and fettled by competitions manager Bert Perrigo; features were a high-level exhaust pipe, greater ground clearance, lower gear ratios, and narrower, chromium-plated mudguards. Price of the B32 Competitions was exactly £100, although purchase tax of £47 had to be added.

A third version of the design, announced for the 1949 season, was a clubman racer known as the B32 Special. This was first of the group to be given a plunger-type rear suspension and it had, also, a light-alloy cylinder barrel and head, plus the option of a close-ratio gearbox. Development of this model had included the entry in the 1947 Junior Manx Grand Prix of an experimental BSA with B29-type engine (including hairpin valve springs), magnesium crankcase and light-alloy cylinder head. Inevitably, the B32 Special was to grow into the B32GS

A 1955 BSA catalogue picture of the B31. At this time three versions of the machine were on sale: rigid frame (£131 plus £26.4s tax); spring or plunger frame (£140 plus £28 tax); and swinging arm (£150 plus £30 tax) as shown here

Gold Star before very long. But let us not become side-tracked . . .

For 1948 the standard B31 had exchanged its original silver-painted tank for one of mid-green lined in gold, possibly the most handsome livery the model was ever to wear, and one that will be well-remembered by those who were on the roads at this period. A rather stronger frame (still rigid, though) was adopted for the following season, recognisable by the forged steel rear-wheel lugs.

As time went by, it appeared to the general public that while development of the B32 Gold Star proceeded apace, its country cousin, the B31, had been left to vegitate. Thus while the Goldie had been fitted with a light-alloy cylinder and head with cast-in pushrod tunnels, the B31 still retained its now elderly engine arrangement of separate pushrod tower, connected to the underside of the integral rocker-box head by a castellated ring nut. In fact the only notable change for 1953 was to the fuel tank which was given chromium-plated side panels and a red instead of green paint finish. The frame still had no rear springing in standard trim but, eventually, plunger-type suspension could be supplied at extra cost. There was even one interim period when the model was listed in rigid, plunger-sprung, and pivoted-fork versions.

Power output was only mediocre, remaining at around 18 bhp, but at least this had the virtue of leaving the working parts to do their job unhurriedly and without fuss or frenzy. In consequence, the machine seemed to have the ability to go on for ever, with little more attention than adding oil and petrol when necessary.

The coming of three-dimensional plastic tank badges, in place of the rather horrid pressed-steel flashes of 1953, and the fitting of a headlamp semi-cowl, restored to the B31 a little of the style it had lost. It was not until 1956 that major changes were made.

The B31 now emerged with a full duplex-tube frame, pivoted rear springing, deep valanced guards at front and rear, and Ariel brakes in full-width hubs. An optional extra, well worth specifying, was total enclosure of the rear chain.

All this was really an extension of the BSA Group policy of gradual rationalisation. In fact, in everything but cylinder bore, the B31 was the same machine as its B33 499 cc sister, and that accounted for the 420 lb weight quoted in the specification panel of the accompanying road test.

Cylinder head of the 1945 BSA B31, showing the integral rocker boxes. In this engine the ohv pushrods were housed in an external, tapered tower (the later Gold Star version had integral pushrod tunnels in the cylinder and head)

From its introduction, the B31 had been capable of a little over 70 mph flat-out, and the 1956 model, with its two-way maximum of 72 mph, carried on the Small Heath tradition.

As the 1950s progressed, BSA felt that there was still a small corner of the market for the B31 and, accordingly, for 1958 the image was updated by abandoning, at last, magdyno electrics and adopting a crankshaft-mounted alternator. They also enhanced the good looks of the model further by fitting a deeper and more graceful fuel tank, and new-style headlamp mounted integral with the fork upper shrouds. The Ariel brakes were superseded by Triumph pattern. There was a new paint finish, too, of polychromatic almond green, although this was not to everybody's fancy.

Alas, the new-look B31 was destined for a production life of only two seasons, and as the 1950s closed, so the model was dropped from the Small Heath programme. The 1960 range still included the 499 cc B33, plus 348 and 499 cc Gold Star singles, but the B31 was gone.

In due course there would be another 350 cc BSA ohv single, a much lighter affair evolved from the 250 cc unit-construction C15 and no doubt a very worthy model, too. But the newcomer never did achieve the same measure of universal affection as that afforded the old, original slogger.

The B31 is admirably proportioned and smartly finished in maroon and chromium. Front and rear mudguards are of deep section.

THE question as to the most suitable type of motor cycle for all-round purposes is almost as old as the industry. Though riders' decisions are inevitably influenced by personal preferences, the three-fifty has long enjoyed a large following as an all-purpose mount. Generally speaking, the attractions of the type are comparatively low initial outlay and running costs, light handling and an engine which blends docility for town work with brisk, open-road performance.

Scaling more than 400 lb, the 348 c.c. B.S.A. B31 is no lightweight; yet it is not heavy to handle. It combines adequate tractability for dense city traffic with a mile-a-minute cruising speed. But probably the brightest of the model's attractions is its fuel economy. As shown by the performance data in the information panel, petrol consumption at 30 m.p.h. was about average for a 350 c.c. machine but the figures obtained at 40, 50 and 60 m.p.h. were remarkably good. In conjunction with a fuel capacity of

Road Tests of New Models

348 c.c. B.S.A. B31 A Most Economical Single, Comfortable
and Fast for Long-distance Touring, Handy in Heavy Traffic : Excellent Steering and Brakes

Rear-suspension units are provided with three-position adjustment for load. Adjustment is effected with a C-spanner. Neat in appearance, the rear chaincase proved most effective.

four gallons, the low consumption rate endows the B31 with an unusually long range.

The model tested was equipped with a rear chaincase (an optional extra). So worth while was this enclosure of the drive in enhancing both the cleanliness of the machine and the condition of the chain that it is reasonable to suppose the chaincase will become a standard item of specification before long.

The B31 engine has manual ignition control and no great skill was called for in its use. A three-fifty cannot be made to slog on a retarded ignition setting as can a machine of 500 c.c. or more. Hence, apart from engine starting, the ignition on the B31 was retarded only for two purposes, namely, to give a slow and regular tickover and to obviate the need for clutch slipping when trickling along at 4 or 5 m.p.h. in heavy traffic. For both conditions a setting of one-half to two-thirds retard was found to be suitable. But for normal running it was best to employ full advance and keep the engine spinning happily by correct use of the gear box.

Engine starting was almost invariably achieved at the first swing of the kick-starter and the preliminary drill was simple. When the engine was cold the air lever was closed, the ignition partially retarded, the carburettor lightly flooded and the throttle set as for fast idling. It was then necessary to ease the piston over compression by using the exhaust-valve lifter before thrusting the kick-starter down smartly. When the engine was warm the only prerequisite for a first-kick start was to ease the piston over compression. If required the engine could be started on full advance but in that case care was needed to employ only a minute throttle opening to avoid a kick back.

The air lever could be opened to its full extent very soon after a cold start and, as implied earlier, a slow, even tickover could be obtained on half retard. When moving off from a standstill, however, it was best to have the ignition at full advance; that pre-

Left: Valve-clearance adjusters are situated at the lower ends of the pushrods. Right: Contact-breaker points are readily accessible

sented no problem for it was easy to thumb the ignition lever forward before releasing the clutch lever.

At low and medium speeds the engine functioned smoothly and reasonably quietly. Mechanical noise was about average for a single, slight piston slap and valve-gear clack being audible, while the exhaust had a full, mellow tone. Use of large throttle openings resulted in a harsher exhaust note but it was not difficult to ride the B31 fast and unobtrusively. At indicated speeds of 53 to 63 m.p.h. in top gear (and corresponding speeds in the indirect gears) engine vibration was perceptible through the dual-seat.

When used for serious touring, the B31 proved capable of maintaining sufficiently fast average speeds to permit large daily mileages to be covered without boredom. Under average conditions, use of half throttle gave an indicated speed of 60 to 65 m.p.h. in top gear. At that throttle setting the engine was working happily but not unduly hard and up to 50 miles could be covered in each hour on fast roads. A similar speed could be

sustained up the majority of main-road hills by increasing the throttle opening. Speedometer flattery increased progressively from 1 m.p.h. at 30 m.p.h. to 5 m.p.h. at maximum speed.

Light to operate, the clutch freed completely and took up the drive smoothly and firmly. With the engine idling slowly, only a negligible click accompanied the engagement of bottom gear. Once the initial stiffness in the gear-control mechanism had worn off, clean gear changes could be effected by gentle, synchronized operation of clutch, throttle and gear pedal without any appreciable pause in pedal movement. On the model tested selection of neutral from second gear was frequently stiff and remained so throughout the test.

Riders of various statures found the riding position uncramped and such as to afford maximum control. Even when a period of several hours was spent awheel no discomfort was felt. The pillion position, too, was comfortable and the dual-seat long enough for two medium-size riders. With the exception of the rear-brake

Information Panel

348 c.c. B.S.A. B31

SPECIFICATION

ENGINE: B.S.A. 348 c.c. (71 × 88 mm) overhead-valve single with fully enclosed valve gear. Crankshaft supported in ball and roller bearings on drive side and in roller and plain bearings on timing side. Roller big-end bearing. Compression ratio, 6.5 to 1. Dry-sump lubrication; oil-tank capacity, 5¼ pints.

CARBURETTOR: Amal Monobloc with twistgrip throttle control; air slide operated by handlebar lever.

IGNITION and LIGHTING: Lucas Magdyno with manual ignition control. Lucas 6-volt, 12-ampere-hour battery. Lucas 7in-diameter headlamp with pre-focus light unit.

TRANSMISSION: B.S.A. four-speed gear box with positive-stop foot control. Gear ratios: bottom, 14.42 to 1; second, 9.82 to 1; third, 6.77 to 1; top, 5.6 to 1. Multi-plate clutch with fabric and cork inserts. Primary chain, ⅜ × 0.305in in oil-bath case. Rear chain, ⅝ × ¼in enclosed in pressed-steel case. Engine r.p.m. at 30 m.p.h. in top gear, 2,200.

FUEL CAPACITY: 4 gallons.

TYRES: Dunlop 3.25 × 19in; rear, Universal; front, ribbed.

BRAKES: Both 7in diameter × 1⅛in wide; fulcrum adjusters.

SUSPENSION: B.S.A. telescopic front fork with hydraulic damping. Pivoted-fork rear springing employing coil springs and hydraulic damping; three-position adjustment for load.

WHEELBASE: 56in unladen. Ground clearance, 5in unladen.

SEAT: B.S.A. dual-seat; unladen height, 31½in.

WEIGHT: 420 lb fully equipped, with full oil tank and approximately one gallon of petrol.

PRICE: £162. With purchase tax (in Great Britain only), £200 17s 8d. Extras: rear chaincase, £2 10s (p.t., 12s); prop stand, 15s (p.t., 3s 8d).

ROAD TAX: £3 15s a year; £1 0s 8d a quarter.

MAKERS: B.S.A. Motor Cycles, Ltd., Small Heath, Birmingham, 11.

DESCRIPTION: *The Motor Cycle*, 13 October 1955.

PERFORMANCE DATA

MEAN MAXIMUM SPEED: Bottom: *32 m.p.h.
Second: *47 m.p.h.
Third: *68 m.p.h.
Top: 72 m.p.h.
*Valve float occurring.

HIGHEST ONE-WAY SPEED: 73 m.p.h. (conditions: still air; rider wearing two-piece plastic suit and overboots).

MEAN ACCELERATION:

	10-30 m.p.h.	20-40 m.p.h.	30-50 m.p.h.
Bottom	4.2 sec	—	—
Second	5 sec	5 sec	—
Third	—	7.4 sec	8.6 sec
Top	—	9.2 sec	9.8 sec

Mean speed at end of quarter-mile from rest: 63 m.p.h.
Mean time to cover standing quarter-mile: 20.4 sec.

PETROL CONSUMPTION: At 30 m.p.h., 110 m.p.g.; at 40 m.p.h., 105 m.p.g.; at 50 m.p.h., 90 m.p.g.; at 60 m.p.h., 68 m.p.g.

BRAKING: From 30 m.p.h. to rest, 32ft (surface, dry tarmac).

TURNING CIRCLE: 14ft 3in.

MINIMUM NON-SNATCH SPEED: 14 m.p.h. in top gear with ignition fully retarded.

WEIGHT PER C.C.: 1.21 lb.

pedal all controls are adjustable for position and can be well set for convenient manipulation. The left footrest rubber forms a stop for the brake pedal which is set a trifle high.

Both front and rear springing allowed an ample range of wheel deflection and combined to take the sting out of the majority of road shocks. The three settings on the Girling rear shock absorbers were ample for all normal loads though a manual adjustment, without the need for using a spanner, would be preferred for casual passenger carrying. The front fork on the model tested was sufficiently damped to prevent undue pitching, with the result that movement around the static-load position was a little firm.

Equipped with a ribbed front tyre and endowed with steering geometry similar to that of the successful Gold Star clubman-racing models, the B31 possesses excellent steering qualities.

Whether the model was following a straight course or being swung stylishly through fast or slow bends it followed the intended path precisely. Heeling the model over required little effort and stability at steep angles of lean was such as to engender every confidence. Though the prop stand could be caused to scrape the road surface lightly by spirited left-hand cornering, the fault was very rarely apparent provided the rear springing was set correctly for the load carried.

Braking efficiency matched the general high standard of the machine. Both brakes are contained in smart, full-width, light-alloy hubs and have generous friction areas. Consequently the need for adjustment (made at the shoe fulcrum and not at the cable adjuster) was infrequent in spite of extensive hard use. Power of the brakes was such that either tyre could be made to squeal loudly and the model could be arrested in a short enough distance to cope with any emergency. There was no significant lessening of braking power when the B.S.A. was ridden for a period of two hours in torrential rain.

The brightness of the main headlamp beam was sufficient to make a mile-a-minute speed quite safe on unlit main roads after dark. But, as is sometimes found with the B.S.A. headlamp cowl, the best setting of the beam required removal of the rubber beading from the front edge of the cowl except when a pillion passenger was carried (which naturally results in a slight raising of the beam).

Considering that the test involved over 1,000 miles of hard riding, external cleanliness of the B31 at the finish was commendable. With the exception of some messiness around the drain pipe from the cylinder head to the crankcase, oil seepage was almost negligible. Leakage past the oil-tank filler cap was not entirely absent when the model was ridden fast. As already implied the rear chaincase made a considerable contribution towards keeping the rear portion of the model free from filth in addition to protecting the chain and thus minimizing wear. By the time the test was concluded the exhaust pipe had blued for a length of seven or eight inches at the cylinder-head end.

Apart from difficulty in removing the high-tension pick-up brush holder, routine maintenance presented no problems. Lifting the model on to its centre stand, however, required appreciable physical effort. Setting the valve clearances did not entail removal of the petrol tank: the two adjusters are incorporated in the tappets and are accessible on removal of the cover at the lower end of the pushrod tunnel. The adjusters for the contact-breaker points, front and rear chains, clutch and brakes are also accessible. Though the battery is concealed beneath the dual-seat, topping-up required only the prior removal of the two bolts holding the seat in place. The standard tool kit proved adequate for making all adjustments. When it becomes necessary to remove the petrol tank, such as for decarbonizing the engine, only one retaining bolt has to be withdrawn after disconnecting the fuel pipe and detaching the bracing strap from the base of the tank.

To sum up, the B31 B.S.A. with rear chain enclosure is an attractive model for the rider who wants a lively, economical, easy-to-handle all-rounder but who is not insistent on an ultra-high maximum speed. Finish is in the customary B.S.A. maroon enamel, with chromium plating for the tank sides as well as for the more usual parts.

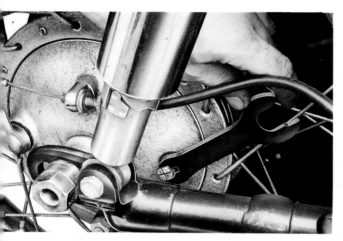

Top: Brake adjustment, made at the shoe fulcrum, was rarely necessary and easily carried out by means of a short spanner.

Above: A lifting handle is conveniently mounted to the left of the seat.

Drive side of the machine. The twin-seat blends well with the B.S.A.'s general lines.

TOE 748

ARIEL
SQUARE FOUR MARK II

Probably one of the best-known legends of motor cycling tells of how a Dulwich (South London) dealer named Edward Turner, who had been building an overhead-camshaft 350 cc single of his own design, thought of a way to build a particularly compact four-cylinder engine, by mounting the cylinders two by two.

That way, the overheating problems that affected an in-line four were bypassed, and at the same time the width problem of an across-the-frame four did not arise. Jotting down the bones of his idea on the back of a cigarette packet – a Wild Woodbine cigarette packet, confirmed Mr. Turner, in later years – he travelled to the Midlands and tried to get first one factory, then another, interested. For a while, it looked as though the AJS firm might be interested; but AJS, in the mid-1920s, were already pretty well extended with recent ventures into the light car, bus chassis, and even radio fields.

At last Turner tackled Jack Sangster, boss of the Ariel factory at Selly Oak, Birmingham. Sangster liked the idea, but refused to commit himself until he had had the chance to study some rather more workmanlike drawings. To that end, though, he was willing to instal Turner in a quiet office away from the bustle of the works and, what is more, he would provide a young assistant draughtsman to help with the detailing. That young man turned out to be Bert Hopwood who, nearly two decades later, would be designing such all-time classics as the Norton Dominator and BSA Golden Flash.

What emerged was an extremely light and lively overhead-camshaft 500 cc four, essentially a pair of vertical twins mounted one behind the other and with their crankshafts geared together in the middle. The design embraced unit-construction, with a three-speed gearbox, with the crankcase split horizontally. It was so light that for development test purposes the engine was mounted in the frame of a 250 cc single.

However, prudency and expediency meant that the Square Four in production form was rather more sedate and weighty. For a start, the Ariel range standardised on Burman gearboxes – so unit construction was out and a separate, heavier gearbox was in. For economy reasons, it had to use the duplex frame already in production for the Val Page single-cylinder sloper (which was fair enough, because although the 250 cc frame could serve for development, it would have been too flimsy to let loose upon the ham-fisted populace at large).

The first, 1931, five-hundred was followed by a 600 cc overhead-camshaft version. Naturally enough, racing types wanted to get rather more performance out of the design, and both Howard Somerville Sikes, and Ben Bickell tried the effect of adding a supercharger. But the curse of the early Square Four was a weak and insufficiently cooled cylinder head which tended to warp and blow a gasket when put under duress. Ben Bickell managed to get his 500 cc four to lap Brooklands at 100 mph – but three laps was about the limit before the head blew once again.

Edward Turner was aware of the drawbacks and so, for 1936, he evolved a totally new engine which retained the Square Four name and cylinder layout, but that was about all. The newcomer was a 997 cc pushrod overhead-valve model, with a chain-driven central camshaft running across the unit between the two pairs of cylinders. The crankshafts were still geared together, but now the gears were located on the left-hand end of each shaft, instead of in the middle.

The maker's advertising claimed '10 to 100 mph in top gear', and that the engine would require only light servicing at 10,000-mile intervals. Very elegant was the 1936 Square Four, for Edward Turner was not only a designer but a stylist with a sure touch, and the flowing lines of the valanced front mudguard, handsome chromium-plated tank with instrument panel in its top face, and lozenge-and-fishtail silencers, made for an harmonious whole. Amazingly, the all-up weight was only 410 lb. Power output was 38 bhp which, for the day and age, was quite something.

Initially, the 600 cc ohc four was continued alongside, but in reality this was just to use up existing stocks of parts, and before 1936 was out the 'cammy' had been replaced by a pushrod ohv model of the same dimensions. There, though, Selly Oak had miscalculated. There was but little demand for the 600 cc, and it was dropped after only one season, while the Mark I iron-engine Model 4G 997 cc continued alone.

First major post-war change for the 998 cc Ariel Square Four came in 1949, when employment of light-alloy cylinder block and head castings reduced overall weight by over 100 lb. This drawing shows the 'two-pipe' light-alloy engine, replaced for 1953 by the final 'four-pipe' model

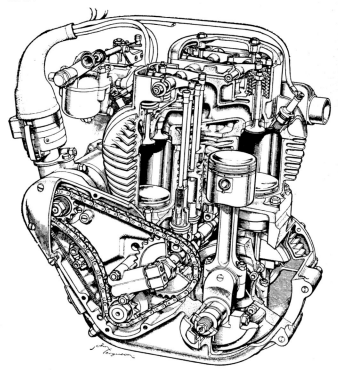

Unusual role for a 'four-pipe' Square Four was this sprinter, built in 1955 by Peter Peters, of the Avon Tyre company. Another Ariel four was sprinted by the Healey brothers at a slightly later period

Compensated-link plunger rear springing, designed to keep the rear chain in constant tension, was available for 1939 (in which year, by the way, the 600 made a surprise re-appearance), and this was again featured when the 4G made its post-war re-appearance – now graced with Ariel's own telescopic front fork – late in 1946.

It could be, of course, that Selly Oak felt that the addition of a pivoted rear fork would lengthen the wheelbase, but in truth the

Another unfamiliar Square Four was this road-racing sidecar outfit, used in 1966 by its constructor, Stan Nightingale. The Ariel, however, is a difficult engine to tune for speed and tends to suffer from camshaft whip which restricts the usable rpm band

production Square Four was to retain compensated-link plunger springing to the end of its day. A prototype with a pivoted fork was indeed built, and is at present in a private collection, but it did not reach the assembly line.

In the next few years, the Square Four found particular favour among USA enthusiasts. Through the efforts of an energetic West Coast importer, some even found their way to local Californian Police Departments (as at Monterey, for example). Police in Australia, too, added the Square Four to their strength.

Nevertheless, there had been very little engine development since the pushrod four was first announced and, in the meantime, the machine had undoubtedly put on a lot of excess weight. So the redesign of late 1948 was well timed.

The bottom-end assembly was hardly altered, but now there was a light-alloy cylinder block and head. Weight-saving was carried on in other directions, too, and as a result the 1949 Square Four (still listed as the 4G Mark I) had shed over 100 lb. That was not all, because the use of the light-alloy block served also to lower the centre of gravity and therefore improve the handling.

The old trouble of overheating was still prevalent, and so a further redesign was undertaken for 1953, resulting in the famous four-pipe Mark II model. Again the cylinder block and head were of light alloy, but in the new model the exhaust manifolds (also light-alloy castings) were bolted to each side of the head instead of being cast integrally, and there was a separate exhaust pipe for each cylinder. Inlet porting was revised and enlarged and, on the 73 octane fuel available at the time, power output was raised to 40 bhp at 5,600 rpm.

Possibly to celebrate the launch of the Mark II model, there was a complete departure from the earlier colour schemes, and the Square Four was presented in a delicate shade of light Wedgwood blue. The colour change was of short duration, for by 1954 it was back to maroon. A few minor changes were yet to come – a one-gallon oil tank, a full-width front hub, a headlamp cowl – but in general the Square Four had served its time, and by 1959 it had gone.

The Square Four was to achieve a kind of posthumous popularity, with Americans, especially, combing the backyards of Britain for examples to ship back to the States. But there cannot be many left now.

ROAD TESTS OF NEW MODELS

997 c.c. Mark II Ariel Square Four

SINCE only two British manufacturers market machines in the 1,000 c.c. class, it might be asserted that the thousand, as a type, has a limited appeal—an appeal restricted to fastidious connoisseurs. However, the latest version of the long-established Ariel Square Four—the 997 c.c. Mark II—by the enhanced versatility of its performance over that of its predecessors, extends the appeal of the 1,000 c.c. machine to the widest possible range of tastes. An outstanding trait of the model is the smoothness and flexibility of its engine torque over an unusually large range of r.p.m. The outcome of more than

The lines of the latest Ariel Four are distinctly sleek and well proportioned. Chromium-plated flashes enhance the appearance of the five-gallon fuel tank

20 years' development of the original concept, the 4G Mark II combines, in large measure, the docility for which Ariel Fours have always been renowned with an open-road potential capable of satisfying the most hardened road burner.

The Ariel's repertoire contains a type of performance to suit a rider's every mood. It may be ridden in top gear at speeds below 20 m.p.h. Alternatively, full use may be made of the engine's high power output in all gears. In either case, acceleration is exceptionally smooth, quiet and unhesitant; if the full performance is used, acceleration has an urgency matched by few road-going vehicles. Intermediately, the Square Four will

cruise quietly and unostentatiously at 50, 60 or 70 m.p.h. on a mere "whiff" of throttle.

For long or short journeys, the Ariel was easy and pleasant to ride. Factors contributing to this characteristic were comfortable wheel suspension, excellent riding position and control layout, a large reserve of engine power, good brakes and—not least in importance—a high degree of exhaust and mechanical quietness. At no period in the performance range does the exhaust note rise above a pleasant, subdued hum. Mechanical noise, except when the engine was idling, was reminiscent of that of a well-oiled sewing machine. On tickover, the only audible noises were in the form of a rumble from the crankshaft coupling gears, and a slight rustle from the valve-gear.

In spite of its weight, the 4G Mark II has a high degree of handleability. On slow and medium-pace corners it could be heeled over confidently until the prop stand or silencers grounded — which could occur readily when the suspension was loaded by the added weight of a pillion passenger. This ease of handling, coupled with the machine's zestful but unobtrusive acceleration, made the Ariel a commendably safe and pleasant machine to use under traffic conditions.

The riding position is a fine compromise between an "armchair" layout for maximum comfort at town speeds and a slight crouch for fatigue resistance at high speeds—with, perhaps, a slight bias towards the former. Relationship of seat and footrests resulted in an agreeably wide knee angle. The shape of the handlebar provided a natural position for the grips. Seat height was such as to enable a rider of average height easily to place his feet on the ground at traffic halts. All controls could be well placed for ease of operation and were silky to use. Those on the handlebar are reduced to a minimum number. The twistgrip has a somewhat longer than usual rotary travel, a feature providing a delicacy of throttle control which enhances the already outstanding sweetness of the engine.

Starting the four-cylinder engine was always simple. No great muscular effort was required to operate the kick-starter, even when the machine had been standing outdoors overnight in the cold weather experienced in March. Under such conditions, three depressions of the starter pedal were normally sufficient to start the engine with the carburettor bi-starter control in operation. This control could be moved to its intermediate stop after a few seconds' running, and moved to its normal-running position when the machine had covered about a quarter of a mile. When warm, the engine could be brought to life by no more than a leisurely movement of the kick-starter. Carburation at very small throttle openings was uneven, particularly when the engine was cold.

With the engine idling, bottom gear could be engaged noiselessly from neutral. Occasionally, partial release of the clutch was required for gear selection. Neutral was at all times easy to locate from either bottom or second gears. Clutch operation was reasonably light and entirely positive. Gear changes, both upward and downward, could be effected with great rapidity. Owing to the engine's unusually quick response to throttle opening and

---

Close-up view of the massive, yet compact, four-cylinder engine. The distributor is seen in front of the oil tank

A Unique High-performance Mount with Gentle Manners and Outstanding Acceleration

Noteworthy features are the neatness of the power unit and the 20-amp-hour battery. The ignition coil and voltage regulator are mounted beneath the seat

closing, it was found that a fast gear-changing technique achieved the best results. Partial clutch and throttle operation, with a simultaneous, light depression of the gear pedal, produced excellent upward changes, though sometimes second and top gear engagement could be felt slightly. Second to third was a particularly sweet change. Clean and ultra-rapid downward changes were easily made.

Both front and rear wheel suspensions possessed an adequate range of movement and worked well at all speeds. A reasonably soft response around the static-load position and a progressively increasing resistance to deflection brought both small and large surface irregularities within the compass of the springing. Only at ultra-high speeds, on surfaces which were not smooth, did a certain amount of pitching set in. Steering was first class, being both light and positive; bend-swinging was quite effortless. A slight tendency to weave was apparent only when travelling at very high velocities on bad surfaces. The top hamper of a full, five-gallon fuel tank was virtually unnoticeable, except under extreme conditions.

Both brakes were pleasantly light to operate, smooth and extremely powerful. Though their hard use incurred frequent need for adjustment in the early stages of the test, the adjustment took only a matter of seconds.

In the matter of ultimate road performance, the figures shown in the panel speak for themselves. In fact, these data were obtained after the machine had been ridden exceptionally hard for 1,500 miles with little attention, and when a gusty, 15-20 m.p.h. three-quarter wind prevailed. There can be little doubt that, under more favourable conditions, a mean maximum speed of 100 m.p.h. would have been recorded. The fastest one-way run in top gear was at 107 m.p.h.

Under suitable road and traffic conditions, speeds of 80-85 m.p.h. could be maintained for as long as required. In a deliberate attempt to tire the engine, the machine was ridden for many miles with the speedometer needle hovering between 90 and 95 m.p.h., but the engine betrayed not the least sign of distress. Its reserve of power enabled high cruising speeds to be sustained against headwinds and up long gradients, thus making high average speeds commonplace. A slight vibration period

sets in between 50 and 55 m.p.h., but is not felt above 60 m.p.h.

The minimum non-snatch speed is of more than academic interest in the case of the Ariel. In the normal course of town riding, it was frequently throttled back below 20 m.p.h. in top gear and accelerated away sweetly.

The speedometer fitted to the test machine had a high standard of accuracy up to 60 m.p.h. There was virtually no error up to 50 m.p.h.; from 60 to 90 m.p.h. the instrument registered four to five m.p.h. fast. Failure of the ammeter necessitated a replacement during the test. When riding on flooded roads, there was a tendency for one sparking plug to cut out.

The main head lamp bulb provided an adequate beam for fast night riding. The dynamo balanced the full ignition and lamp load at 30 m.p.h. in top gear.

The discerning Ariel Four owner will appreciate the 20-amp-hour battery and its accessibility for topping-up purposes. Another praiseworthy feature is the fuel-tank capacity, which enables 200-250 miles to be covered at high cruising speeds without refuelling. In spite of the machine's weight, it is a relatively easy matter to place it on its rear stand. The accessible prop stand is excellent for use on cambered roads.

Information Panel

997 c.c. Ariel Square Four Mark II

SPECIFICATION

ENGINE : 997 c.c. (65 × 75 mm) four-cylinder o.h.v. Aluminium-alloy cylinders cast *en bloc* in square formation. Detachable light-alloy cylinder head embodying cruciform induction manifold ; totally enclosed and positively lubricated valve gear, with push-rod operation ; separate exhaust manifolds. Twin crankshafts coupled by hardened and ground gears. Light-alloy connecting rods with plain, shell-type big-end bearings. Compression ratio, 7.2 to 1. Dry sump lubrication ; oil-tank capacity, 6 pints.
CARBURETTOR : Solex, Bi-starter type ; twistgrip throttle control.
IGNITION and LIGHTING : Coil ignition. 70-watt, voltage-controlled Lucas dynamo incorporating distributor with automatic timing variation. 7 in-diameter headlamp with sealed-beam light unit. 6-volt, 20-amp-hour Lucas battery.
TRANSMISSION : Burman four-speed gear box with positive-stop foot control. Bottom, 11.07 to 1. Second, 7.1 to 1. Third, 5.46 to 1. Top, 4.18 to 1. Multi-plate clutch with Neoprene inserts, operating in remote case. Primary chain, ½ 0.305 in. in oil-bath case. Secondary chain, ⅝ × ⅜ in., lubricated by adjustable bleed from primary chaincase ; guards over top and bottom runs. R.p.m. at 30 m.p.h. in top gear, 1,675.
FUEL CAPACITY : 5 gallons.
TYRES : Dunlop. Front, 3.25 × 19 in Ribbed. Rear, 4.00 × 18 in Universal.
BRAKES : 7 × 1⅛ in front ; 8 × 1⅛ in rear. Fulcrum adjusters.
SUSPENSION : Ariel telescopic front fork with hydraulic damping. Ariel link-action rear springing.
WHEELBASE : 56½ in unladen. Ground clearance, 4¾ in unladen.
SEAT : Ariel dual-seat. Unladen height, 30 in.
WEIGHT : 460 lb fully equipped, with no fuel and full oil tank.
PRICE : £225. With purchase tax (in Gt. Britain only), £271 17s. 6d. Extras : Spring frame, £16 (with P.T., £19 6s 8d).
ROAD TAX : £3 15s a year ; £1 0s 8d a quarter.
MAKERS : Ariel Motors, Ltd., Selly Oak, Birmingham, 29
DESCRIPTION : *The Motor Cycle, 6 November, 1952.*

PERFORMANCE DATA

MEAN MAXIMUM SPEED : Bottom :* 40 m.p.h.
Second :* 62 m.p.h.
Third :* 79 m.p.h.
Top : 97 m.p.h.
* Valve float occuring.

MEAN ACCELERATION :

	10-30 m.p.h.	20-40 m.p.h.	30-50 m.p.h.
Bottom	2 secs	2 secs	—
Second	3.2 secs	2.6 secs	2.5 secs
Third	4.4 secs.	3.8 secs	3.4 secs
Top	—	5.4 secs	5 secs

Speed at end of quarter-mile from rest : 85 m.p.h.
Mean time to cover standing quarter-mile : 15.4 secs.
PETROL CONSUMPTION : At 30 m.p.h., 57 m.p.g. At 40 m.p.h., 55 m.p.h. At 50 m.p.h., 54 m.p.g. At 60 m.p.h., 50 m.p.g.
BRAKING : From 30 m.p.h. to rest, 26ft 6in (surface, dry tarmac).
TURNING CIRCLE : 15ft.
MINIMUM NON-SNATCH SPEED : 13 m.p.h. in top gear.
WEIGHT Per C.C. : 0.46 lb.

Velocette

MSS

It is one of the facts of motor cycling life that 'Velocette' is a misnomer. The name of the manufacturer was Veloce Ltd (from the Latin word for 'speed') and, indeed, the first products of the company carried Veloce tank badges. However, just before the First World War a small two-stroke was added to the range, and to emphasise the different nature of the machine it was described as a Velocette, or 'little Veloce'.

The return of peacetime saw the Veloce firm – or to put it another way, the Goodman family – concentrating initially on an all-two-stroke programme and, naturally, these were continued under the Velocette name. But the coming of the 350 cc overhead-camshaft Model K engine in 1926 gave the factory a chance to get back to bigger stuff and, accordingly, the first batch of 350 cc bikes had 'Veloce', once more, on the tank sides.

'Take them away', said the dealers. 'Motor cyclists have forgotten what Veloce means by now'. And so the Goodmans had no choice but to label every bike from then on as a Velocette, regardless of engine size!

Still, that is by the way. The overhead-camshaft model was supplemented, in 1933, by a neat little pushrod overhead-valve 250 cc from the drawing board of Eugene Goodman. To reduce the weight of the valve operating gear, and so make for higher revs, the cams were located high in the timing chest and driven by a train of gears (initially straight-cut but later, in order to cut down clatter, with helical teeth).

This was the MOV, a success right from its introduction, and it was swiftly followed by a corresponding ohv 350 cc known as the MAC. Two years later, and especially for the family sidecar man, the third of the M-series machines arrived – the 495 cc Model MSS. This was the first British bike to embody automatic ignition advance and retard, and which soon built up a healthy export trade. Indeed, as related by the late Len Moseley (*My Velocette Days*; Transport Bookman Ltd) some were sent as far afield as Japan.

Production continued up to the outbreak of the Second World War, and when the Hall Green works resumed motor cycle manufacture in 1945, the big MSS was still in the programme. Surprisingly, however, the very first peacetime machines to leave the Hall Green assembly line were about two-hundred Model GTP two-strokes featuring magneto ignition instead of the pre-war coil ignition. Ostensibly these were all earmarked for overseas markets, although a dozen travelled no further overseas than the Channel Islands.

The 495 cc MSS, together with other Velocette singles, ceased production in 1948, the reason being that the Goodman family were by then totally commited to the revolutionary flat-twin 150 cc Model LE side-valve. The LE was the 'everyman runabout' of dreams, the archetypal clean and quiet commuter machine for the masses.

Yes, well . . . Oh, certainly the potential commuter market existed. It was just that the LE was not the model for which commuters had been waiting, and the true answer was the chic little scooter as exemplified by the Vespa and Lambretta.

In the end the LE did find a niche, as silent transport for the pre-Panda beat policeman. But the numbers required for this work were insufficient to keep the factory in full production, and so the 350 cc MAC returned, initially in rigid form, but later with

Died-in-the-wool sidecar men swear that there never has been a bike to match the 499 cc MSS Velocette for sheer slogging power. A typical outfit was this 1954 marriage of an MSS and a Watsonian Monarch sidecar. Tested by Motor Cycling, *it achieved a top speed of 64 mph*

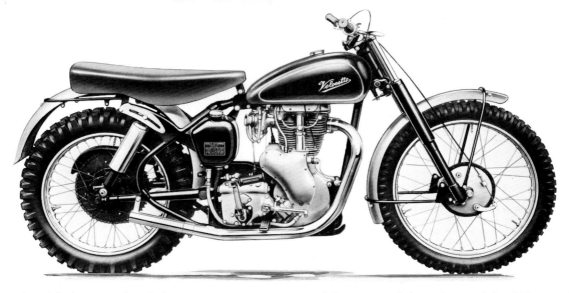

A model catalogued for some years but which never quite came up to expectations was the 499 cc MSS Scrambler, here seen in 1955 form

pivoted rear springing of unusual type. The fork itself was conventional, but the upper mountings of the rear damper units could be moved through a curved slot, to soften or harden the springing in accordance with the load on the machine.

The frame was the old traditional pattern, built by the hearth-brazing method with malleable-cast lugs, and conceding nothing to modern practice, with the rear fork grafted on.

For 1954 the MSS returned, too, but this was not the earlier MSS, even if it looked much the same. The cylinder barrel and head were now of Al-Fin light-alloy construction with bonded-in iron liner (Al-Fin was a proprietary process, operated by Wellworthy's of Lymington) but, more important still, bore and stroke dimensions had changed from the old longstroke format of 81 × 96 mm, to the fashionable 'square' 86 × 86 mm. Valve springs were of hairpin pattern.

Had Velocette's chief designer, Charles Udall at last decided to move towards modernity? In a way, maybe; but as Udall himself disclosed in an interview, the real reason was that the factory had decided to standardise on the MAC sprung frame

Far better known as a road-racer, the late John Hartle tackles a snow gulley at Panpunton, in the 1964 national Victory Trial. Most unusually, his mount is an adapted MSS Velocette

out of sheer economic necessity – and the old longstroke 495 c MSS was just that fraction too tall. They merely shortened it t fit.

Peak power output of the MSS, on a compression ratio of 6· to 1, was only 23 bhp at 5,000 rpm, but the torque curve was flat one, and a useful helping of urge was available from as lov as 2,500 rpm. Which was fair enough, because the machine wa designed as a slogger with the family sidecar man in mind.

For all that, the MSS found a ready sale among USA enthusiasts, who tended to skim the head, take off the lights an other non-essentials and ride flat-out across the dusty desert i the type of mass-start enduro racing of which they seeme inordinately fond.

More or less in self-defence, Hall Green had to evolve a official cross-country racer from the MSS, and this duly took it place in the catalogue as the MSS Endurance. In fact there wer *two* off-road variants, the other being the MSS Scrambler; th Endurance could be considered as the Scrambler with lightin set fitted. For both, introduced in 1955, there was a high compression engine with Amal TT9 racing carburettor an BTH racing magneto. Wheels were shod with competition-typ 'knobbly' tyres and the frames, though still of time-honoure brazed lug construction, were given an extra helping of groun clearance.

On British circuits the Scrambler never did achieve very mucl fame or fortune (although on one occasion Billy Nicholson usee one at an Easter Monday Redmarley freak hill-climb), but th Endurance version built up quite a sizeable following i America. Moreover, Tex Luce used an MSS Endurance engine with reworked cylinder head porting and lightened and polishee internals, as the basis of a very successful half-mile dirt tracl model; but Hall Green drew the line at adding a dirt-tracker t the now lengthy list of MSS variants.

Two more variants came into the list for 1956. Both based o the MSS engine, these were the sports-roadster 499 cc Venon and 349 cc Viper. It might be thought more feasible to have based the smaller machine, the Viper, on the existing 349 c MAC, but in fact the same crankcase assembly was employee for both newcomers. So it made economic sense, after all.

In the years ahead, it was the Venom which took the glory – ir production-machine racing and, most glorious feat of all, ir capturing the 24-hour world 500 cc record at 100·05 mph. Late still there would be the Venom Thruxton, an even more rort variation on the MSS theme. During this time, the MS continued in production until the Velocette factory ceased bik manufacture during 1971.

499 c.c. High-Camshaft MSS Velocette

INCLUSION of the 499 c.c. MSS model in the Velocette range of machines for 1954 marked the return of an old favourite rather than the introduction of an entirely new model. Nevertheless, though the latest version of the Velocette five-hundred bears an unmistakable affinity with its precursor, the new model has been modernized and re-designed in many respects.

Twenty-one years have passed since the high-camshaft, pushrod-operated overhead-valve Velocette engine made its first appearance—as a two-fifty. Two years later, following the introduction of the 349 c.c. MAC, the MSS was born to complete a trio of high-camshaft Velocettes. Those machines considerably extended the popularity of a marque already famous for the excellence of its overhead-camshaft touring and racing machines and for its high standard of engineering.

Post-war production considerations led to the discontinuance of the MSS six years ago. It re-emerges as an up-to-the-minute, single-cylinder five-hundred of exceptional quality and fine finish. It provides a high degree of riding comfort for one or two people, exemplary steering and road-holding, and an engine performance which is remarkable for the lusty power produced with complete smoothness at low and medium speeds.

Riders of various statures found that the relationship between seat, footrests and handlebar afforded a riding position which was comfortable and relaxed, even when many consecutive hours were spent in the saddle. The width across the handlebar grips, their height and their angle were such that the rider's hands rested on them naturally. All the controls on the bar could be well sited for ready operation and were smooth in use. With the footrest hangers in the 12 o'clock position, the brake and gear pedals were ideally situated and could be manipulated while the rider's insteps remained on the rests. For continued high-speed cruising the next rearward position of the footrests gave an even more suitable riding position but, with that setting, the reach to the pedals was too great for convenience. With the footrests in either position, the inside of the rider's right ankle was against the folding kick-starter crank.

Of unusual, two-level design, the dual-seat is of generous proportions, well shaped, and comfortably upholstered. With its overall length of 26½in and maximum width of 12in, it provided ample accommodation for two adults dressed in wet-weather riding kit. The pillion passenger's riding position was no less comfortable than that of the rider.

Complementary to the well-tailored riding position in furnishing a smooth and fatigue-free ride is a highly efficient system of front and rear springing. The adjustable-for-load, pivoted-fork rear suspension gave results which place it among the very best of contemporary layouts. For solo riding, the adjustment was set in its softest position. Road irregularities of all types normally encountered were absorbed without shock to the rider, whether the machine's speed was low or high. No pitching was experienced at any time, and roadholding on bumpy or undulating surfaces was of the highest order. In fact, it can truly be said of the MSS that its rider was at all times unconscious of the rear wheel. The range of adjustment provided was found to be more than adequate for pillion work.

Judged by the high standard of the rear springing, the action of the telescopic front fork was felt to be just a trifle hard, though by no means uncomfortably so. The comparative firmness became less perceptible as road speed mounted.

As is appropriate in a machine from a factory whose products have, in the past, achieved meritorious racing successes, the MSS almost steered itself. Straight-ahead steering was positive under all conditions, but it was cornering and bend-swinging which best revealed the Velocette's racing ancestry. The utmost confidence was quickly inspired by the unwavering way in which the front wheel would turn inward by just the right amount when the machine was banked into a bend or corner. This self-steering characteristic was evident at all speeds from a comparative crawl to the machine's maximum, and it operated for all normal degrees of lean. There was never any tendency for the front wheel to deviate from its allotted path, and corners of all types could be negotiated in safety faster on the MSS than on most contemporary machines. At low and medium speeds the footrest rubbers could be grounded, but that did not seriously limit cornering technique.

Left : well proportioned lines are enhanced by chromium-plated wheel rims and polished-aluminium engine and gear-box castings

Following pages: 1966 Venom Thruxton

A Light-alloy Single With Remarkably Smooth
Power Delivery : Race-bred Steering
and Road-holding Qualities

*The external throttle-stop control on the carburettor provides settings
for normal running and for starting*

In its latest guise, the MSS engine exhibited in marked degree those pleasant attributes which characterize the well-designed single and which endear the type to a large number of riders. The low- and medium-speed torque was quite exceptional. Added to good engine balance, effectively heavy flywheels and extraordinarily sweet transmission, the excellent torque resulted in an outstandingly tractable top-gear performance.

Though the engine is no sluggard in mounting the r.p.m. scale, a great deal of its charm lies in its smooth and rapid acceleration from low speeds. Whether the machine was ridden solo or two-up it was frequently throttled back to 20 m.p.h. in top gear in the normal course of traffic negotiation and was accelerated from that speed smartly and without pinking merely by opening the throttle. On steep, main-road gradients the same technique could be employed, if desired, from a speed of 20 to 25 m.p.h.

Efficient cooling is a feature of the light-alloy engine. On fast, main-road journeys no amount of hard riding tired the power unit. An extremely pleasant continuous cruising speed was 60 to 65 m.p.h., a pace which required a throttle opening of one-half or less, according to wind conditions; when main-road hills were encountered the MSS would take them in its stride without appreciable loss of speed and without need for increased throttle opening. At no engine speed was vibration perceptible through the footrests or fuel tank; a slight tremor could be felt at the handlebar but was almost unnoticable.

Mechanical noises were well subdued. A rhythmic clack from the valve gear could be identified but was not obtrusive. At small throttle openings the exhaust note was blameless. During brisk acceleration, however (though the note possessed a deep, clean-cut quality delightful to the ears of a single-cylinder enthusiast), it was considered to be too loud, particularly for built-up localities.

Achievement of prompt engine starting required a rather precise technique. When the engine was cold it was sensitive to mixture strength and, consequently, to the degree of carburettor tickling employed. A first-kick start could be effected by closing the air lever, turning the external throttle-stop control on the carburettor to the starting position, depressing the tickler lightly for a second and then, with the twistgrip in the closed position, spinning the engine rapidly by means of a long, powerful thrust on the kick-starter.

Insufficient or too much tickling were equally detrimental to easy starting. The remedy in the latter case was to open the throttle wide during operation of the kick-starter. As soon as the engine was running the air lever could be opened fully and the throttle-stop control turned to its normal running position. When the engine was warm, spinning it quickly was no less essential to a ready response though, in that case, the throttle-stop was set in its normal running position, the air lever left open and the tickler ignored. Whether hot or cold the engine would tick over reliably at a speed so low that individual power strokes could easily be counted.

Information Panel—499 c.c. High-Camshaft MSS Velocette

SPECIFICATION

ENGINE: 499 c.c. (86 x 86 mm) single-cylinder o.h.v. with fully enclosed valve gear; Duralumin pushrods, hairpin valve springs. Aluminium-alloy cylinder and cylinder head. Roller-bearing big end; crankshaft supported on taper-roller bearings. Compression ratio, 6.8 to 1. Dry-sump lubrication; oil-tank capacity, 4 pints.

CARBURETTOR: Amal with twistgrip throttle control; air slide operated by handlebar lever. Air filter.

IGNITION and LIGHTING: Lucas magneto with auto-advance. 36-watt Miller dynamo. 7½in-diameter Miller headlamp with sealed-beam light unit.

TRANSMISSION: Velocette four-speed gear box with positive-stop foot control. Bottom, 11.18 to 1. Second, 7.74 to 1. Third, 5.86 to 1. Top, 4.87 to 1. Multi-plate clutch with fabric inserts. Primary chain, ½ x 0.305in, in oil-bath case. Rear chain, ⅝ x ¼in, with guard over top run. Engine r.p.m. at 30 m.p.h. in top gear, 1,970.

FUEL CAPACITY: 3 gallons.

TYRES: Dunlop Universal, 3.25 x 19in front and rear.

BRAKES: 7in-diameter front and rear.

SUSPENSION: Velocette telescopic front fork with hydraulic damping. Pivoted-fork rear springing employing coil springs and hydraulic damping; adjustment for load.

WHEELBASE: 54¼in unladen. Ground clearance, 5in unladen.

SEAT: Velocette dual-seat. Unladen height, 31in.

WEIGHT: 392 lb fully equipped, with full oil tank and one gallon of petrol.

PRICE: £175 10s. With purchase tax (in Great Britain only), £210 12s.

ROAD TAX: £3 15s a year; £1 0s 8d a quarter.

MAKERS: Veloce, Ltd., York Road, Hall Green, Birmingham, 23.

DESCRIPTION: The Motor Cycle, 29 October 1953.

PERFORMANCE DATA

MEAN MAXIMUM SPEED:
Bottom: *37 m.p.h.
Second: *53 m.p.h.
Third: *71 m.p.h.
Top: 80 m.p.h.
*Valve float occurring.

HIGHEST ONE-WAY SPEED: 82 m.p.h. (Conditions: moderate three-quarter wind; rider wearing two-piece suit and overboots.)

MEAN ACCELERATION:

	10-30 m.p.h.	20-40 m.p.h.	30-50 m.p.h.
Bottom	3.4 secs	—	—
Second	4.6 secs	4.2 secs	4.8 secs
Third	—	5.8 secs	5.8 secs
Top	—	7.2 secs	7.2 secs

Mean speed at end of quarter-mile from rest: 72 m.p.h.
Mean time to cover standing quarter-mile: 17.8 secs.

PETROL CONSUMPTION: At 30 m.p.h., 94 m.p.g. At 40 m.p.h., 82 m.p.g. At 50 m.p.h., 72 m.p.g. At 60 m.p.h., 52 m.p.g.

BRAKING: From 30 m.p.h. to rest, 31ft (surface, dry tarmac).

TURNING CIRCLE: 18ft.

MINIMUM NON-SNATCH SPEED: 16 m.p.h. in top gear.

WEIGHT PER C.C.: 0.78 lb.

The 499 c.c. MSS Velocette

Left : detaching the tail of the rear mudguard gives access for removal of the quickly detachable rear wheel

Of average lightness in operation, the clutch was smooth and very positive in taking up the drive. A slight tendency for the clutch plates to drag was perceptible in the form of a faint clonk which could be heard and felt when bottom gear was engaged with the engine idling. All gear changes, both upward and downward, were a delight to execute. Pedal travel was short. Quick, light and simultaneous operation of the throttle, clutch and gear pedal invariably produced clean, noiseless changes.

Advantage has been taken of the engine's exceptional low-speed torque to employ closely grouped gear ratios. The 4.87 to 1 top-gear ratio enables the engine to reach its peak-power speed of 5,000 r.p.m., and the bottom-gear ratio of 11.18 to 1, though uncommonly high for a machine of this type, is in no circumstances disadvantageous; indeed, in the standing-start quarter-mile test, the Velocette put up a performance which was above average for a 500 c.c. single.

Both brakes were adequately powerful, though not so light in operation that either wheel would be locked inadvertently on wet roads. There was no trace of sponginess in the controls, and no adjustment was called for throughout the test. Incidentally, adjustment of the MSS brakes necessitates the use of spanners.

Intensity of the headlamp beam was considered insufficient for fast night riding. When the machine was ridden in rain the voltage-control unit was vulnerable to the ingress of water. As a result, when the engine was stopped, the ammeter showed a full-scale discharge and it was necessary temporarily to remove the dynamo plug to obviate running down the battery.

The speedometer fitted to the Velocette was checked for accuracy and was found to read fast progressively from 1 m.p.h. at 30 m.p.h. and 3 m.p.h. at 50 to 60 m.p.h. to 8 m.p.h. at an indicated 90 m.p.h.

For parking purposes the prop stand was considered to be among the best contemporary fittings of its type. It was accessible to operate, and it supported the machine safely on level surfaces and on all normal degrees of camber. A centre stand is provided for maintenance purposes.

Two minor criticisms arose during routine maintenance. To eliminate backlash from the throttle control it was necessary to remove the dual-seat and fuel tank to gain access to the cable adjuster. During primary chain adjustment the gear-box top front clamping nut was found to be difficult of access. The toolkit was of average quality, though a more suitable sparking-plug spanner would have been appreciated in view of the extent of the cylinder-head finning around the plug.

The highly polished surfaces on engine and gear-box castings facilitated cleaning of those units. At the conclusion of a strenuous test the engine remained completely oil-tight and only a smear of oil had found its way on to the outside of the gear box in the vicinity of the pedal pivot.

The finish of the machine is in keeping with its fine all-round performance. The new MSS unquestionably occupies a position in the forefront of single-cylinder five-hundreds.

Above : clutch adjustment is by means of a peg passed through the final-drive sprocket. Right : the dynamo is driven by a flat belt

TRIUMPH
TIGER 110

The advice chalked on the blackboard thrust out from the pits was clear enough, if somewhat superfluous. 'Slipstream Mac', it ran; and young Mike Hailwood, flat on the tank, nodded to his pit attendant father. He knew well enough that his chief opponent was the seasoned Bob McIntyre and he was, already, doing his best not to lose sight of the flying Scot.

A road-racing scene typical of the late 1950s period, perhaps? Indeed so. But in this instance the race was the gruelling Thruxton 500-mile production-machine marathon of 1958, first event of the series to carry that label (earlier meetings, run by the clock and not the milometer, had been known as the Thruxton Nine-Hour). And Mike, sharing a Triumph Tiger 110 with Dan Shorey, not only slipstreamed the 692 cc Royal Enfield

Triumph's famous Tiger 110 engine was a sportier version of the 649 cc Thunderbird seen here. In turn, the Thunderbird engine was itself a development of the original Speed Twin design, enlarged to suit American market requirements

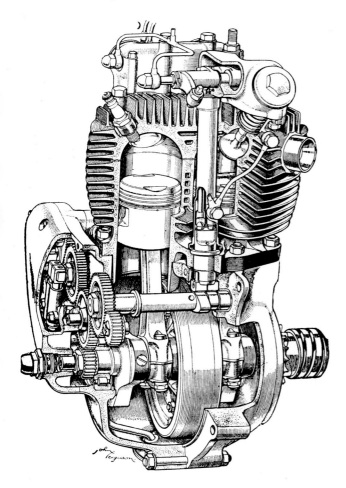

Constellation of Bob Mac and Derek Powell but, eventually, finished one lap ahead with an overall average speed of 66 mph. It is worth noting, too, that fifth place in the same event was taken by another T110 with, as one of its co-riders, a certain Percy Tait who was not exactly unknown in Triumph circles . . .

For that matter, 1958 was turning out to be a very good vintage for the 'Tee-One-Ten', because over on the far side of the Atlantic one Bill Johnson – already a record-breaker on other Triumphs – pushed a twin-carburettor-head version of a Tiger 110 through the speed trap at Bonneville Salt Flats, Utah, at 147.32 mph, to claim a new USA Class C (650 cc stock-machine) national record.

Yet that Johnson effort carried the seeds of the T110's eventual eclipse. Meanwhile, a super-sports variant of the 650 cc was on the stocks, code-named the T120. And what better catalogue name for the newcomer could there be but Bonneville!

However, to return to the beginning. Triumph got going in the immediate post-war market with the Speed Twin and Tiger 100 twins, but although these 500 cc models were perfectly acceptable to the British, the Americans were soon demanding something with more performance. Edward Turner obliged with the 649 cc Thunderbird and then, following his usual practice of allowing a design to settle down in unstressed touring form before developing it further, evolved from that basic model a high-performance edition to which he gave the name Tiger 110.

The development prototype T110 made its appearance in the 1953 International Six Days Trial, where it was ridden by Jimmy Alves, a member of the British Trophy team. That year, Britain took the main award, and no bike could have had a tougher baptism. A month later, the production version took its bow, at the Paris Salon, where it was said that the machine was primarily for export only, and very few would be released to the home market.

Right from the beginning, the T110 adopted pivoted fork rear suspension, together with an alternator to supply lighting current (although a magneto, with hand-operated advance and retard, was retained for ignition purposes). By snuggling the gearbox cosily behind the crankcase and fitting a shortened primary chaincase, the Meriden engineers had managed to keep the wheelbase only 0.5 in longer than the rigid-frame Thunderbird.

Engine changes included a beefed-up crankshaft, larger inlet valves, a compression ratio of 8.5 to 1 (instead of the Thunderbird's 7 to 1), and an increased volume of oil in circulation. Power output was 42 bhp at 6,500 rpm, notwithstanding the cast-iron cylinder block and head. From personal experience, however, I can say that the early T110 was not the sweetest of models to ride, and the power delivery was harsh, especially at low engine rpm, unless the rider juggled with the advance-retard ignition lever – and, in heavy traffic, that was not always possible.

Be that as it may, the Americans seemed to like the new Tiger 110, and were soon entering it in all kinds of events for which it

Well before his days of international racing fame, a very young Mike Hailwood here pilots an unlikely-seeming model in the production-machine Thruxton 500-mile Race of 1958. It is the 649 cc Triumph Tiger 110 which Mike and co-rider Dan Shorey took to a magnificent win, a lap ahead of the Royal Enfield twin of Bob McIntyre and Derek Powell

was never intended, strictly speaking – such as the Cambridge (Minnesota) Enduro, where, in July, 1954, it took the Light-heavyweight class award.

In Britain, the T110 found its niche in production-machine racing, finishing first, second and third in the 1955 Thruxton Nine-Hour 750 cc class, but there were better things to come with the introduction, for the 1956 season, of a new die-cast light-alloy cylinder head with cast-in austenitic iron valve seats; new, too, were steel-backed thin wall big-end bearing shells.

This time Percy Tait took 750 cc honours at Thruxton though it must be confessed that the honour was a fairly empty one, with a solid wedge of at least half a dozen BSA Gold Stars finishing ahead of him in the overall reckoning. BSA riders were the principal opposition, also, at America's unique Catalina Grand Prix meeting – a combination of road race and moto-cross – but three Tiger 110s finished fourth, fifth, and sixth. For something just a little different, Triumph provided a batch of five Tiger 110s as mounts for the TT Race travelling marshals in the Isle of Man, and the machines, collectively, covered 7,000 high-speed miles during the practice and race weeks.

One year later, Geoff Hughes and Syd Stevens brought their model home second overall in what was to be the last of the

Thruxton Nine-Hour races, albeit two laps behind a three-fifty BSA Gold Star. In general the T110 had been giving good service, but at racing speeds cracks had tended to develop in the cylinder head, between the valve seat edge and holding-down-stud holes; this was put right for 1958, by providing additional metal, and by slightly reducing the valve diameter. A twin-carburettor cylinder head was offered at extra cost, but in fact this option was to remain in the catalogue for only one year, and with the coming of the Bonneville for 1959 the T110 reverted to a subsidiary role, as the halfway house between the touring Thunderbird and the super-sports Bonnie.

It was the beginning of the end for the Tiger 110, and although it did survive into the 1961 range (by which time separate engine and gearbox construction had given way to unit-construction, and the voluminous rear wheel enclosure panels known irreverently as the 'bathtub' had been adopted), by that time it was almost indistinguishable from the Thunderbird. It had a compression ratio of 8·5 to 1, as against the Thunderbird's more modest 7·5 to 1 ratio, and magneto ignition – now, at long last, with automatic advance and retard – instead of coil; but that, apart from colour schemes, was all.

In any case, another newcomer had been added to the Meriden programme. This was the 649 cc TR6 Trophy, virtually a single-carburettor version of the Bonneville, and in the years ahead it would take over the role originally allotted to the T110. In time, too, the TR6 Trophy would become the Tiger 650 then, as engine size increased, the Tiger 750. Faithful shadow to the Bonneville 750, it remains in production to this day.

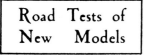

Road Tests of
New Models

649 c.c. Triumph Tiger 110

Impressive O. H. V. Twin Combining Light Steering and Powerful Braking with a Performance to Delight the Sporting Rider

THE 649 c.c. Triumph Tiger 110 owes its existence largely to the demands of the American market where the primary requirement, within reasonable limits, is the highest possible power output from a given engine capacity. A tuned variant of the six-fifty Thunderbird, the T110 was introduced for 1954. Its specification included the then-new Triumph pivoted-fork rear springing and an engine incorporating a cast-iron cylinder block and cylinder head.

Most notable development for the current year is a light-alloy cylinder head of entirely new layout. The casting incorporates air passages to assist cooling; valve-seat inserts are of austenitic iron. An incidental improvement on the new head is that oil from the valve gear drains via the pushrod tubes, thus eliminating the need for external pipes. Combining a superb road potential with light handling and smooth, powerful braking, the T110 is a machine which cannot fail to impress the sporting rider. Few road burners, in truth, would ask for a higher cruising speed than the Triumph eagerly provides. Indeed, its capacity for searing acceleration and tireless, ultra-high cruising speeds is second only to the higher-performance 1,000 c.c. models of current and recent vintage.

But the Tiger 110 is not unduly obtrusive in its behaviour, for its exhaust note is reasonably well subdued no matter how hard the machine is ridden. Nor is it too intractable for use in heavy city traffic. Naturally, the high compression ratio, sporting valve timing and large port sizes necessary for such outstanding acceleration and speed from six-fifty roadsters involve some sacrifice of docility at low engine revolutions. Discreet use of the manual ignition control, however, tames the engine to a considerable degree and if, in addition, liberal use is made of the indirect gear ratios, negotiating heavy traffic need involve no irritation for the rider. Engine starting was dependable and relatively easy even in extremely cold weather, while petrol consumption was remarkably economical. In short, the T110, though primarily a high-powered sports model, is sufficiently well-mannered, manageable and economical to be employed for more modests duties without compromise.

Passing from a general survey of the model's qualities to a specific analysis of the various facets of its behaviour, it is logical to deal first with its most outstanding attribute—high open-road performance. The figures shown in the information panel speak for themselves. Yet it should be emphasized that the mean maximum speed and the quarter-mile acceleration figures would probable have been fractionally better still had less-windy conditions prevailed at the time the data were obtained. Though a very stiff wind blew only about 15 degrees off the direction of the stretch of road used, the speed loss upwind in such circumstances was not compensated by the downwind advantage.

Acceleration through the gears was scintillating and carburation clean. Even at an indicated 80 m.p.h. an exhilarating

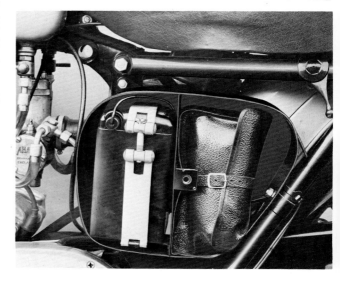

Battery and tool kit are housed in a single, partitioned container. The tool kit is adequate for routine adjustments

Finish of the Tiger 110 is shell-blue and black enamel. With many light-alloy castings polished and the usual components chromium plated, the model is very smart

TNX 749

Left: Elimination of external pipes for valve-gear drainage results in a cleaner appearance of the engine. Right: Concealed between the oil tank and the battery box, the air filter did not restrict engine performance to any appreciable degree

surge forward could be produced simply by snapping the throttle wide open. To the Tiger 110, cruising at 75 m.p.h. was child's play and required only a small throttle opening. A speed of 80 m.p.h. could be held on half throttle, while a sustained 90 m.p.h. proved to be quite within the model's capabilities. The highest speedometer reading obtained with the rider sitting upright was 100 m.p.h. with a following wind.

The carrying of a pillion passenger did not substantially reduce cruising speed. With two adults (each clad in winter riding kit) occupying the dual-seat, the Triumph hummed along at a speedometer 80 m.p.h. for many consecutive miles on little more than half throttle. Opening the twistgrip fully sent the speedometer needle quickly round to the 90 m.p.h. mark. When checked for accuracy, the speedometer was found to register about 5 per cent fast at all speeds from an indicated 30 m.p.h. to the highest reading obtained—114 m.p.h. As a matter of interest the maximum-speed checks were repeated with the air filter disconnected, a bell-mouth fitted to the carburettor and the main-jet size increased from 250 to 270. No difference in speed was perceptible.

Engine vibration was detectable through the petrol tank from about 80 m.p.h. upward (or from a lower speed when the tank was full). Though pronounced, the tremor was not objectionable so long as the rider refrained from gripping the tank between his knees.

Maintenance of a steady 30 m.p.h. in built-up areas required a partially retarded ignition setting if top gear was used. Alternatively, third gear could be employed with the ignition control at full advance. Idling, once the engine had reached its normal working temperature, was slow and regular with the throttle closed and the ignition fully retarded or nearly so. With these conditions fulfilled, bottom gear could be engaged almost noiselessly; but the first bottom-gear engagement after a cold start was accompanied by an audible scrunch as a result of the relatively fast idling speed necessary to prevent stalling.

Ignition is controlled by a lever on the left side of the handlebar, though the lever is of the pattern normally used on the right side of a bar. After engagement of bottom gear on full retard, it was found desirable to advance the ignition partially or fully (by pulling the lever to the rear) before feeding in the clutch. For that reason a left-hand-pattern ignition lever would have

---

Information Panel

SPECIFICATION

ENGINE: 649 c.c. (71 × 82mm) overhead-valve vertical twin. Fully enclosed valve gear. Aluminium-alloy cylinder head. Light-alloy connecting rods; plain big-end bearings. Crankshaft supported in two ball bearings. Compression ratio: 8.5 to 1. Dry-sump lubrication; oil-tank capacity, 6 pints.

CARBURETTOR: Amal Monobloc with twistgrip throttle control; air slide operated by lever situated under seat. Air filter.

IGNITION and LIGHTING: Lucas magneto with manual control. Separate 60-watt Lucas dynamo and 6-volt, 12-ampere-hour battery. 7in-diameter headlamp with pre-focus light unit.

TRANSMISSION: Triumph four-speed gear box with positive-stop foot control. Gear ratios: bottom, 11.2 to 1; second, 7.75 to 1; third, 5.45 to 1; top, 4.57 to 1. Multi-plate clutch with Neolangita insert operating in oil. Primary chain, ½ × 0.305in in oil-bath case. Rear chain, ⅝ × ⅜in lubricated by bleed from primary chaincase; guard over top run. Engine r.p.m. at 30 m.p.h. in top gear, 1,760.

FUEL CAPACITY: 4 gallons.

TYRES: Dunlop: front, 3.25 × 19in with ribbed tread; rear, 3.50 × 19in Universal.

BRAKES: 7in-diameter rear; 8in-diameter front with ventilating scoops; finger adjusters.

SUSPENSION: Triumph telescopic front fork with hydraulic damping. Pivoted-fork rear springing employing coil springs and hydraulic damping; three-position adjustment for load.

WHEELBASE: 57in unladen. Ground clearance, 5in unladen.

SEAT: Triumph Twinseat; unladen height, 31in.

WEIGHT: 420 lb fully equipped, with full oil tank and approximately one gallon of petrol.

PRICE: £214; with purchase tax (in Great Britain only), £265 7s 3d. Extras: quickly detachable rear wheel, £3 (p.t., 14s 5d); prop stand, 15s 6d (p.t., 3s 9d); pillion footrests, 16s (p.t., 3s 11d).

ROAD TAX: £3 15s a year; £1 0s 8d a quarter.

MAKERS: Triumph Engineering Co., Ltd., Meriden Works, Allesley, Coventry.

DESCRIPTION: "The Motor Cycle", 27 October 1955.

PERFORMANCE DATA

MEAN MAXIMUM SPEED:

Bottom:	* 51 m.p.h.
Second:	* 73 m.p.h.
Third:	94 m.p.h.
Top:	101 m.p.h.

*Valve float occurring.

HIGHEST ONE-WAY SPEED: 109 m.p.h. (conditions: strong near-tail wind; rider wearing two-piece riding suit and overboots).

MEAN ACCELERATION:

	10-30 m.p.h.	20-40 m.p.h.	30-50 m.p.h.
Bottom	2 sec.	2.8 sec.	2.8 sec.
Second	3.2 sec.	3 sec.	2.4 sec.
Third	—	4.6 sec.	4.6 sec.
Top	—	6 sec.	6.4 sec.

Mean speed at end of quarter-mile from rest: 82 m.p.h.
Mean time to cover standing quarter-mile: 16 sec.

PETROL CONSUMPTION: At 30 m.p.h., 100 m.p.g. At 40 m.p.h., 92 m.p.g. At 50 m.p.h., 80 m.p.g. At 60 m.p.h., 70 m.p.g.

BRAKING: From 30 m.p.h. to rest, 33ft (surface, dry tarmac).

TURNING CIRCLE: 14ft 6in.

MINIMUM NON-SNATCH SPEED: 18 m.p.h. in top gear with ignition fully retarded.

WEIGHT PER C.C.: 0.65 lb.

A ribbed drum and ventilation scoops are features of the 8in-diameter front brake. Stopping power was excellent

been preferred so that it could be pushed forward with the left thumb for advance while the clutch lever was still grasped.

Though temperatures below freezing point were frequently experienced during the test, engine starting was nearly always achieved at the first kick. Naturally, a vigorous thrust on the kick-start was necessary to spin the engine over compression. Prerequisites for cold starting were half retard, closure of the air lever, liberal flooding of the carburettor and a small (but not critical) throttle opening. Because of the very cold weather it was found necessary to leave the air lever closed or partially closed for the first mile or so. Situated beneath the seat, the lever was not too easy to operate with thickly gloved fingers.

Except for the common fault of a longish reach to the clutch and front-brake levers, all the other controls were quite convenient to operate and were smooth in action. (When a chain link was fitted between the lever and pivot-block of both the clutch and front-brake controls to reduce the reach required, there was still an ample range of lever movement.) The clutch was sweet yet firm in taking up the drive, and the gear pedal was pleasantly light to operate. Upward gear changes required a leisurely movement of the pedal if the dogs were to engage noiselessly. Provided engine speed was appropriately increased by slight blipping of the throttle, clean downward changes could be achieved without any pause in control movement. No difficulty was experienced in selecting neutral from bottom or second gear whether the machine was moving or at rest.

The riding position proved to be very comfortable for low and medium speeds. There was ample room on the dual-seat for a pillion passenger, though the width of the seat between the passenger's thighs was slightly too great to permit him comfortably to place his feet as far inboard on the rests as was desired. For sustained high-speed cruising, particularly against a strong wind, a position giving a more forward inclination to the rider's body would have been preferred in order to lessen the tension

in his arms caused by wind pressure. Strapping luggage across the dual-seat to support the base of the rider's spine proved helpful in this connection.

As is characteristic of modern Triumph twins, steering and general handling were extremely light. This trait, coupled with the armchair riding position and the machine's smooth response to the controls, made the T110 particularly delightful to ride at speeds up to say, a mile a minute. Confidence was soon engendered and stylish riding became automatic. Stability on wet city streets was first class. Unusually little effort was needed to heel the model over and, in consequence, it could be ridden round slow- and medium-speed bends in very slick fashion. At high speeds a greater degree of heaviness in the steering would have been appreciated, especially on bumpy road surfaces and in strong, gusty winds. In such circumstances a turn or two of the steering damper had a marked steadying effect on the steering, but was by no means essential.

Both front and rear springing were distinctly firm, a feature not uncommon on high-speed machines. As a result of the firmness no components fouled the ground when the model was banked steeply on corners; that was the case whether the machine was ridden one-up with the rear springing at its softest setting or with a pillion passenger and the springing adjustment at its hardest.

Matching the machine's speed capabilities, braking efficiency was higher than the relevant figure in the performance data suggests. The reason is that the front brake was more effective at high speeds than at 30 m.p.h. Even from near-maximum speed, firm application of the brake easily evoked a squeal of protest from the tyre. Leverage in the rear-brake control was high; consequently pedal travel was longer than average and the wheel could readily be locked. After dark, main-road cruising speeds of 60 to 70 m.p.h. were possible by the light of the headlamp beam.

As a result of the extensive full-throttle riding involved when compiling the performance figures, an appreciable amount of oil leaked past the gear-box mainshaft on to the rear tyre. Also when performance data were being obtained the ammeter failed, possibly as a result of vibration. When the machine was ridden in London traffic in particularly heavy rain, some misfiring was caused by water finding its way inside the sparking-plug covers. Long main-road journeys in similar weather, however, were quite free from the bother. The firm action of the taper-cock petrol taps was appreciated (the left-hand tap controls the reserve supply), as was the fact that four gallons of fuel could be put in the tank after a few miles had been covered on reserve. Both petrol and oil tanks have large, quick-action filler caps.

With its shell-blue and black finish, the Tiger 110 is extremely smart in appearance. Possessing a performance which suggests the analogy of an iron hand in a velvet glove, it is one of the most impressive Triumphs yet produced and is justly popular among sporting riders.

Though possessing exhilarating road performance, the T110 is not unhappy in heavy traffic. The manual ignition control can be used to obtain docile engine behaviour, while manœuvrability is very good

TRIUMPH
TIGER CUB

In the years immediately following the Second World War, the British motor cyclist had become so accustomed to linking the words 'Triumph' and 'twin', that he had almost completely forgotten the lively little 149 cc Model XO overhead-valve single of the hungry mid-1930s. So visitors to the 1952 Earls Court Show were most surprised to see, displayed among the vertical twins, a little maroon-painted lightweight described as the Terrier.

However, although the Terrier had some superficial resemblance to the pre-war model, in design it was quite new. From the drawing board of Edward Turner, it was a 149 cc (57 × 58·5 mm) unit-construction four-speeder with a most unusual bottom-half arrangement whereby the gearbox and crankcase formed a single casting; the crankshaft was inserted through the open drive-side of the unit, and the aperture was then closed by a circular door forming part of the primary chaincase inner half.

To publicise the newcomer and, at the same time, show sceptics that the factory top brass had faith in their own product, an ACU-observed round-Britain ride was put in hand, the riders being Edward Turner himself, works manager Bob Fearon, and service manager Alex Masters. Agreed, the riding schedule was none too strenuous, and each day's run somehow managed to end at a five-star hotel – but it was the thought that counted.

It was Turner's usual policy to produce a 'cooking' model, then follow it up a year later with a sportier version (Speed Twin: Tiger 100, Thunderbird: Tiger 110, 3TA: Tiger 90, and so on) but for 1954 there was a departure in that the sports lightweight, to be called the Tiger Cub, was not only 199 cc, but had a longer stroke (actual dimensions were 63 × 64 mm). That meant a different crankshaft, cylinder barrel, and head. Like the Terrier, the new Cub had plunger rear springing, but there was a dual seat instead of a saddle.

The Terrier and Cub remained in the range for the next two years, sharing such developments as a reinforced fuel tank, an improved clutch, heavier-duty oil pump, and die-cast light-alloy cylinder head. But there were signs that the Terrier was losing face (notably when 3·25 × 16 in wheels were adopted for the 1956 Cub, while the Terrier continued in unchanged form with 19 in wheels and single saddle), and it was not really a surprise to see, in the 1957 programme, that the 199 cc model reigned alone.

Well no, not exactly alone, because now there were *two* Tiger Cubs, roadster and competition, and for each there was a new frame with pivoted fork rear springing. The engine still employed plain big-end and timing side main bearings, but these were now of copper-lead on steel backings.

Back in the previous autumn, Ken Heanes had ridden a Cub to a gold medal placing in the International Six Days Trial, and the new T20C Competition Cub, equipped with lower gear ratios, higher ground clearance, and trials tyres, was a production version of the Heanes model. And at last Triumph had a competitive trials model on which to mount their works squad.

A batch of Cubs was prepared for the 1957 Scottish Six Days Trial, in which event they were ridden by Roy Peplow, Ken Heanes, John Giles, and (you had better believe it!) Mike Hailwood, but although they did reasonably well, there were still a few bugs to be shaken out.

In the following year's Scottish, the Cubs were yelping to good effect, with Artie Ratcliffe finishing third, Roy Peplow sixth, and John Giles tenth. And that was just the start, because in national trials from that point on the Tiger Cub men were to be a truly formidable force. Roy Peplow was probably the best of the early squad of Cub tamers, but in due course there would be many more – Gordon Blakeway, Ray Sayer, Scott Ellis, Gordon Farley – before the Meriden works abandoned trials support.

For a season or two, Zenith carburettors replaced Amal units, the single primary chain gave way to a duplex type, and the barrel and head were given deeper finning. For 1959 midriff enclosure panels (but, thankfully, not the full bathtub treatment of the twins) afflicted the Cub. There was a bigger (three gallon) tank, too.

And talking of enclosure, across in Utah Bill Martin constructed a long, cigar-like shell, powered it with a 199 cc Tiger Cub engine running on dope, and returned a fantastic two-way speed of 139·82 mph.

First really drastic revision of the Tiger Cub design happened in May, 1960, when the whole lower end was completely

Compact indeed was the 199 cc Tiger Cub unit. The same basic design was employed until 1966, when a completely different crankcase arrangement was adopted, mainly for manufacturing convenience. Shown here is the 1953 version, with special angled Amal carburettor

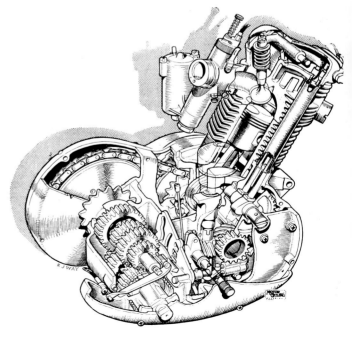

The touring 199 cc Tiger Cub of 1956, with plunger-type rear springing and the small (16-in diameter) wheels new in that year's programme

redesigned. Now, there were only two main castings, joined on the longitudinal centre line. The timing-half crankcase incorporated also the gearbox shell, while the drive-half crankcase was integral with the primary drive casing. It was primarily an engineering department change, aimed at reducing production costs and speeding up assembly, and it certainly had no detrimental effect on the Cub's popularity worldwide.

Worldwide indeed, because now came a scrambles version (with 9 to 1 compression ratio, and energy-transfer ignition) and, for the USA market, an enduro model. As season followed season, so a pastoral model was added (for such agricultural duties as sheep-herding in Australia and South America); and the Mountain Cub, a trail model for the USA market – which had to be painted bright yellow so that trigger-happy hunters would not mistake it for a moose on the loose.

An addition to the roadster model was the T20SH Sports Cub, which could nip along so smartly that it earned the nickname of the 'Baby Bonnie'. The engine of the T20SH was virtually that of the scrambler with 9 to 1 compression ratio, beefed-up bottom end, increased oil supply, etc. Other desirable features included a quickly-detachable headlamp with plug-in

harness, and a two-way-damped front fork (derived from that of the BSA C15).

Understandably, youngsters were soon road-racing them, and it was the clamour for Tiger Cub races which gave rise to the British Formula Racing Club.

In the scrambles field it suffered slightly, in that it had to compete in the 250 cc class. Still, what else was a BSA C15 than an enlarged Cub with the cylinder vertical instead of sloping? But the road-going public loved the Cub, and in a 1964 *Motor Cycle* survey, 90 per cent of the contributors declared that they would readily buy another. Yet there were a number who had reservations. The Cub, it seemed, was reliable enough if given reasonable treatment. But if driven hard, it tended to knock out its main and big-end bearings.

That could have been overcome, of course, but towards the end of its life the Cub was becoming uneconomical to produce, even when it discarded its Meriden frame for that of the BSA Bantam. It had gone by 1968 . . . hadn't it? Yes, of course it had. But just imagine a Tiger Cub with an overhead camshaft instead of pushrod overhead valves, and with a capacity of 125 instead of 199 cc. That, after all, is what Honda did.

199 c.c. Triumph Tiger Cub

A Lively Overhead-valve Light-weight with Remarkable All-round Performance : Outstanding Economy and Powerful Brakes

Well revealed in the lower photograph is the neat, functional appearance of the Tiger Cub. In the view above are shown the accessible contact breaker and the rocker-box finning, a 1957 modification

WITHOUT fear of contradiction, the latest Tiger Cub can be described as an impressive lightweight. It impresses not merely by its performance against the watch but by the balance of its qualities. There is no particular difficulty in extracting plenty of power from an overhead-valve two-hundred; but that so lively a model should also have a top-gear minimum non-snatch speed of 12 m.p.h. and really brisk low-speed acceleration is cause for admiration. And when this flexible performance is coupled to good road manners and a very meagre thirst the result is an outstanding little mount which, at under £144, is remarkable value.

First impressions of the Cub are of a small, low machine although at 50¼in the wheelbase is about normal for the capacity. The low build, however, is real enough and the 16in wheels give a 29in seat unladen height which is below average. Nevertheless, the riding position is not cramped even for a tall rider, thanks to the low footrest location permitted by the narrowness of the engine unit. The relationship between seat, rests and handlebar is a happy one affording full mastery of the model, and all controls are conveniently sited save for the dip-switch which has to be located too far from the right thumb owing to the fixed pivot block of the brake lever. Hand span to brake and clutch levers is commendably short.

Although no air slide is embodied in the carburettor, the Cub was a certain first- or second-kick starter during the admittedly mild weather of the test period. The only prerequisites were light flooding and a small but not critical throttle opening. Mechanical and exhaust noise formed one of the few points of criticism. Valve-gear clatter was audible and wide throttle openings evoked a hard, flat exhaust note of considerable volume. Unlike the other Tiger Cubs ridden, the test model had a slightly erratic tickover which could not be rectified by normal carburettor adjustments.

Once on the move carburation was satisfactory save that when the throttle was opened suddenly there was a momentary hesitation before the engine responded. The high degree of economy obtained in the steady-speed tests, and quoted in the data panel, was paralleled in normal running: in spite of extensive town work and full use of the Cub's agility, consumption averaged around 100 m.p.g.

Provided the clutch plates were freed before starting, by actuating the kick-starter with the handlebar lever raised, bottom-gear engagement was quiet. The clutch has bonded-on Neolangite facings and was as sweet and light in action as one expects of a Triumph. Synchronized operation of the controls gave delightfully quick gear changes except upward between second and third when a slight pause was necessary if the meshing of the dogs was not to be felt; pedal travel was a good compromise between lightness of action and convenience. There was no detectable gear noise in the indirect ratios. Neutral was easy to find from either bottom or second gear but the gear-position indicator on the nacelle left no room for doubt.

It would be difficult to envisage a more enjoyable machine to ride in traffic than the Tiger Cub. The combination of light weight, a trials-type steering lock and admirable low-speed punch made it more nippy under such conditions than the majority of two-wheelers. Such is the flexibility that second-gear starts necessitated no undue clutch slipping and it was, in fact, felt that a closer-ratio gear box would be an improvement. In selecting the ratios, however, the manufacturers have borne in mind the desirability of easy steep-gradient restarts with two up.

One of the most remarkable features of the Cub is its ability to climb quite steep gradients in top gear. Muswell Hill, probably North London's most severe main-road acclivity, was tackled at the legal 30 m.p.h. and even on the steepest section there was no difficulty in maintaining speed—a feat which many machines of more imposing capacity can scarcely equal.

So brisk was the top-gear acceleration that only when absolute maximum pick-up was required was third gear engaged at derestriction signs, yet if desired that ratio could be retained up to an indicated 50 m.p.h. or more (the speedometer recorded 1 m.p.h. fast at 30 m.p.h. and the optimism increased to 4 m.p.h. at 60 m.p.h.). The eagerness apparent in traffic was well maintained outside built-up areas and was coupled with complete tirelessness. As a result the model was habitually cruised at a genuine 55 m.p.h., a speed which enabled averages of 40 m.p.h. or more to be readily attained. No matter how hard the model was driven it never pinked on premium-grade fuel and remained almost completely oil tight. Only when pulling hard at low engine speeds was there any roughness in the power delivery and the engine was particularly sweet at the cruising speed just mentioned. The additional weight of a pillion passenger caused little falling-off in performance.

The low weight and light steering makes for some sensitivity to gusty cross winds, but the handling qualities are, in general, fully up to the performance. Such are the cornering abilities that on really sinuous going there can be few quicker and less tiring mounts. The stands and exhaust system are well tucked away and the footrests could be grounded on corners only if extreme methods were employed. An innovation for 1957, the pivoted-fork rear suspension proved an excellent compromise for solo or two-up riding and the Girling units had ample rebound damping to control any pitching tendency. In comparison the front fork was on the firm side and its action was audible on rough surfaces. Slight oil leaks from the fork legs developed during the test.

Both brakes were thoroughly reassuring in their progressive response but their great power was not truly revealed until the crash-stop tests were carried out. That such a creditable mean stopping distance should have been recorded with drums of only 5½in diameter may seem surprising but such drums are, in fact,

The new rear sub-frame and pivoted-fork springing are of sturdy design and the rectifier and coil are located under the seat

some 13 per cent more effective with 16in-diameter than with 19in rims. Wet roads did not cause any deterioration of the brakes and revealed that the mudguarding was of rather higher-than-average efficiency.

Though its shape is a big improvement over the earlier pointed-nose pattern, the twin-seat gave the impression of being on the hard side after riding spells of much over two hours, and for a long-legged rider the upper edges of the knee grips became noticeable. It was considered that the grips could with advantage project less from the narrow but commendably capacious tank.

The nacelle-mounted horn had a pleasant, arresting note. The ample power of the headlamp would have been more effective if it were possible to set the beam higher. Accessibility of valve-clearance adjusters and contact breaker is noteworthy, and the coil and rectifier are reached after removal of the seat, a task involving merely the slackening of three nuts. Equally accessible is the battery; for topping-up it has only to be withdrawn from its compartment in the tool box. The prop stand could hardly be bettered for its accessibility, neat stowage and stability on cambered surfaces; very little effort is needed to bring into use the low-lift centre stand.

INFORMATION PANEL

The Triumph Tiger Cub

SPECIFICATION

ENGINE: Triumph 199 c.c. (63 x 64mm) overhead-valve single. Steel connecting rod with plain big-end bearing. Crankshaft supported in ball bearing on drive side and plain bearing on timing side. Compression ratio, 7 to 1. Dry-sump lubrication; oil-tank capacity, 2¼ pints.

CARBURETTOR: Amal Type 332, without air slide. Oil-wetted gauze-element air filter.

IGNITION and LIGHTING: Lucas RM13 alternator with coil ignition; auto-advance and emergency-start switch position. Lucas 6-volt, 8-ampere-hour battery charged through a rectifier. Lucas 5½in-diameter headlamp with 30/24-watt bulb in pre-focus light unit.

TRANSMISSION: Four-speed gear box in unit with engine; positive-stop foot control. Gear ratios: bottom, 19.0 to 1; second, 13.1 to 1; third, 8.35 to 1; top, 6.35 to 1. Multi-plate clutch with bonded-on moulded inserts running in oil. Primary chain, non-adjustable, ⅜ x 0.205in in oil-bath case. Rear chain, ½ x 0.205in with guard over top run. Engine r.p.m. at 30 m.p.h. in top gear, 2,830.

FUEL CAPACITY: 3 gallons.

TYRES: Dunlop 3.25 x 16in studded front and rear.

BRAKES: 5½in diameter x 1in wide front and rear.

SUSPENSION: Telescopic front fork with hydraulic damping. Pivoted-fork rear springing with Girling hydraulically damped suspension units.

WHEELBASE: 50⅛in unladen. Ground clearance, 4⅛in.

SEAT: Triumph dual-seat; unladen height, 29in.

WEIGHT: 231 lb fully equipped, with full oil tank and approximately ⅓ gallon of petrol.

PRICE: £116. With purchase tax (in Great Britain only), £143 16s 10d.

ROAD TAX: £1 17s 6d a year; 10s 4d a quarter.

MAKERS: Triumph Engineering Co., Ltd., Meriden Works, Allesley, Coventry.

DESCRIPTION: *The Motor Cycle*, 25 October 1956.

PERFORMANCE DATA

MEAN MAXIMUM SPEED: Bottom: *29 m.p.h.
Second: *42 m.p.h.
Third: 55 m.p.h.
Top: 63 m.p.h.
* Valve float occurring.

HIGHEST ONE-WAY SPEED: 67 m.p.h. (conditions: moderate tail wind; rider wearing two-piece suit and overboots).

MEAN ACCELERATION:

	10-20 m.p.h.	20-30 m.p.h.	30-40 m.p.h.
Bottom	1.5 sec	—	—
Second	1.8 sec	2.0 sec	3.0 sec
Third	3.0 sec	3.4 sec	4.1 sec
Top	—	4.8 sec	5.4 sec

Mean speed at end of quarter-mile from rest: 56 m.p.h.
Mean time to cover standing quarter-mile: 21.8 sec.

PETROL CONSUMPTION: At 30 m.p.h., 130 m.p.g.; at 40 m.p.h., 111 m.p.g.; at 50 m.p.h., 90 m.p.g.

BRAKING: From 30 m.p.h. to rest, 32ft (surface, dry tarmac).

TURNING CIRCLE: 11ft 6in.

MINIMUM NON-SNATCH SPEED: 12 m.p.h. in top gear.

WEIGHT PER C.C.: 1.16 lb.

Norton
MODEL 99

One of the experiments carried out by Edward Turner during his spell at the Ariel works in the 1930s, was to remove the front crankshaft of an Ariel Square Four, and run the engine as a vertical twin. The experiment, which gave considerable food for thought, was watched by two other members of the Ariel design staff of the time, Val Page and Bert Hopwood; and it could well be claimed that it was the inspiration for many of the British vertical twins which were to follow in subsequent years – Page's 550 cc Model 6/1 Triumph, and post-war 498 cc Ariel KH, Bert Hopwood's 497 and 597 cc Norton Dominators and 648 cc BSA Golden Flash, and Edward Turner's own 498 cc Triumph Speed Twin and derivatives.

Hopwood had served a lifetime in the Midlands motor cycle industry, starting as tea-boy in the Ariel foundry, but in due course he graduated to the drawing office, and when Edward Turner was put in charge of Triumph in 1936, Bert went with him as assistant designer and, therefore, had a considerable hand in the detailing of the Speed Twin, the machine that was to set a fashion to the world.

Bert's opportunity of stepping out from Turner's shadow

The main characteristic of the Norton twin was the front-mounted single camshaft; with all four pushrods rising at an angle between the two cylinders. This is the 1958 version of the 597 cc Dominator 99 engine, in which year a crankshaft-mounted alternator was first employed

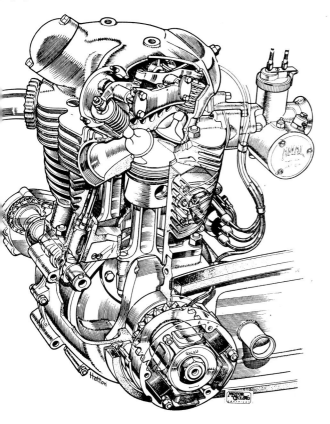

came in 1947, when he took up the position of Norton chief designer. There, his first task was to bring out a new Norton gearbox, followed by a redesign of the ES2 and 16H engines. Immediately after came the first engine for which Hopwood was wholly and personally responsible, the 497 cc Norton Dominator introduced in 1948. And then it was off to Small Heath, to produce the famous A10 Golden Flash. A busy man . . .

He was, however, back at the Norton works by 1955, and within a few months the 597 cc version of the Dominator twin was under way. Between times, the road-racing Manx Nortons had been grabbing the limelight, with their McCandless-designed duplex-loop Featherbed frames, and the Norton firm cashed in on track success by evolving a roadster edition of the Featherbed layout, using commercial-quality tubing instead of the more expensive Reynolds 531 material.

First Dominator to emerge in Featherbed guise was the 497 cc Model 88, joined for 1956 by the 597 cc Model 99. These were the original 'wideline' twins, the nickname derived from the broad spacing of the frame top tubes. In later years there would be 'slimline' versions, the top tubes being cranked inward in the region of the dual seat nose, to afford a more comfortable riding position.

Early Dominators employed all-iron engines, but the 497 cc Dominator 88, on joining the range for 1955, introduced such features as a light-alloy cylinder head and full-width wheel hubs. These were inherited by the 597 cc Dominator 99 of the following year.

To this point a chromium plated fuel tank with frosted silver top and side panels had been fitted, but an economy was effected for 1957 by using all-painted tanks adorned with separate, chromium-plated side panels framed in plastic beading. Traditionalists might well have mourned, too, the change from the D-shape footrest rubbers used since vintage days, to ordinary round rubbers.

Magneto ignition and separate direct-current dynamo had sufficed for the Dominator's electric equipment thus far, but modernity in the form of the crankshaft-mounted alternator was waiting around the corner, and was adopted for the 1958 season. In order to avoid expensive redesign work, Nortons kept the changes to a minimum, eliminating the front-mounted dynamo, but retaining the magneto drive chain which now served to drive a distributor with advance-and-retard unit incorporated. To save making a new drive-side crankcase half, the stator of the Lucas RM15 alternator was carried on a spider spigoted to a boss on the crankcase exterior.

Among the extras listed by Nortons was a 'full rear chaincase' but in practice this was a snare and delusion because a gap existed between the fore part of this chaincase, and the gearbox sprocket, and into this gap an accumulation of assorted road muck found its way. In any case, an inadequate rear chain had always been the Achilles heel of the Norton (they persisted in using a $\frac{1}{2}$-in wide chain, despite constant pleas from customers) and one customer who specified the 'full chaincase' came to the

The world-renowned 'featherbed' duplex tubular frame is shown to good effect in this view of the 1961 597 cc Dominator 99 Standard. A further model (the 99 de Luxe) featured large, pressed-steel enclosure panels, shrouding the carburettor and extending rearward to the registration plate

cynical conclusion that its effect was to shorten rear chain life from its usual 8,000 miles to something nearer 4,000 miles.

From the USA came the inevitable demand for more and yet more performance, and so the early part of 1958 saw the announcement of a twin-carburettor set-up, for which an increase of some 8 to 10 per cent in performance was claimed. The Bracebridge Street works were prepared, also, to polish Dominator cylinder heads internally, and fit larger-diameter inlet valves to order.

Lineal descendant of the Dominator was the Norton Commando, which remained in production into the 1970s. The engine was eventually enlarged to 850 cc, canted forward from the vertical and carried on a rubber mounting system

But the Americans wanted more, and to satisfy them the Nomad Enduro was evolved. This machine employed the old brazed-lug Norton cradle frame, into which was slotted a 597 cc Dominator 99 engine souped-up by the fitting of twin $1\frac{1}{16}$-in Amal Monobloc carburettors, a more sporting camshaft, and high-compression pistons which gave a compression ratio of 9 to 1.

The 'Slimline' Featherbed frame, mentioned earlier, was one highlight of the 1960 range, and with it came a new-style fuel tank, painted all over and with a long, die-cast styling flash (incorporating miniature knee-grip rubbers) on each side. Nor was that all, because the Norton folk had become caught up in the craze for tinware draped around the rear wheel. This embellishment was first seen on the 250 cc Jubilee twin, and the disease then spread to the vertical twins, and the 1960 catalogue illustrated the Norton 88 de Luxe, and 99 de Luxe. Fortunately more discerning customers could still order the standard 88 and 99, undraped at the rear – and, what's more, with a saving of around £6 on the cost.

Previously offered at extra cost, the bigger inlet valves were now fitted as standard, but the major engine change was a new cylinder block and head for the 597 cc model, featuring an increased area of finning.

In Britain, the Dominator had not been considered to date as a machine with a racing potential, even though American users had begun to chalk up victories. Especially for the USA market Nortons brought out the 597 cc Manxman (and without even a passing nod to the Excelsior firm, either) with a special racing camshaft and flat-based cam followers, plus two-rate valve springs, and barrel-shaped tubular light-alloy pushrods. This was soon followed by a European version known as the 597 cc Dominator Sports Special, in essence the Dominator 99 with Manxman modifications, geared to a top speed of 115 mph.

Joe Craig, the legendary Norton race chief, had been killed in a car accident, and racing development was now in the hands of Doug Hele; but Doug's hands were tied because the AMC Group, in overall command of Norton destiny, were running into a trading loss and wanted to cut back on what they saw as a drain on their capital.

Could the Dominator design be used as the basis of a new, and cheaper, racer? To find out, Doug tweaked a 497 cc Dominator unit and mounted it in a Manx frame, then entered Tom Phillis on the resulting Domiracer for the 1961 Senior TT. It is a part of TT history that Tom finished an astonishing third, having turned in a lap at 100·36 mph.

But the sands were now running out fast, and 1962 saw the end of the Bracebridge Street works. Soon, AMC themselves had gone, but at least the Dominator concept survived eventually to become NVT's Norton Commando of the 1970s.

THE MOTOR CYCLE

ROAD TESTS OF NEW MODELS

597 c.c. Norton Model 99

Flashing Acceleration, Hairline Steering, Tremendous Braking Power : A Notable Sports Twin

THERE has never been any doubt as to the rôle of the 597 c.c. Norton Model 99 twin: it is a high-performance roadster intended primarily for solo use. The wide popularity of vertical-twin five-hundreds shortly after the war soon led to the introduction of models of similar layout but larger capacity. Most of the newcomers were dual-purpose machines, equally suitable for fast solo touring or hauling a sidecar. But the Model 99, first marketed in 1956, is not intended to woo the sidecarrist. Its duplex-loop frame has no sidecar lugs and is of the type made famous first on the factory racing models (in 1950) and subsequently on the Manx production racers and the Model 88, forerunner and smaller brother of the 99.

Superb steering, extraordinarily powerful braking and a delightful gear change combine with surging acceleration to justify the Norton's claim to be a sporting roadster. From its inception the Model 99 took advantage of the development of the smaller twin in having the so-called Daytona camshaft and a light-alloy cylinder head. The cumulative effect of improvements made in the past two years furnishes a good example of the way a sports model's manners can be enhanced by detail changes. The raucous exhaust of the early models has been subdued to a note which, though throaty, is not offensive. Use of light alloy for the pushrods and elimination of the dynamo and its drive (a crankshaft-driven A.C. generator is standardized for 1958) have contributed to a reduction in mechanical noise. Detail appearance has been tidied up. Finally, a scarcely noticeable but much appreciated refinement is the use of plastic covering for the control cables. The covering ensured that the initial sweetness of the controls was maintained in spite of many hours of riding in vile weather.

The adoption of an alternator was naturally accompanied by a change to coil ignition and the easy starting claimed for that system was very evident. Provided the air lever was closed and the

carburettor well flooded under cold conditions, no more than one swing of the kick-starter was required to set the engine running. After a cold start in chilly weather the air lever was opened in two of three stages covering the first mile or so to ensure unhesitant response to throttle opening during the warming-up period. An emergency position for the ignition switch is provided to enable the engine to be kick-started if the battery is flat. With the switch in that position the only additional requirement for a sure start was a really hearty thrust on the pedal.

Behind the crankcase mouth may be seen the distributor cover which conceals the contact breaker and auto-advance unit

Idling was slow and even once the engine was warm and, though petrol consumption was a little heavier than average in the lower speed ranges, carburation was clean at all throttle openings. There was no tendency to blurred running at 30 m.p.h. in top gear and pick-up from that speed was brisk as, indeed, it was right up the scale.

As would be expected, the most vivid acceleration was obtained by using the gear box to the full, and although the 99 had no vices for town riding it was on the open road that it showed up to best advantage. On full throttle, with the rider sitting upright, the model quickly reached its level-road top speed of an indicated 90 m.p.h.—quickly enough, that is, to outstrip a number of sleek sports cars of comparable or slightly higher top speed. Half throttle was sufficient to cruise at 75 m.p.h. or a little more while a throttle setting of two-thirds kept the speedometer needle in the 80 to 85 m.p.h. range as long as road conditions permitted. (Speedometer flattery was roughly constant throughout the range at five per cent.)

The engine was utterly tireless and, within its compass, the only considerations which dictated the speed to be sustained on long journeys were a vibration period and the riding position (unless a backrest was improvised). Felt through the handlebar and tank, the tremor became noticeable just before 65 m.p.h. was reached (in top gear), peaked at about 70 m.p.h. and faded out at 75 m.p.h. Beyond reasonable criticism for low and medium speeds, the riding posture was rather upright owing to the upward sweep of the handlebar and to the forward positioning of the footrests relative to the seat. Hence the rider had to exert an appreciable pull on the bar to counter the effect of wind pressure on the body. In the same context, the lower frictional characteristics of the plastic handlebar grips (as compared with rubber) served to increase the effort required, especially in wet weather. A considerable improvement resulted from a change to rubber grips but it was felt that a similar effect could be achieved with plastic grips if the material were more resilient or the knurling deepened.

Width of tank and seat between the rider's thighs is above average (11½in) and made it slightly awkward for riders of average height to put their feet to the ground. The rear part of the seat is of ample proportions for a pillion passenger and is well shaped for comfort. With the exception of the horn button (which is set rather low on the left side of the handlebar), all controls are excellently sited and proved smooth in operation.

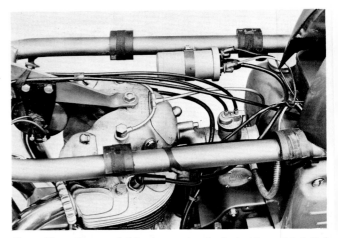

Above: Normally concealed by the petrol tank, the ignition coil is bolted to a lug welded to the upper run of the right-hand frame tube. Below: The 597 c.c. engine has a light-alloy cylinder head

INFORMATION PANEL

SPECIFICATION

ENGINE: Norton 597 c.c. (68 × 82mm) overhead-valve vertical twin with light-alloy cylinder head. Valve gear operated from a single camshaft. Light-alloy connecting rods with steel-back, micro-babbitt shell big-end bearings. Crankshaft supported in roller bearing on drive side and ball bearing on timing side. Compression ratio, 7.4 to 1. Dry-sump lubrication; oil-tank capacity, 4½ pints.

CARBURETTOR: Amal Monobloc; air slide operated by handlebar lever.

IGNITION and LIGHTING: Coil ignition with automatic advance. Lucas RM15 60-watt A.C. generator driven by left end of crankshaft. Lucas 6-volt, 12-ampere-hour battery charged through rectifier. Lucas 7in-diameter headlamp with pre-focus light unit.

TRANSMISSION: A.M.C. four-speed gear box with positive-stop foot control. Gear ratios: bottom, 12.1 to 1; second, 8.03 to 1; third, 6.04 to 1; top, 4.53 to 1. Multi-plate clutch with moulded inserts running in oil. Primary chain, ⅜ × 0.305in in oil-bath case. Rear chain, ⅝ × ⅜in with guard over top run. Engine r.p.m. at 30 m.p.h. in top gear, 1,750.

FUEL CAPACITY: 3¾ gallons.

TYRES: Avon; front, 3.00 × 19in Speedmaster; rear, 3.50 × 19in Safety Mileage.

BRAKES: Front, 8in diameter × 1⅛in wide; rear, 7in diameter × 1⅛in wide; finger adjusters.

SUSPENSION: Norton telescopic front fork with hydraulic damping. Pivoted-fork rear springing employing Girling hydraulically damped shock absorbers with three-position adjustment for load.

WHEELBASE: 55½in unladen. Ground clearance, 5½in unladen.

SEAT: Norton dual-seat; unladen height, 31½in.

WEIGHT: 413 lb fully equipped, with full oil tank and approximately half a gallon of petrol.

PRICE: £235. With purchase tax (in Great Britain only), £293 3s 3d.

ROAD TAX: £3 15s a year; £1 0s 8d a quarter.

MAKERS: Norton Motors, Ltd., Bracebridge Street, Birmingham, 6.

DESCRIPTION: *The Motor Cycle*, 5 September 1957.

PERFORMANCE DATA

MEAN MAXIMUM SPEED: Bottom: *45 m.p.h.
Second: *68 m.p.h.
Third: *91 m.p.h.
Top: 93 m.p.h.
*Valve float occurring.

HIGHEST ONE-WAY SPEED: 96 m.p.h. (conditions: moderate side wind; rider wearing two-piece plastic suit and overboots).

MEAN ACCELERATION:

	10-30 m.p.h.	20-40 m.p.h.	30-50 m.p.h.
Bottom	2.4 sec	2.2 sec	—
Second	4.2 sec	3.4 sec	3.2 sec
Third	—	4.4 sec	4.4 sec
Top	—	7.2 sec	6.8 sec

Mean speed at end of quarter-mile from rest: 80 m.p.h.
Mean time to cover standing quarter-mile: 16 sec.

PETROL CONSUMPTION: At 30 m.p.h., 78 m.p.g.; at 40 m.p.h., 73 m.p.g.; at 50 m.p.h., 68 m.p.g.; at 60 m.p.h., 60 m.p.g.

BRAKING: From 30 m.p.h. to rest, 27ft (surface, dry tarmac).

TURNING CIRCLE: 17ft.

MINIMUM NON-SNATCH SPEED: 20 m.p.h. in top gear.

WEIGHT PER C.C.: 0.69 lb

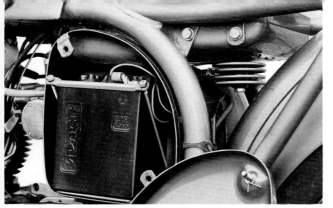

The alternator charges the enclosed battery through a rectifier which is bolted to the underside of the tool tray beneath the seat

In the matter of wheel suspension the makers have compromised in favour of short firm movements, especially at the front, to obviate all possibility of pitching. At the expense of a hard ride on bumpy surfaces the rider has the advantage of precision handling at very high speeds. Once initial overtightening of the head races had been rectified, steering was absolutely first rate. In all circumstances it inspired the highest confidence; indeed, it was one of the most prominent factors in the joy of riding the 99. On a straight path the Norton steered itself irrespective of speed or surface irregularities. And all that was necessary to cut a stylish line on any variety of bend or corner was to heel the model over by leg pressure. There was never a waver from the front wheel nor a chop from the rear, so that a line could be chosen almost to the breadth of a hair. But a more generous steering lock would have been appreciated when turning about in a narrow road or manhandling the model in a confined space.

Braking power was more than a match for the speed of the 99. Either wheel could be locked by panic action but the controls were sensitive enough to preclude such a mistake otherwise. The slight heaviness in front brake operation which resulted from the use of an unusually thick cable on earlier models has been eliminated by a change to a cable of normal weight. Travel of the rear-brake pedal is a shade long. On the debit side, comparatively frequent adjustment for wear was required on both brakes and the finger adjuster on the rear control was awkward to use owing to the proximity of the left-hand silencer.

Gear changing was a joy. No deliberation was called for in the movement of the controls. Pedal operation was light and text-book methods gave text-book results: rapid, smooth and noiseless changes. The slight stiffness in engaging bottom gear which was a feature of some of the earlier A.M.C. boxes has been cured by an alteration in the rating of the selector spring. Neutral selection from bottom or second gear was simplicity itself whether the model was rolling or stationary.

The only criticism of the box concerned rather wide spacing of

the third and top ratios and a slight whine when the engine was pulling in either of the intermediate gears. However, the lowish third gear gave a very useful burst of acceleration from 40 to 65 m.p.h. As is shown by the mean maximum speed figures in the information panel, the 99 is overgeared in top. Indeed, in one direction the model was just as fast in third gear as in top. But although the mean maximum speed would doubtless be raised and top-gear flexibility enhanced by use of an engine sprocket having one tooth fewer, the overgearing was not really obtrusive, for the engine pulled lustily in the middle speed ranges.

Extremely light to withdraw, the clutch took up the drive abnormally quickly in the last fraction of lever movement. But the delicacy required for a smooth getaway was soon mastered and was subsequently quite automatic. In a rapid succession of four full-throttle quarter-mile sprints from a standing start, the free movement in the control cable increased perceptibly as a result of expansion of the friction material; but there was never the slightest trace of slip or drag and cable clearance returned to normal as soon as the clutch had cooled down. Since the clutch adjuster is situated in the centre of the pressure plate (there is also an external cable adjuster on the gear-box cover), a detachable panel in the rear dome of the primary chaincase would be a boon, so that adjustment could be effected without removing the left footrest, brake pedal and chaincase outer half. Incidentally, removal of the outer half of the case does not disturb the alternator.

During a test comprising just under 1,000 miles of hard riding the engine and gear box retained their oil well, there being only faint smears at some of the joints at the end of the test. Slight seepage occurred from the oil-tank filler cap and chaincase inspection cover. A small pool of oil formed under the crankcase breather when the model was parked at the end of a run. At 1,200 to 1,500 m.p.g. oil consumption was rather high. The rear chain ran dry and required adjusting and oiling at frequent intervals. Intensity of the headlamp beam was well up to average and the offset of the dipped beam precluded offence to oncoming traffic.

Most routine maintenance tasks were easily carried out with the standard tool kit (which is carried in a shallow tray under the dual-seat). The exception was adjustment of the contact-breaker points. The auto-advance and contact-breaker unit is situated behind the crankcase mouth in the place previously occupied by the magneto; the adjustment is inaccessible and thereby liable to invite neglect by owners who are not fastidious. When raising the 99 on to its centre stand for maintenance work it was found helpful to use the left footrest as one lifting point. The foot of the prop stand operates close to the machine's centre line and hence a firm, level surface is necessary if the risk of toppling is to be avoided.

In appearance the Model 99 is a winner. Its lines are handsome and the polychromatic grey finish blends tastefully with the polished aluminium and chromium plating. Framed in plastic beading, the separate chromium side panels give a distinctive aspect to the petrol tank, while the cleaning-up process mentioned earlier results in a pleasing absence of bittiness.

The 597 c.c. Norton Model 99 twin

Velocette

VIPER

Although, in general, the motor cycling public looked upon the Velocette as a sturdy machine built by conscientious engineers for a connoisseurs' market, one gets the sneaking feeling that the company (in other words, the Goodman family) would have sold many more bikes, if only they could have added a touch of modernity to the design.

By the 1950s, for example, other makers were using lighter, all-welded tubular frames; and yet Velocette, right to the bitter end, stuck with the malleable-lug, hearth-brazed heavy frame that echoed 1920s practice. To take another point, the peculiar Velocette clutch, located inboard of the final-drive sprocket, no doubt worked very well when set correctly; but to riders not steeped in Velo lore the design was distinctly off-putting, and it is interesting to speculate on how many possible purchasers decided, instead, to buy a BSA, or an Ariel, or something else with a clutch that looked familiar.

To be brutally frank, the electrics were pathetic (an alternator-equipped model was on the stocks, but the factory closed down before it could be put into production). And what other British single needed a special paragraph on starting technique in the rider's handbook?

A remote ancestor of the Viper was the 248 cc MOV which appeared in the summer of 1933, a Eugene Goodman design and the first of the M-range of pushrod, overhead-valve Velocette singles. This was followed for 1935 by the 349 cc MAC. By June of the same year (Velocette never were particularly fussy about reserving new models or production changes for autumn announcement) the 495 cc MSS had arrived, and so the family of high-camshaft singles was complete.

In the course of time the MOV would disappear, and the remaining MAC and MSS would acquire pivoted-fork rear springing and a telescopic front fork, but there were few other changes and, externally at least, the 1955 Velocette singles looked much as they had done for the past 20 years.

By this time, however, demand was rising for something with a more spirited performance than the MAC or MSS could produce. In earlier days, the answer would have been the overhead-camshaft KSS, but post-war economics had caused this model to be dropped.

Designer Charles Udall set to work and the result, unveiled in October, 1955, was a pair of sporty overhead-valve models, the 349 cc Viper and 495 cc Venom, each benefitting from the factory's road-racing experience by the adoption of a bi-metal Al-fin cylinder with cast-iron liner, and by a cylinder head in light alloy.

The two models were really one, because the Viper was not based on the touring MAC but, instead, employed the same bottom-end assembly as its bigger Venom sister. Viper bore and stroke dimensions were 72 × 86 mm (compared with the 68 × 96 mm dimensions of the MAC). Other specification details included a high-compression, split-skirt piston, and enclosed hairpin valve springs. A chromium-plated fuel tank and mudguards, set off by black or willow green paintwork, made the Viper a handsome machine indeed.

With its over-90 mph potential, the new Viper would have been a possible answer to the overwhelming BSA Gold Star dominance of the Isle of Man Clubmans TT – if only it had been introduced a year or two earlier. But the Clubmans TT had folded. Still, production-machine racing was beginning to catch public imagination, and in the 1957 Thruxton Nine-Hour Race a Viper co-ridden by Eddie Dow and John Righton held a creditable third place until a dropped-in valve brought retirement.

The classic high-camshaft layout of the pushrod overhead valve Velocette engine is seen to good effect in this cutaway drawing of the 349 cc Viper, which featured a light-alloy cylinder barrel and head, and totally-enclosed hairpin valve springs

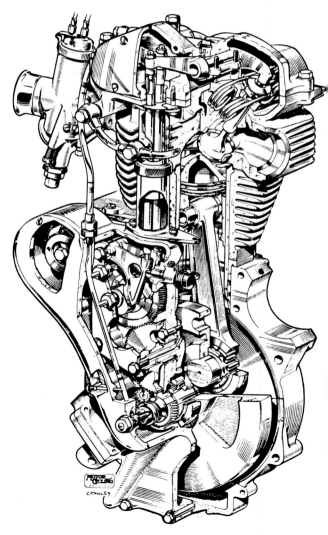

Preceding pages: 1965 Viper Veeline

In later years the Viper was indeed to achieve a modest degree of racing success, but it was fated to be overshadowed by the 495 cc Venom, and in the end it was the Venom which was given further development to produce the ultimate in super-sports Velocettes, the Venom Thruxton.

One move which met with little enthusiasm from the motor cycling fraternity, and with even less from die-hard Velocette fans, was the adoption of glass-fibre panels which encased everything below cylinder-base height. This was an economy measure, the covers obviated the need for polishing the light-alloy castings of the timing cover and gearbox end cover. In fact New Hudson had tried something similar (but in pressed steel) as far back as 1932, with a notable lack of success and only Francis-Barnett, with their pre-war Cruiser, had scored any sort of hit with engine enclosure.

Still, the message must have got through, because although the covered-up Viper and Venom were continued, from 1960 they were now partnered by the Viper Clubman and Venom Clubman, in which the lower works were once again left naked and unashamed. And there was rather more to it than that, because, in the interests of clubman and production-machine racing, these were equipped with TT Amal carburettors, BTH racing magnetos, and close-ratio gearboxes. Compression ratio was raised (9·3 to 1, on the Viper), a solid-skirt piston replaced the split-skirt type, and rear-set footrests were provided.

The following year brought yet another variant, the Viper Veeline which featured a roadster-type dolphin fairing. When applied to the tuned model, the fairing gave rise to the Viper Clubman Veeline, which was quite enough of a mouthful for anyone. Up to this time, both the Viper and Viper Clubman had been fitted with a chromium-plated fuel tank, and Velocettes were certainly the last British firm to do so. Now, however, the Viper Clubman had a new and rather ugly 4½-gallon tank with square lines, painted all over, bearing the Velocette name in a rectangular clear-plastic panel, and trimmed by a horizontal band of corrugated, anodised alumium.

For two more years, the chromium-plated tank was listed for the standard Viper, but by 1962 that model, too, was using the big square tank.

Meanwhile, a Venom had gained the world 500 cc 24-hour record at Montlhéry, and in July, 1963 an attempt was made on the 350 cc long-distance records at the same venue, with Velocette sales director Bertie Goodman again as a member of the riding team. Unhappily, ignition bothers set in after the first six hours (at which time the average speed was just over 105 mph), and with no hope of achieving the target 12-hour or 24-hour records, the attempt was abandoned for the day. A restart was made next morning, but speed was down, and after an hour and a half the engine failed.

Another attempt was made to produce an economy model in the early 1960s, using the old-style three-gallon fuel tank and an all-painted finish but, somehow, a Velocette in grey-blue with a horizontal cream band on the tank did not look right.

Motor Cycle road-tested the Viper again in 1966, and found it to be much as it had been in 1958, so far as all-out performance was concerned, a shade less lively in acceleration, but rather better on fuel economy. But for the Viper, and for Velocettes as a whole, time was fast running out. Coil ignition at last replaced the time-honoured magneto in July, 1968. A Velocette range was announced for 1970, but it no longer included a 350 cc model, and before long the factory had ground to a complete halt.

Previously available on the Clubman version only, the squared-off 4½-gallon fuel tank with anodised-alloy styling band became a standard fitment on the Velocette Viper from 1963 onward

Ambassador Three Star Special

The pre-war motor racing scene would appear to have been peopled by characters who were slightly larger-than-life, among whom could certainly be classed Kaye Don. In his younger days Kaye had been a regular member of the Brooklands motor cycling brigade, but by the mid-1920s he had switched to four wheels.

His particular field was record-breaking, and with a little car named the Avon-JAP, using alternative engines of 495, 731 and 986 cc, he established a variety of records; those in the 500 cc class were unbroken when Brooklands closed for good and, therefore, stand in Kaye Don's name in perpetuity.

He had his eyes on higher things, too, nothing less than the World Land Speed Record, for which reason he persuaded the Sunbeam Motor Car Company (who had constructed Major Henry Segrave's record-holder, Golden Arrow) to build him a suitable challenger, named Silver Bullet.

Regrettably, the Silver Bullet did not have quite enough energy to allow it to reach the set target, although Kaye Don did gain some consolation by taking the World Water Speed Record with his boat, *Miss England*. To finance such ambitions, Kaye had established the firm of US Concessionaires, based at Ascot, to import and service American-built Pontiac cars.

That line of business folded abruptly on the outbreak of the Second World War, but Pontiac Works were kept fully occupied with the overhaul and repair of all kinds of road transport, under governmental direction.

The return of peace saw little hope of a resumption of the import of vast and expensive American cars. Quite the opposite, indeed, for Britain now found itself desperate for foreign currency. This was 'Export or Die' time, with the limited stocks of steel and other metals being allocated only to those with a flourishing export trade.

Kaye Don felt that he could find a market for a simple and uncomplicated British lightweight motor cycle in the more far-flung areas of the world and so, in mid-1946, he registered the appropriate trade-mark of Ambassador. Not everybody in the existing British industry was happy to see a newcomer muscling-in on the scene. For example, the old-established Zenith, Cotton, and AJW factories were struggling to get back into production, using a new 500 cc side-valve vee-twin engine from J. A. Prestwich. Supplies were slow in coming through, and on a visit to the JAP works, Mr. J. O. Ball, of AJW, was not at all pleased to see one of these units being fitted to a bike bearing the hitherto-unknown name of Ambassador on the tank.

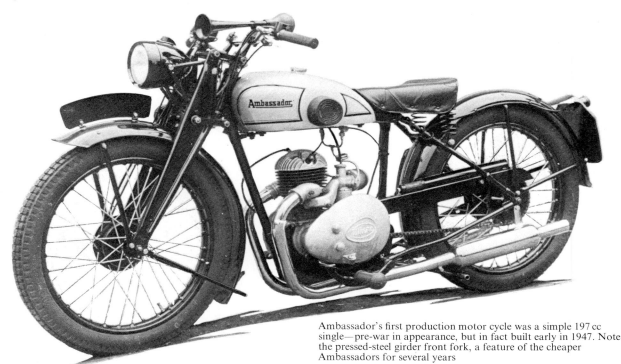

Ambassador's first production motor cycle was a simple 197 cc single—pre-war in appearance, but in fact built early in 1947. Note the pressed-steel girder front fork, a feature of the cheaper Ambassadors for several years

Nevertheless, it was not with a JAP but with a 197 cc Villiers power unit that Ambassador went into production in December, 1946. Answering the 'Export or Die' call, the makers had earmarked the entire first batch for overseas customers, the first consignment going to Argentina and the second to Ceylon.

Simple, agreed, but nobody could call that first 197 cc Ambassador pretty. It had a distinctly 'pre-war' appearance, even to the use of a pressed-steel Webb girder front fork, and rigid brazed-lug frame, and was so low-built that it looked to have negative ground clearance.

Villiers had first announced the 197 cc unit-construction engine-gear assembly—at that time called the Double Century, because it was roughly 200 cc—back in 1938, as a follow-up to their first venture into unit-construction with the 125 cc Mk. 9D. It was fitted with hand gear-change, and only James had taken it up, but few were made before the coming of war.

The new version which made its debut with the Ambassador was the Mk. 5E, still with twin exhaust pipes but now featuring foot gear-change. It was to prove one of the most successful Villiers designs of all time, not only progressing through various developments to the well-remembered Mk. 9E unit which powered a number of trials and scrambles models of the late-1950s/early-1960s period, but also forming a basis for the later 250 cc singles.

Alec Frick was the Ambassador designer, and within a year or so he had devised a rather better, welded tubular frame and, moreover, he arranged for the frames to be built in Birmingham by the Reynolds Tube Company. Previously, Reynolds' had supplied tubing only, leaving it to the motor cycle factories to make their own frames. However, during the war they had undertaken the manufacture of tubular mounting assemblies for the aircraft industry, and it was this experience that was now put to good use in the motor cycle field. What is more, Alec Frick now left Ambassador, and joined the Reynolds Tube works as a motor cycle frame designer, devising and building frames for the majority of the smaller British factories.

The Ambassador range expanded to accommodate a 147 cc Popular model and, at the other end of the scale, a 249 cc Villiers 2T twin. It was probably the last British factory to retain (on the bargain-basement Popular) a girder fork and rigid frame, albeit enterprising enough in other directions, exhibiting at Earls Court what was claimed to be (and probably was) the first British machine with electric starting—employing a starter motor mounted under the tank, and vee-belt drive to a groove around the periphery of the Villiers flywheel magneto.

Meanwhile, Ambassador noted the scooter trend, and made arrangements to import and distribute the German-made Zündapp Bella scooter and the Zündapp Combinette moped and, ostensibly, went into moped manufacture on their own account by producing, for the 1962 season, an Ambassador model with somewhat overdressed bodywork and a 50 cc Villiers 3K engine (it was, of course, just a Zündapp imported without power unit, and fitted with the Villiers at Pontiac Works).

Design by this time was under the charge of former Norton technician, Edgar Franks, and by 1960 a very attractive house-style had been achieved, as is seen on the Three Star Special of the following pages. The then-current fashion was for semi-enclosure of the rear wheel, but Ambassador did not go the whole hog (as did Francis-Barnett, with the full-skirted Cruiser 84) and, instead. evolved a kind of mini-skirt rear pressing which, in conjunction with the deeply valanced front guard, is still pleasantly eye-catching, even now.

Following pages: Fred Hibbert's 1960 Super S has the 249 cc Villiers 2T engine, but is otherwise similar to the 197 cc Three-Star single

Close-up of the 197 cc Villiers Mk. 4E engine-gear unit of the 1947 Ambassador, a revamp of the 1938 Mk. 3E unit, retaining twin exhausts but now with foot instead of hand gear change

The Ambassador story was not entirely one of unqualified success, and their reason for introducing (in October, 1960) their own 172 cc Villiers-powered scooter is a little obscure. Styling, not unnaturally, was based on the Zündapp Bella, which the firm was still importing. It was about £20 cheaper than the Bella, but that is as much as can be said for it.

Unlike most other British small manufacturers, Ambassador shunned the sporting side, and did not add a trials or scrambles model to the programme. In fact, as time went by the firm's enthusiasm for motor cycles went into a decline as, more and more, the import from France of giant Latil earth-moving equipment for open-cast mining took precedence.

The sale of the Ambassador name, jigs, and manufacturing rights to DMW, of Dudley, in 1962 was not really a surprise. The 197 cc Three Star Special was to remain available for two more seasons, still with its pressed-steel tail but now featuring a DMW-style square-tube frame loop. It was more or less badge-engineering, because towards the end the two ranges were identical, except that if you ordered a DMW it came with the familiar humpty-style tank and DMW badges, whereas the Ambassador fancier got the same bike but equipped with the more rounded tank and diamond-shape badges of the former Ascot-based marque.

During a 1930 visit to the Isle of Man TT races, Kaye Don—later the founder of the Ambassador factory—rounds Signpost Corner on a Norton

ROAD TESTS of new models

197 c.c. Ambassador

VERY ATTRACTIVELY STYLED TWO-STROKE CAPABLE OF TIRELESS PULLING: GOOD SUSPENSION, STEERING AND HANDLING: FULL MUDGUARDING

★

★

★

WITH the increased flow of two-fifties on the British market in recent times, a new rôle has fallen on the one-nine-seven. Hitherto the most powerful of the "true lightweights," it now caters for riders prepared to settle for slightly less power than they might have in order to take advantage of a lower initial price. Viewed in that light —as a sort of keen buyer's two-fifty—the latest Ambassador Three Star Special earns full marks.

The outstanding impression after several hundred miles' riding was of the 197 c.c. Villiers Mark 9E engine-gear unit's untiring capacity for hard work. One- or two-up, buzzing along main roads or pulling hard on steep country upgrades, the Ambassador seemed capable of going on indefinitely. A Villiers silencer is fitted which means that the exhaust is commendably quiet; this tended to emphasize induction roar, particularly at wide throttle openings. Mechanical noise was confined to mild piston slap at low engine speeds.

Power delivery was smooth but marred by flutter from the rear chain at around 45 m.p.h. in top gear and at corresponding speeds in the intermediate gears. The engine has a wide torque spread and pulled well throughout the range. Two-stroking was good, even at ultra-high engine revolutions in the intermediate gears—an indication of good breathing. Threading city traffic at walking pace could be accomplished with the clutch fully home, while the model would pobble along in top gear on a fractionally open throttle without transmission snatch.

On one occasion the test model was ridden hard on a 120-mile non-stop trip, during which long main-road hills were taken on full throttle in top or third gear as necessary. There was no sign of distress. The power unit remained oil-tight throughout. Calibrated to 70 m.p.h. the Smiths speedometer (which has no trip recorder) read 2 m.p.h. fast at 30 m.p.h. and 3 m.p.h. fast at 50 m.p.h.

Closing the carburettor strangler ensured first-kick starting from cold, after which the strangler could be opened immediately. Starting when the engine was warm required no particular technique.

Fuel consumption, overall, worked out at about 80 m.p.g. Tank capacity, at 3½ gallons, therefore permitted 250-mile runs to be completed without a refuelling stop. The filler cap is commendably large and, positioned centrally, allows the fuel level on both sides of the tank arch to be readily seen. The cap is effectively sealed, so that the top of the tank remained

Above: The handlebar is concealed by a metal pressing. The tank filler cap is sensibly large, enabling the level to be easily checked. Right: Underseat view showing the battery and tool roll neatly stowed. Note the ingenious rubber mounting for the rear of the tank

Three Star Special

pleasantly free from oil stains. The pull-on fuel tap, which incorporates a reserve position, was difficult to operate with a gloved hand.

Robust and with wide-spaced feet, the centre stand was easy to operate and supported the model safely, even on steepish cambers. Rear-chain adjustment was required only once during 900 miles. Though not "oil bath," the enclosure is markedly effective.

The riding position would be improved if the footrests were about three inches farther to the rear, to allow the rider's feet to take a greater proportion of his weight than is possible with the present location. Adjustment is provided, but results in the footrests being lower, thus allowing them to ground on corners. The handlebar shape gives a satisfactory wrist angle, and the generously dimensioned dual-seat is comfortable whether it is used one- or two-up. Removal of the seat (by withdrawing two screws with a coin) exposes the top of the battery and the recess containing the tools.

Rear springing is by a pivoted fork controlled by Girling spring-and-hydraulic units with three-position adjustment. The front fork is undamped. Characteristics of both the front and rear systems were such that there was no pitching even on undulating surfaces. Changes of lock could be made swiftly and with remarkably little conscious effort.

Braking was progressive, and adequate, although the front brake was a shade spongy. The rear-brake pedal is so positioned that its pad lies directly beneath the rider's left foot. Front-brake and clutch levers, the pivot blocks for both of which are welded to the handlebar, needed a long reach.

The gear-change pedal could be moved by merely pivoting the right foot on its footrest. Gear changing was positive and noiseless—at all times simplicity itself.

Pedal movement was short and light. Neutral could be selected without fumbling from bottom or second gear when the machine was stationary and the engine idling. The ratios proved excellently matched to the power characteristics and the closeness of third and top (7.74 and 6.2 to 1) enabled third to be used

Left: Access to the contact breaker is easily gained by removal of three screws and a cover. Right: A detail shot of the rear-brake cross-over shaft and braker-light mechanism

immediately traffic, gradient or headwind brought a drop in speed.

An indicated 45 m.p.h. suited the model best when journeys of any length were undertaken. Main-road hills normally needed no gear lower than third. On steep upgrades encountered on minor roads it was rarely necessary to use bottom gear except for restarting or when baulked two-up.

Restarting on a 1 in 6 hill was accomplished in bottom gear with very little fuss. Indeed, the clutch could be fully engaged as soon as the machine was under way. Heavier in operation than was strictly necessary, the clutch freed at all times,

even after a number of standing-start tests. It took up the drive progressively and required no adjustment.

After-dark riding was very pleasant. The driving beam ensured that daylight cruising speeds could be maintained, and that held good whether the direct or battery lighting was in use. With the handlebar-mounted dip switch in the dipped position, the cut-off was well-defined and dazzle-free. Mounted simply in two ears on the top fork covers, the headlamp is easily adjustable. Twin electric horns are located in the rear panelling (one on each side facing forward); they were adequately powerful

The ammeter is located on the left upper face of the headlamp shell; it indicated that the flywheel generator balanced the maximum load (all lights on) at 30 m.p.h.

Protection from road filth was first-class. The valancing of the front mudguard extends almost to the bottom of each fork leg. That feature, and the rear enclosure, did much to trap water thrown up by the tyres. More than that, the valancing and mid-section enclosure, combined with the smart black-and-white finish, a "three-dimensional" tank motif and the discreet use of chromium plating, all contribute towards making the Ambassador a most eyeable model.

▲▲▲▲▲▲▲▲▲▲▲▲▲▲▲▲▲▲▲▲ *Specification* ▲▲▲▲▲▲▲▲▲▲▲▲▲▲▲▲▲▲▲▲▲▲

ENGINE: Villiers 197 c.c. (59 x 72 mm) Mark 9E single-cylinder two-stroke. Roller big-end bearing; crankshaft supported in a roller bearing on the right-hand side and two ball bearings on the left. Light-alloy cylinder head; cast-iron barrel. Compression ratio, 7.25 to 1. Petroil lubrication; mixture 20 to 1.

CARBURETTOR: Villiers S.25 with wire-gauze air filter incorporating a strangler.

TRANSMISSION: Villiers four-speed, foot-controlled gear box in unit with the engine. Gear ratios: bottom, 17.95 to 1; second, 10.85 to 1; third, 7.74 to 1; top, 6.2 to 1. Multi-plate clutch with bonded, moulded linings running in oil. Primary chain, ⅜ x 0.225in in oil-bath case; rear chain ½ x 0.305in enclosed in pressed-steel case. Engine r.p.m. at 30 m.p.h. in top gear, 2,650.

IGNITION AND LIGHTING: Villiers flywheel magneto with lighting coils. Exide 6-volt 7.5 ampere-hour battery charged through rectifier; 5½in-diameter Miller headlamp with prefocus light unit; 30 24 watt main bulb.

PETROIL CAPACITY: 3½ gallons.

TYRES: Dunlop 3.25 x 17in studded front and rear.

BRAKES: 6in diameter front and rear.

SUSPENSION: Ambassador undamped telescopic front fork with two-rate springing. Pivoted rear fork controlled by Girling adjustable spring-and-hydraulic telescopic units.

WHEELBASE: 51in unladen. Ground clearance 6½in unladen.

SEAT: Ambassador dual-seat; unladen height 31in.

WEIGHT: 272 lb fully equipped and with one gallon of petroil.

PRICE: £137 10s; with purchase tax (in Great Britain only) £165 15s 2d.

ROAD TAX: £1 17s 6d a year.

MANUFACTURERS: Ambassador Motor Cycles, Ltd., Pontiac Works, Ascot, Berks.

PERFORMANCE DATA

MEAN MAXIMUM SPEED: Bottom: 26 m.p.h.
Second: 39 m.p.h.
Third: 49 m.p.h.
Top: 55 m.p.h.

HIGHEST ONE-WAY SPEED: 60 m.p.h. (conditions: strong following wind; rider wearing two-piece suit and overboots).

MEAN ACCELERATION:	10-30 m.p.h.	20-40 m.p.h.	30-50 m.p.h.
Second	10.2 sec	—	—
Third	—	14 sec	—
Top	—	16 sec	18.2 sec

Mean speed at end of quarter mile from rest: 53 m.p.h.
Mean time to cover standing quarter mile: 23.2 sec.

PETROIL CONSUMPTION: At 30 m.p.h., 96 m.p.g. At 40 m.p.h., 82 m.p.g.

BRAKING: From 30 m.p.h. to rest, 38ft (surface dry tarmac).

TURNING CIRCLE: 12ft 6in.

MINIMUM NON-SNATCH SPEED: 18 m.p.h. in top gear.

WEIGHT PER C.C.: 1.32 lb.

Matchless G12 de Luxe

They always were a contrary lot, down at the AMC factory in Plumstead Road, Woolwich. For years they scorned the services of the specialist suspension firms and when, at long last, they did adopt proper Girling rear damper units, AMC insisted that these should be made with special yoke ends to fit their frames, rather than modify their frames to accommodate standard dampers.

Except on their two-stroke engines used by James and Francis-Barnett (and even then, AMC gave up eventually and shipped the parts up to Wolverhampton, so that Villiers could put them together properly), they never did go in for full unit-construction of engine and gearbox.

When it came to following the lead set by Triumph, and adding a vertical twin to the range, they had to be different by giving theirs a centre bearing, so that the engine 'could operate to very high rpm while remaining rigid'. Don't you believe it! Former Midland editor of *Motor Cycling*, Bernal Osborne had one of the first Matchless twins—indeed, *the* first one ever to be sold on the home market—as his staff machine, and the vibration was far worse than that of any Triumph, Ariel, BSA or Norton twin.

The crankshaft was a massive one-piece casting in nodular iron, supported at each side in roller main bearings, but the centre bearing (which served to locate the shaft) was a Vandervell thin-wall shell through which was fed oil under pressure, to be delivered through drillways to the big-end bearings.

The designer was Phil Walker, and the first of the range was the 498 cc Model G9 Super Clubman introduced as a 1948 Earls Court Show surprise. Unfortunately, AMC were under the delusion that their bottom-end assembly, designed for touring work, would serve equally well for racing purposes, but they were given a rude awakening when the engine of the first G45 racer (essentially a beefed-up G9 unit, installed in the rolling chassis of an AJS Model 7R Boy Racer) was undergoing final bench-testing, prior to being despatched to the Isle of Man so that Robin Sherry could ride it in the 1951 Senior Manx Grand Prix. When the motor was given full throttle, the cast-iron crankshaft snapped just behind the driving sprocket, and the broken shaft, complete with test-bed coupling, went whizzing

Paddy Driver (646 cc Matchless) leading Phil Read on a battered-looking 650 cc Norton damaged in a spill, at the 1963 Oulton Park 1000 km race

round the test shop carving chunks out of the concrete walls. A steel crankshaft was hurriedly substituted, and Robin Sherry finished a creditable fourth in the race, but admitted to being shaken to a jelly by the vibration.

However, the shimmy-shakes were brought under control in later seasons, and for 1956 a bigger roadster twin, the 592 cc G11, joined the programme. The reason, said the makers was 'a demand for increased power from overseas markets, particularly the USA, and from sidecar drivers at home who require greater torque than is available from 500 cc'. The stroke of both models was retained at 72·88 mm, but the bore of the bigger engine was 72 mm, as against the 66 mm of the G9.

As explained earlier, AMC's own rear damper units were exchanged for Girling units (with special yoke ends) in 1957, and the next season brought a new cast-light-alloy primary chaincase.

In April, 1958, *Motor Cycle's* technical editor, Vic Willoughby, had a lot of fun hurtling around the Motor Industry Research Association's banked-bends test track near Nuneaton on a fully-equipped 592 cc Matchless G11 Sports Twin—headlamp, registration plates, even a licence holder—to cover 102·926 mph in an hour from a standing start.

Even so, the Americans wanted yet more power, and that set the AMC factory a poser. Because the cylinder centre lines are a set distance apart, there is a limit on how far one can bore-out a cylinder, and that limit had been reached with the G11. The only alternative was to retain the 72 mm bore of the G11, but fit a crankshaft with a longer (79·3 mm) stroke.

So, at last, in 1959 the 646 cc G12 family was evolved—four models, comprising G12 Standard (with alternator electrics), G12 de Luxe, G12CS, and G12CSR, the last two featuring higher compression ratio, siamese pipes, and titivated porting. The major change for 1960 was a new duplex frame.

Around this time, marketing of AJS and Matchless models in the USA was left to the tender mercies of the Joe Berliner

South African racing star of the 1960s, Paddy Driver pilots a G12 Matchless twin prepared by Tom Kirby in the 1964 Thruxton 500-miler

Corporation, at whose door can be laid the blame for the horrific juke-box tank badges which erupted in 1962. Nor was that all, because the catalogue became spattered with model names—which, naturally, the faithful public flatly refused to use. The de Luxe and G12CS variants were dropped and, instead, there were just the G12 Majestic, and G12CSR Monarch—the latter better known to the lads of the village as the Sportstwin or, from its catalogue designation letters, the 'Coffee Shop Racer'.

For 1963, the wheel diameter was reduced to 18 in and there was a choice of 10·25 to 1 pistons, 'suitable for marathon racing'. That was significant, because by then the G12CSR was featuring in long-distance production machine racing. Quite notably, too, with Paddy Driver and Joe Dunphy as the winning co-riders in the Bemsee 1000-kilometre event of May, 1963. They might well have made it a double by winning the Thruxton 500-Miles, had not a broken chain put them out of the reckoning. (Success had come at Thruxton in 1960, when Ron Langston and Don Chapman romped home with a 646 cc AJS twin—which was just a Matchless with a different timing cover motif.)

In the 1964 Thruxton 500-Miles, Paddy Driver was again the hero, this time sharing the saddle of Tom Kirby's G12CSR with Roger Hunter. For hour after hour the Matchless was involved in a thorough ding-dong with Triumph testers Percy Tait and Fred Swift, on a Bonneville. But at just after 4 pm, with 159 laps completed and having led for four hours, the Matchless was pushed into the pits. Paddy Driver thought that the primary chain had broken; an ominous hole in the crankcase told a different tale.

Because of dire financial troubles, the writing was now on the wall for Matchless, and 1966 was the final year of production of the vertical twin. With the collapse of the AMC empire, Norton Villiers stepped in to pick up some of the pieces, and for a short time the Plumstead works came back to a semblance of life under the new subsidiary name of Norton-Matchless Ltd. But the twin had gone, and the Matchless name survived on just one model, a single-cylinder scrambler. Then that, too, vanished.

Alone among British vertical-twin four-strokes, the Matchless employed a centre crankshaft bearing, housed in a divider plate sandwiched between the two crankcase halves. Cylinder barrels, and cylinder heads, were independent castings

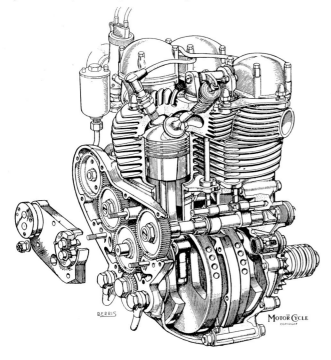

646 c.c. Matchless G12 de Luxe

Fast but Tractable Super-touring Parallel Twin with a Liking for the Open Road

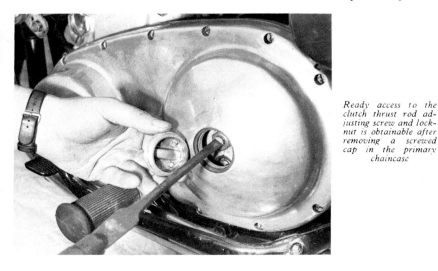

Ready access to the clutch thrust rod adjusting screw and locknut is obtainable after removing a screwed cap in the primary chaincase

DOCILITY and high performance make a rare combination. Top-gear tractability you can have, speed you can have; but both? Yes, both! In the latest 646 c.c. Matchless G12 de Luxe you can. A bulldog with all the get-up-and-go of a greyhound, this is a twin to which everything comes alike, whether it be a gentle potter around the lanes at 30 m.p.h. or a blast along M1 at 80 m.p.h. on half throttle.

From a near-walking pace in bottom gear, juicy, beefy power is on tap right through the range—and that is a characteristic which diehards say vanished with the big vee-twins of old. Above all, the charm of the Matchless lies in the way such urge is developed. There is commendably little fuss, and speed builds up smoothly and with deceptive rapidity.

With such ample power in hand high point-to-point averages could readily, and safely, be maintained; a mere whiff more of gas and the model would sail past slower-moving traffic, so that full advantage could be taken of gaps in the vehicle stream.

Response to the throttle was instantaneous. From 25 m.p.h. in second, a tweak of the grip was sufficient to send the speedometer needle scurrying round to the 50 mark; then up to third gear, and 70 would arrive in a satisfyingly short time before top was engaged. On the other hand, if there was no urgency about the ride, top could be held to well down below 30 m.p.h.—and the engine would pull away smoothly, unobtrusively, with not a hint of transmission roughness.

Long main-road gradients meant not a thing. Steeper hills were a joy to tackle. Second gear sufficed for the really severe stuff, while a standing start on the 1 in 3 test hill at the M.I.R.A. proving ground was easily accomplished in bottom.

Though the engine was exceptionally smooth at speeds up to 60 m.p.h. (or 63 m.p.h., if the speedometer reading was accepted) beyond that some vibration could be felt through the handlebar and footrests—though it was not serious enough to deter one from holding the eighties for mile after mile; for some unaccountable reason the tremor seemed to disappear when accelerating hard. By allowing the model sufficient time to gather speed, a genuine 100 m.p.h. was reached on M1 on several occasions with the rider adopting a slight crouch to reduce windage.

The engine seemed perfectly willing to take harsh treatment indefinitely, with the only external evidence of hard driving a slight seepage from the oil-tank filler cap. If the tank was topped up much

Drive-side aspect of the well-proportioned, six-fifty twin power unit

Layout of the handlebar looks particularly clean. Lighting and ignition switches are in the headlamp shell

above the minimum level, excess oil blown out through the crankcase breather left a film on the rear of the machine. (However, in 750 miles, only a pint of oil was required to restore the level in the tank.)

From the twin megaphone-type silencers came a deep-throated growl which, though pleasing to an enthusiast's ears, was perhaps a shade too loud for these days.

As to be expected with a coil-ignition model, starting was "first time, every time" provided that, when cold, the carburettor was flooded lightly and the air lever closed; within a few seconds the lever could be fully opened, when the engine would settle down to a slow and reliable tickover. One minor crib concerned the very light action of the ignition switch of the test model. Mounted

A roomy box on the left of the model, with hinged lid and coin-slot Dzus fastener, contains the battery and tool roll

on the right of the headlamp shell, it was possible to brush against the switch, unknowingly turn it on and so cause the battery to run flat.

So that the full performance of the G12 may be enjoyed, some care should be taken in tailoring the riding position to suit, and for that reason the very wide range of adjustment of the footrests, rear-brake pedal and gear lever was appreciated.

The controls are well laid out and convenient to operate. Horn push and dip switch are within easy reach of the left thumb (though a more far-reaching horn blast would be an advantage on such a roadburner as this). Handlebar grips are of plastic, and it was felt that a bolder patterning might have been more comfortable, in addition to affording greater friction.

Following pages: the 650 cc G12 Matchless twin was a development of the 600 cc design, of which this is a 1958 G11CS example (*National Motorcycle Museum*)

The dual-seat is generously dimensioned and after a non-stop two-up trip of over 200 miles, neither the rider nor female passenger felt any trace of stiffness or fatigue—and when the passenger volunteers a remark that her half of the seat is comfortable, that can be counted as high praise indeed!

A man-size mount, the Matchless tips the scales at 420 lb and so is a little too bulky to be thrown around as though it were a two-fifty. Nevertheless, once a line through a corner was chosen, it would adhere to that line without deviation and was particularly stable if the power was fed in through the corner. Low-speed balance was good, and it was easy to weave the model through slow-moving traffic.

Straight-ahead steering was impressively positive, though at speeds below 35 m.p.h. a trace of front-wheel flutter could be felt on very smooth surfaces. Cornering on unusually bumpy surfaces produced slight (although never troublesome) yawing, but in general the suspension was well up to the job of ironing-out road shocks without pitching.

Like the engine, the clutch did not object to abuse, and engaged the drive smoothly with a pleasantly light handlebar-lever action. When the engine was allowed to idle slowly, bottom gear engagement was noiseless. Movement of the gear lever was rather heavier than is usual with an A.M.C. gear box; this was noticeable on the upward change from second to third. The ratios matched the engine characteristics perfectly.

Smooth, powerful, and reasonably

Handsome fast tourer from a famous stable, the Matchless G12 de Luxe has a duplex cradle frame

light to operate, the brakes were capable of making the tyres squeal without locking the wheels. The rear brake drum was unaffected by water, but a downpour lessened the effectiveness of the front brake; however, the full power returned after a few minutes of running with the brake lightly applied.

Rather more intensity of light from the main beam of the headlamp would have permitted higher cruising speeds to be maintained at night. The cut-off on dip was adequate and prevented oncoming drivers from being dazzled.

The only maintenance required during the test period was one adjustment of the rear chain after 600 miles. Accessibility to the power unit and cycle parts is first class and normal routine tasks could be carried out quickly and simply. The Matchless has one of the most comprehensive tool kits to be found on any machine.

That's the Matchless G12 de Luxe, a really robust twin with well-bred manners but all the punch of a prizefighter. The beef is pedigree, and handsome enough to win all the rosettes that may be going.

SPECIFICATION

ENGINE: Matchless 646 c.c. (72 x 79.3mm) overhead-valve parallel twin. Crankshaft supported in one plain and two roller bearings; plain big-end bearings. Aluminium-alloy cylinder heads. Compression ratio, 7.5 to 1. Dry sump lubrication; oil-tank capacity, four pints.

CARBURETTOR: Amal Monobloc with air slide operated by lever on handlebar.

IGNITION and LIGHTING: Coil ignition. Lucas RM15 alternator driven by crankshaft, charging 6-volt, 13 amp-hour battery through rectifier; emergency start switching. Lucas 7in-diameter pre-focus light unit with 30/24-watt main bulb and integral pilot light.

TRANSMISSION: A.M.C. four-speed gear box with positive-stop foot control. Gear ratios: bottom, 12.23 to 1; second, 8.15 to 1; third, 5.85 to 1; top, 4.79 to 1. Multi-plate clutch with bonded friction faces; Primary chain, $\frac{3}{8}$ x $\frac{1}{4}$in chain in cast-aluminium oil-bath case. Final drive by $\frac{5}{8}$ x $\frac{3}{8}$in chain with guard over top run. Engine r.p.m. at 30 m.p.h. in top gear, 1,825.

FUEL CAPACITY: 4¼ gallons.

TYRES: Dunlop; front, 3.25 x 19in ribbed; rear, 3.50 x 19in Universal.

BRAKES: 7⅛-diameter front, 6½in rear; finger adjusters.

SUSPENSION: A.M.C. Teledraulic front fork with two-way hydraulic damping. Pivoted rear fork controlled by adjustable Girling spring units with hydraulic damping.

WHEELBASE: 55⅜in unladen. Ground clearance, 6in unladen.

SEAT: A.M.C. dual-seat; unladen height, 31in.

WEIGHT: 420 lb fully equipped with full oil tank and approximately one gallon of petrol.

PRICE: £221 6s 11d; with purchase tax (in Great Britain only), £267.

ROAD TAX: £4 10s a year; £1 13s for four months.

MAKERS: Matchless Motor Cycles, Plumstead Road, London, S.E.18.

PERFORMANCE DATA

(Obtained at the Motor Industry Research Association's proving ground Lindley Leicestershire.)

MEAN MAXIMUM SPEED: Bottom: *50 m.p.h.
Second: *75 m.p.h.
Third: 88 m.p.h.
Top: 95 m.p.h.
* Valve float occurring.

HIGHEST ONE-WAY SPEED: 97 m.p.h. (conditions: light three-quarter breeze; rider wearing two-piece suit and overboots).

MEAN ACCELERATION:

	10-30 m.p.h.	20-40 m.p.h.	30-50 m.p.h.
Bottom	2.6 sec	2.8 sec	3.4 sec.
Second	3 8 sec	3.6 sec	3.6 sec
Third	—	5.0 sec	5.6 sec
Top ...	—	7.2 sec	6.6 sec

Mean speed at end of quarter-mile from rest: 82 m.p.h.
Mean time to cover standing quarter-mile: 16.4 sec.

PETROL CONSUMPTION: At 30 m.p.h., 64 m.p.g.; at 40 m.p.h., 62 m.p.g.; at 50 m.p.h. 59 m.p.g.; at 60 m.p.h., 51 m.p.g.

BRAKING: From 30 m.p.h. to rest, 34ft (surface, dry tarmac).

TURNING CIRCLE: 15ft 6in.

MINIMUM NON-SNATCH SPEED: 18 m.p.h. in top gear.

WEIGHT PER C.C.: 0 65 lb.

Royal Enfield Constellation

For many years the biggest-capacity vertical twin in production in Britain, Royal Enfield's mighty Constellation never quite made it to the top of the Superbike league, although that was not for lack of effort on the part of Scotland's heroic Bob McIntyre. More about that later, but first a look at the Connie's family tree.

It was a matter of evolution rather than design, and it all began with the Royal Enfield 500 Twin (by Ted Pardoe and Tony Wilson-Jones) which was first shown at the 1948 London Show. Keeping to the same conception of a nodular-iron, one-piece crankshaft, independent cylinder barrels so deeply spigoted into the crankcase that they were almost oil-cooled, and independent cylinder heads, the original 496 cc design was stretched to 692 cc for 1953, so producing the Meteor, a rather woolly animal intended primarily for sidecar haulage.

However, there was a demand, particularly from the USA, for a machine with more performance. And so the Super Meteor was introduced in 1956, while at the same time the Redditch technicians were evolving something rather better.

Although the British public first heard of the 692 cc Constellation in April, 1958, in fact it had been in production for export markets for nearly a year, and the bugs had already been shaken out. The Connie was more than a revamped Super Meteor, for it employed shell-type big-end bearings running on $1\frac{7}{8}$-in diameter crank throws (instead of running the rods directly

on the pins as before). This design change had meant a bigger crankcase, but since the old crankcase dies were starting to wear out, anyway, it was as good an opportunity as any to invest in new dies. Larger valves, sportier cams, a higher compression ratio and a single Amal TT carburettor all helped to boost the power output to 51 bhp at 6,250 rpm, and to cope with all this extra power there was a hefty clutch, operated by scissors-action levers housed within the primary chaincase.

April may have seemed the wrong time to announce a new model, but the reason was that the prestigious Thruxton 500-mile race was due to be run in June, and success there would have given the Connie a flying start. Five machines were entered for the race, each being shared by a pair of riders: Bob McIntyre and Derek Powell; Brian Newman and Ken James; Alan Rutherford and Ernie Washer; Don Williams and Geoff Shekell; and Don Chapman and Jack Hill.

In the early stages of the event Royal Enfield hopes were high, with Bob Mac going straight into the lead, and taking the award for the first machine to cover 100 miles. But coming up fast was the determined pairing of Mike Hailwood and Dan Shorey, on a Triumph Tiger 110. Despite slicker pitwork by the Triumph's crew, the Constellation seemed to have the race in the bag, until

Ultimate vertical twin from Royal Enfield was the sporting 736 cc Interceptor, enlarged from the Constellation and seen here in 1964 trim with chromium-plated tank and mudguards

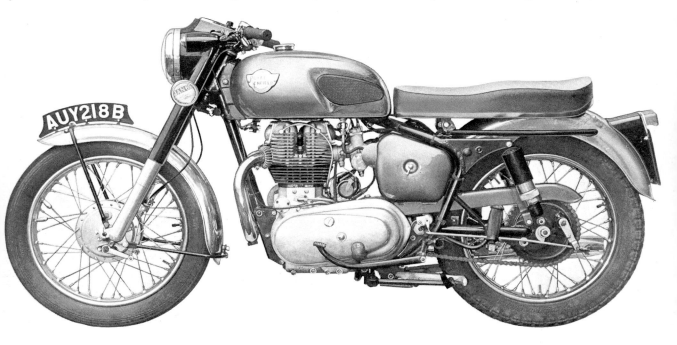

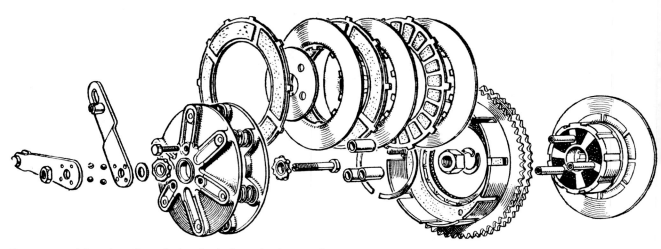

Components of the unique Constellation clutch. Operation is external through scissors-action levers, one fixed and one moving; when the outer lever is operated four interposed balls ride up the ramps of their indents and so the lever moves laterally also

the bike came into the pits for work to be done on a leaking fuel tank.

The stop was of 3 min 15 sec duration, and when Bob got back into the race he began to claw back 3 sec a lap on the Triumph. The only snag was that there was not enough race distance left, and so the Royal Enfield had to settle for runner-up spot, just half a minute astern of the winning Tiger 110. Behind McIntyre and Powell, Brian Newman and Ken James claimed third. The Williams/Shekell and Chapman/Hill teams both finished, and only the Rutherford/Washer machine dropped out.

There was no major change for 1959, except that an Airflow-fairing version was listed. Came the Thruxton 500-Miles again, with Bob McIntyre partnered now by Eric Hinton. Again the Constellation went straight into the lead, but became an early casualty when Bob dropped the model, coming through the chicane.

For the 1960 Thruxton 500-Miles, Bob took Alan Rutherford as his partner. This time it really did look like success for the Royal Enfield, and Bob and Alan were leading the field by *two laps* when trouble struck. Earlier, the nipple had pulled off the lower end of the clutch cable, but Bob pressed on, clutchless, until the end of the cable somehow tangled itself in the primary chain, locked the transmission, and pitched off poor old Bob at high speed.

There was no better luck in the 1961 event, which took place the same week as the road test which follows was published. Now Bob Mac had, as his riding mate, fellow-Scot Alastair King. Yet again the Royal Enfield took an immediate lead, with Bob in the saddle, until a connecting rod decided to come up for air—through the sump—at an estimated 110 mph. Again Bob Mac was sent skating down the track, and this time enough was enough. It was his final try for Thruxton honours.

Although all single-cylinder Royal Enfields were built at Redditch, all twin-cylinder engines had been made, almost from the start, deep underground in the factory converted from old quarry workings at Upper Westwood, near Bradford-on-Avon, Wilts. There, from 1960 onward, all Constellation crankshafts were balanced both statically and dynamically, which accounts for the smooth running of the big engine. But it was more than that because, in the interests of free-revving, lighter pistons were now in use, while a pair of Amal Monobloc carburettors looked after induction, and a new flap-valve crankcase breather was incorporated in the drive-side crankshaft end.

Changes for 1961 included a return to a conventional clutch

operating mechanism. Also, there was a rear mudguard-cum-seat base in glass fibre, wide enough to shroud the upper horizontal tubes of the seat sub-frame. Only minor changes were listed for the 1962 season, probably because the Constellation was by then on its way out.

October, 1962, brought a still bigger Royal Enfield twin, the 736 cc Interceptor, and this too had been in production for export for several months before its release to home purchasers. Ostensibly, the Constellation remained in the catalogue, but in sidecar trim only, and presumably just as a means of using up existing stocks of parts.

The last twin of all (indeed, the last British-built machine to carry the Enfield name) was Reg Thomas' completely rede-signed Interceptor Series 2 of 1969. But by then, the Redditch works had already closed and production was concentrated at the Bradford-on-Avon caverns. The makers were now Enfield Precision Engineers Ltd, an offshoot (like NVT) of the Manganese Bronze empire. With Norton Commando front forks and instrumentation, Amal Concentric carburettors, 12-volt electrics, wet-sump oiling and searing performance, it was the finest Enfield of them all. But it was much, much too late.

Massively constructed, the Royal Enfield Constellation engine was not true unit-construction, the separate gearbox being bolted to the rear of the crankcase assembly. The two camshafts were driven by chain, tensioned by a jockey sprocket on an adjustable quadrant

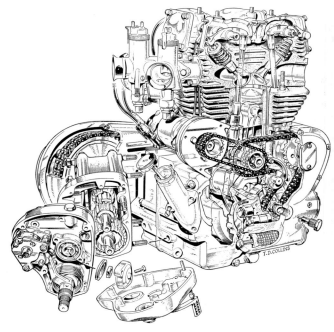

ROAD TESTS OF NEW MODELS

692 c.c. Royal Enfield Constellation

A Well-mannered Roadburner with Tremendous Punch and Ultra-high Cruising Speeds

FIND a connoisseur with sporting tastes and the widest possible experience and you have a rider who knows and loves the incomparable thrill of a high-geared big twin. A few years ago enthusiasts of that ilk were satisfied with nothing but the now-obsolescent 1,000 c.c. vee-twin. Its mighty punch made smaller machines seem puny while the effortlessness of its hill climbing and 90 m.p.h. cruising had to be experienced to be believed. Crisp and stirring, its exhaust note was an ever-present melody, devoid of offence for bystanders.

For those who crave that level of performance there is nothing in the present-day crop of parallel twins that approaches it more closely than the 692 c.c. twin-carburettor Royal Enfield Constellation. True, with comparable power from a smaller engine, the Royal Enfield pulls a lower top gear than the vee-twins; even so, its 4.44 to 1 ratio is higher than that of any other big parallel twin—and the Constellation is not overgeared. Indeed its low- and middle-range punch is its most endearing trait; which is high praise in a machine capable of holding 100 m.p.h. with the rider normally seated.

Tweak the grip on the Constellation and

you get instantaneous, full-blooded acceleration even though the initial revs may be little above idling speed. And though the high gearing lends deception to the pickup, the power is not vicious. Surging and abundant, yes; but smooth and easily controlled. There is as much power on tap as most ordinary riders can handle but no excuse for embarrassment; you get as much as you call for with the twistgrip.

Slick getaways require no great clutch slipping. Even on the quarter-mile

standing-start acceleration tests the clutch was fully home in next to no time. And the same went for a restart on a 1 in 3 climb, so much torque has the engine at low revs.

Much of the test mileage was covered in strong winds but except for absolute maximum speed and the ultimate 5 m.p.h. of cruising speed, the practical effect on the Constellation's performance was negligible. Ridden two-up into a moderate wind, the Enfield held 85 to 90 m.p.h. indefinitely on half throttle with 96 to 98 m.p.h. on tap

Just behind the timing chest is the oil filler cap (with dip stick attached). The valve covers can be removed without disturbing the tank

Left: The dual-seat is large and well shaped; below it is a sturdy lifting handle on each side. On the right can be seen the exhaust-pipe layout. The contact breaker is very accessible and the chaincase cover retained by one nut. Extreme right: Control layout. Particularly appreciated for signalling one's approach was the large and easily reached headlamp switch

whenever the grip was fully opened.

Without a passenger, similar results were obtained against a very stiff wind; while with a following wind the length of M1 was covered at 95 to 100 m.p.h. on half throttle. Maintaining speed on long main-road climbs was simply a matter of using more throttle.

When the performance data were logged at the M.I.R.A. proving ground there was a very strong cross wind gusting to 32 m.p.h. The mean and fastest speeds of 104 and 106 m.p.h. recorded in those conditions are equivalent to still-air speeds of 109 and 111 m.p.h. respectively. Incidentally, an electronic check on the speedometer showed it to be near-enough accurate at 30 m.p.h., 1 m.p.h. fast at 40 m.p.h. and 2 m.p.h. fast from 50 to 90 m.p.h.

Peak-power engine revs of 6,250 are equivalent to 40, 60, 81 and 112 m.p.h. in the four gears, and valve-float speeds some 20 per cent higher in bottom, second and third. Normally, however, upward changes were made at speeds no higher than about 30, 50 and 70 m.p.h. because of unpleasant vibration felt through the seat. The tremor could also be felt from 95 m.p.h. upward in top gear but was not troublesome when a passenger was carried.

Though petrol consumption was on the heavy side at low speeds it dropped to an average level from 50 m.p.h. upward. When the machine was ridden really hard the all-in rate of a shade under 50 m.p.g. was about what one would expect, though oil consumption rose to approximately 1,000 m.p.g.

For a roadburner, the Constellation has an unusually low third gear—some 36 per cent below top. Both performance and the downward change into third would benefit from a reduction of the gap to about 20 to 25 per cent. When made at high speed, the change required a good blip of the throttles and firm pressure on the pedal if engagement was to be certain.

That apart, all changes were positive and clean; pedal movement was short and slightly stiff. A heel-operated neutral finder is fitted but was not normally used because no difficulty was experienced in selecting neutral with the gear pedal. Only the faintest jerk accompanied the engagement of bottom gear with the engine idling slowly. A trifle heavy to withdraw, the clutch took up the drive very sweetly, freed completely and never showed any sign of overheating.

Even when set in the lowest position consistent with not fouling the right footrest hanger on upward changes, the gear pedal was slightly too high for downward changes to be made without lifting the foot from the rest. Putting a downward set in the pedal shank cured the bother.

All the other controls were well sited except for the horn push—too far inboard on the left side of the handlebar to be reached really quickly. Since the separate dip switch is very handy to the left thumb, a combined horn button and dip switch would solve the problem. The horn note, however, was much too feeble to be effective at any but very low speeds.

By and large the riding position proved comfortable; the set of the handlebar gave the very slight forward lean required for really high speeds while a useful chock was formed by the raised rear half of the dual-seat. For all that, a more rearward footrest setting would be a boon in relaxing the grip needed on the handlebar at sustained high speeds.

At the cost of passing on some of the more severe road jolts to the rider, the very firm front and rear springing combined to make wallowing almost unknown and to keep it well in check even when the Constellation was forced round fast, bumpy bends at high speeds with a passenger and full fuel load. Bend swinging was first class and only the most exuberant banking

Below left: The front-brake control casings are anchored in a pivoted bracket on the lever. In the middle is the full-width hub housing the dual brakes. The remaining picture shows one of the snail-cam chain adjusters and the knurled sleeve for adjusting the Armstrong suspension strut

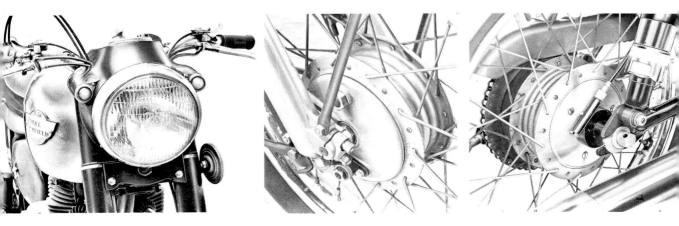

caused the footrest rubbers to graze the road.

For a machine of such speed and weight a little more bite in the brakes would be appreciated—and slightly lighter operation. When the Enfield was ridden in continuous rain or on drenched roads it was necessary to dry out the rear brake by periodic application if its efficiency was to be kept up to par.

Provided the carburettors were neither over- nor under-flooded, cold starting was generally achieved at the first kick. In extremely hot weather it was sufficient merely to close the air lever and not touch the float tickler; at other times a dab on the tickler was a good thing. Either way the ignition was best half retarded to prevent a kick-back and the twistgrip opened a shade towards the end of the pedal swing. No excessive effort was required to spin the engine over compression and the air lever could be opened wide as soon as the engine fired.

Once the engine was thoroughly warm,

full retard was needed to bring idling speed down to the tick-tock level; and precise setting of the throttle stops was essential if the cylinders were to share the running equally.

The Constellation is one of the last few super-sports machines to retain manual ignition control; and since the lever was used solely for starting and idling, auto-advance would be a welcome simplification. Pinking was never experienced on the super-premium petrols used throughout the test.

Routine maintenance was simpler than average, the contact-breaker points and valve-clearance adjusters being particularly accessible. Unusually, the valve clearances can be checked and adjusted easily without lifting the petrol tank.

It was no surprise that the duplex primary chain called for no adjustment in nearly 1,000 miles of hard riding (had it done so the outer half of the chaincase would have had to be removed for access to the adjustable slipper). But the fact that the

exposed rear chain needed resetting by only one notch on the snail cams in the same period (and 300 miles were covered in rain) speaks well for the rubber cush-drive in the rear hub.

For the most part the whole machine remained admirably oiltight; but towards the end of the test oil began to leak from the cast-in pushrod tunnels (where they cross the cylinder-head join face) and from the front-fork filler screws. A more serious leak from the timing cover was cured by replacing three fixing screws which had vibrated out. The only blemish remaining on the Constellation after a few minutes' cleaning was some blueing of the siamezed exhaust pipes. But it is only fair to add that the machine had done some 4,000 miles of high-speed hack work with precious little attention.

Finished in black and polychromatic blue, with chromium-plated front mudguard and tank sides, the Constellation looks the part—a massive, lovable mile-gobbler.

Specification

ENGINE: Royal Enfield 692 c.c. (70 x 90mm) overhead-valve parallel twin. Crankshaft supported in ball bearing on drive side and roller bearing on timing side; steel-backed white-metal big-end bearings. Separate light-alloy cylinder heads; compression ratio, 8 to 1. Dry-sump lubrication; 4-pint oil tank cast integrally with crankcase.
CARBURETTORS: Two Amal Monoblocs fed from float chamber on left-side instrument. Air slides operated by handlebar lever.
IGNITION and LIGHTING: Lucas magneto with manual timing control. Lucas RM15 alternator, with rotor on left end of crankshaft, charging six-volt, 9-amp-hour battery through rectifier. Lucas 7in-diameter headlamp with pre-focus light unit.
TRANSMISSION: Royal Enfield four-speed gear box bolted to rear of crankcase. Gear ratios: bottom, 12.35 to 1; second, 8.19 to 1; third, 6.05 to 1; top, 4.44 to 1. Multi-plate clutch with cork-base friction facings running in oil. Primary chain, ⅜in duplex in cast-aluminium oil-bath case. Rear chain, ⅝ x ⅜in with guard over top run. Engine r.p.m. at 30 m.p.h. in top gear, 1,700.
FUEL CAPACITY: 4¼ gallons.
TYRES: Dunlop: front 3.25 x 19in ribbed; rear 3.50 x 19in Universal.
BRAKES: 6in-diameter dual front, 7in-diameter single rear; finger adjusters.
SUSPENSION: Royal Enfield telescopic front fork with hydraulic damping. Pivoted rear fork controlled by Armstrong spring-and-hydraulic units with two-position manual adjustment for load.
WHEELBASE: 54in unladen. Ground clearance, 6in unladen.
SEAT: Royal Enfield dual-seat; unladen height, 31in.
WEIGHT: 427 lb fully equipped, with full oil tank and approximately one gallon of petrol.

PRICE: £248 5s 10d; with purchase tax (in Great Britain only), £299 10s.
ROAD TAX: £4 10s a year; £1 13s for four months.
MAKERS: The Enfield Cycle Co., Ltd., Redditch, Worcs.

PERFORMANCE DATA

(Obtained at the Motor Industry Research Association's proving ground at Lindley, Leicestershire.)

MEAN MAXIMUM SPEED: Bottom: *48 m.p.h.
Second: *72 m.p.h.
Third: *98 m.p.h.
Top: 104 m.p.h.
* Valve float occurring.

HIGHEST ONE-WAY SPEED: 106 m.p.h. (conditions: very strong cross wind gusting to 32 m.p.h.; rider lightly clad).

MEAN ACCELERATION:

	10-30 m.p.h.	20-40 m.p.h.	30-50 m.p.h.
Bottom	2.1 sec	1.8 sec	—
Second	2.8 sec	3 sec	2.8 sec
Third	—	4 sec	4.2 sec
Top	—	6.6 sec	6.4 sec

Mean speed at end of quarter-mile from rest: 88 m.p.h.
Mean time to cover standing quarter-mile: 15 sec.
PETROL CONSUMPTION: At 30 m.p.h., 70 m.p.g.; at 40 m.p.h., 74 m.p.g.; at 50 m.p.h., 75 m.p.g.; at 60 m.p.h., 63 m.p.g.
BRAKING: From 30 m.p.h. to rest, 35ft (surface, dry tarmac).
TURNING CIRCLE: 16ft 9in.
MINIMUM NON-SNATCH SPEED: 20 m.p.h. in top gear on full retard.
WEIGHT PER C.C.: 0.62 lb.

Following pages: one of the most handsome machines of its day, the 1961 692 cc Royal Enfield Constellation (*National Motorcycle Museum*)

Norton Dominator 650SS

Any bike which won Britain's two most prestigious production-machine marathons of the day (in this case, the Bemsee 1000-kilometre and the Thruxton 500-Miles) within a few months of its introduction has just got to be a classic. In fact the Syd Lawton-prepared Norton 650SS, co-ridden by Brian Setchell and Phil Read, very nearly achieved a double-double . . .

The pedigree of the Dominator range of vertical twins can be traced back to the 497 cc Model 7, designed by Bert Hopwood and announced late in 1948. Personally, I was not too impressed with the Model 7; it had plunger springing at the rear and an almost-solid Norton Roadholder telescopic fork, which combined to make a ride on my brother's model down Worcester's ripply and war-neglected Tything something to make one's eyeballs revolve in opposite directions.

Be that as it may, it was not too long before the roadster twins adopted the world-renowned twin-loop Featherbed frame. The 497 cc Dominator 88 was joined by the 597 cc Dominator 99, and by the 1961 season there were standard and de luxe versions in each capacity, the de luxe models having their nether ends draped around with tinware.

Early in 1961, Bracebridge Street began production of yet another twin, this time a 647 cc model reserved for export only and labelled the Norton Manxman. The name was an affront to Excelsior fans, of course, and anyway no 650 cc Norton twin had ever raced in the Isle of Man, but the blame lay with Norton's USA distributors, and not with the manufacturers.

The 650 cc model was put on the home market during September, 1961. There were now *three* models in each capacity, for an SS (super sports) trim had been added to the standard and de luxe versions. The main difference between the models was that the SS bikes used twin carburettors instead of one, and magneto ignition instead of coil ignition.

The new 647 cc models were not just overbored Model 99s. They retained the 68 mm bore of the Dominator 99, but had a new crankcase wherein was a shaft affording a stroke of 89 instead of 82 mm, so providing the 647 mm capacity. With the shaft came a wider flywheel, and larger-diameter ($1\frac{3}{4}$-in)

crankpins. The light-alloy cylinder head was derived from that of the works Domiracer, and featured wide-splayed exhaust ports, and parallel inlet tracts. In Dominator 650SS form, the engine had twin $1\frac{1}{16}$-in choke Amal Monobloc carburettors, and developed 49 bhp at 6,800 rpm.

A flat and rather short handelbar was supplied, and the specification included a 150 mph speedometer, but there were various optional extras to be had, embracing a rev-meter, folding kick-start, siamese exhaust pipes, chromium-plated mudguards, and a fully-enclosed rear chain—the latter a rather odd option for what was essentially a production-machine racing model. Unlike the standard and de luxe versions, the 650SS had the traditional Norton finish of black frame and silver tank.

By May, 1962, Nortons had added rearset rests complete with brake and gear levers and gear linkage (at £9 16s 7d, tax included) to the catalogue, and within weeks the first race-equipped 650SS models were in action at Silverstone in the Bemsee 1000-kilometre race. During the practice period, Phil Read had flung the Lawton Norton into a muddy field, but it seemed little the worse for its adventure. As the race got going in rain and high winds, so another 650SS, shared by Ron Langston and Bruce Main-Smith built up a useful lead over the Read/Setchell model in second place, but the Langston/Main-Smith effort ended when the Norton's con-rod made a departure, through the crankcase. From then on, Read and Setchell were never headed.

A month later, the same two machines were engaged in battle at the Thruxton 500-Miles, but this time Read and Setchell led throughout apart from a brief moment or two of glory for Langston and Main-Smith, who eventually had to settle for fifth place after Bruce had rammed the straw bales at the chicane.

Not even the boost to 647 cc could satisfy the power-hungry

Cotswold farmer and motor cycling all-rounder, Ron Langston sweeps his six-fifty Norton past John Griffiths' similar mount, in the 1962 Thruxton 500-mile marathon

Americans, and already Nortons had a still bigger twin under way for export only. This was the 745 cc Atlas, giving the same maximum power output as the 650SS, but possessing a lot more low-down torque. But that was not the only news from Bracebridge Street. The AMC group, in financial trouble, was consolidating and by the end of the year Norton production in Birmingham ended and the famous Bracebridge Street factory was put up for sale.

The last bikes to emerge from the historic premises were 85 Dominator 650SS models ordered by the Queensland Police, for escort duties in connection with the forthcoming visit of Her Majesty the Queen and Prince Philip, to Australia.

Tools and dies having been transferred to Woolwich, production of the Norton twins restarted, and soon there were whispers that nothing fitted properly! Of course not; the Londoners were trying to make parts according to drawing, whereas everybody in Birmingham knew that Old Bill, or Old Fred had ignored the drawings for years and made the bits and pieces by instinct.

The Norton range was much abbreviated for 1963. Not only had the 597 cc Dominator 99 been dropped, but the de luxe Dominator 650 had gone, too, leaving just the standard and SS versions. By May, the 497 cc Dominator 88 de luxe had disappeared, too, and thenceforth there would be no more tail-faired Dommies.

May, too, meant it was time once again for the Bemsee 1000-Kilometre race, the venue for which had been moved from Silverstone to the more interesting circuit of Oulton Park. Again, Phil Read and Brian Setchell took the Lawton Norton into an early lead, but the effort came unstuck when Brian skidded off-course at Druid's Corner. Repairs were affected at

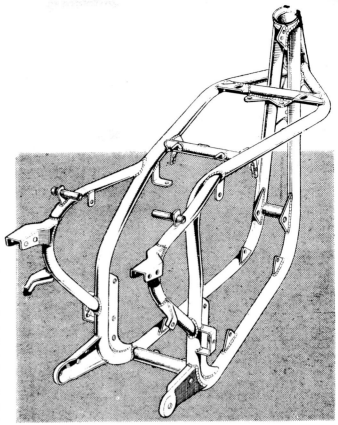

The famous 'featherbed' frame comprised two complete tubular loops which crossed over at the steering head. In the earlier 'wideline' frame the top tubes were parallel. The 'slimline' version was narrowed at the seat nose, for greater comfort and controllability

All Norton twins, from the first 500 cc Dominator up to and including the 850 cc electric-start Norton Commando of the 1970s, were derived from Bert Hopwood's original design featuring a chain-driven front-mounted single camshaft. This is the 1958 597 cc version, with crankshaft-mounted alternator

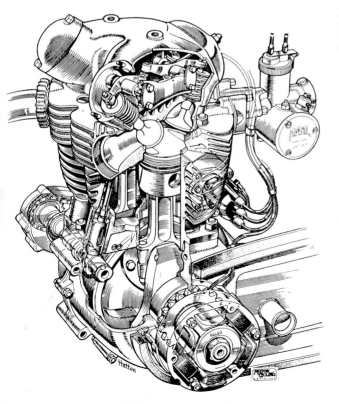

the pits, but the lost time could not be clawed back, and the pair had to settle for second place, with Langston and Main-Smith third in the class.

Still, Thruxton lay ahead, and honour was restored when Read and Setchell took the chequered flag for the second year running. Indeed, the Lawton Norton was to become almost as famous as a course winner as Slippery Sam, the production TT Triumph, because it was to win for the third time at Thruxton in 1964, although on that occasion Setchell was partnered by Derek Woodman.

By 1964, the only version of the Dominator 650 to be listed was the 650SS. It now had 12-volt electrics, and a steering lock on the front fork. But AMC were rapidly heading for obscurity, and in the next two years there was considerable interchanging of components; for example, Norton Atlas engines were inserted into Matchless frames, Matchless singles into Norton frames, and goodness knows what else. An overhead-camshaft Norton twin had been scuttling around the MIRA test track for some considerable while, but it was destined never to see the production line. From the inevitable collapse, Dennis Poore and his new Norton-Villiers concern rescued the 745 cc Atlas engine (which was really the 650SS bottom end married to a 73-mm bore cylinder block). In due course it would be inclined forward, put into a frame with an Isolastic engine mounting system, and given yet another new name—the Norton Commando. But what happened after that is a tale for later in this book.

Useful note for restorers—The official tank colour of the Dominator 650SS was Norton Quicksilver, but in case this is unobtainable the Norton Owners Club recommends Ford Silver Fox as a substitute.

Following pages: 1964 Norton Dominator 650SS fitted with 12-volt electrics, but generally akin to the 1962 road test version (*National Motorcycle Museum*)

Road Tests of New Models

NORTON DOMINATOR 650 SS

Above: A strong candidate for marathon-race honours, the Dominator 650 SS combines race-bred handling with a power output of 49 b.h.p. There is considerable potential for further development, too, for the inlet tracts can be opened up to 1⅛in by removing sleeves. Below is the handlebar-control and instrument layout

Latest and largest

WORSHIPPERS of high performance must be blessing the growth in popularity of production-machine racing. Since the marathon series—led by the Southampton Club's 500-miler—gained a foothold in the sporting calendar, compression ratios and carburettor choke sizes have climbed; cam contours have become more purposeful and, on many a twin, carburettors have doubled up.

In short, super-sports roadsters have acquired speed and acceleration comparable with those of the production racers of not so long ago; and, where necessary, transmission, braking and suspension have been improved to suit.

As fine an example of the trend as any, and better than most, is Norton's ace sportster and marathon racer—the Dominator 650 Sports Special. Though Nortons were the last to push the capacity of their vertical twins beyond the 600 c.c. mark, they have obviously used the time to good advantage. A mean top speed of 111 m.p.h. and a fastest timed run of 118 m.p.h. speak for themselves.

Indeed, considering the tester was wearing a one-piece waterproof riding suit on top of winter muffling, and that the day was wet and windy with gusts of 25 to 30 m.p.h., those figures do more than speak—they shout. There is little doubt that close-fitting leathers, the rear-set footrests allowed for marathon racing and kinder weather would boost top speed by 3 or 4 m.p.h.

Though some features of the engine reflect the influence of the racing five-hundred twin that Tom Phillis rode into

The carburettor downdraught of 20 degrees is apparent here. Ports and cylinder heads are polished and the sports cams actuate flat-base followers

in famous range approaches two miles a minute yet eats out of your hand

...ird place in last year's Senior T.T., there ... nothing freakish about the Dominator 50 SS. Its high performance stems from ...und, straightforward development. As ... result the machine is pleasantly tractable ...ven for town work (thanks in part to the ...se of auto-advance for the magneto and ...balance pipe connecting the two induc-...on tracts); and it cannot be faulted for ...xhaust noise. Provided super-premium ...etrol is used, the engine is free from ...inking; and no great effort is needed to ...wing it over compression for starting.

By parallel-twin standards the engine is ...moother than average. Up to the stipu-...ated r.p.m. limit (6,800) vibration never ...othered the rider, although at peak revs ... caused the petrol tap to shut off until ...he cork-sleeved plunger was renewed. ...esponsible for this comparative smooth-...ess is the extra-stiff crankshaft. Though ... is basically similar to the smaller Dom-...nator crankshafts, the crank throw is 3½ ...mm longer to give the greater stroke of ...9 mm (at 68 mm, cylinder bore is the ...ame as on the six-hundred); the flywheel ... wider and so more effective; and, most ...mportant, crankpin diameter is increased ...o 1⅛in, making the assembly more rigid.

An optional extra, a chronometric rev-...meter was fitted to the test machine. With ...he needle around the 2,000 to 3,000 r.p.m. ...ector the Norton might have been any ...irst-class six-fifty. At 4,000 r.p.m. there ...ere indications that the engine was some-...hing out of the ordinary. By the time the ...ointer had swung round to the 5,000 ...p.m. mark the engine was well and truly ...n the groove; and from there on there ...as a plain challenge to all comers.

Cruising at a speedometer 90 to 95 m.p.h.

(true speed approximately 5 per cent less) was something the Norton was ready to do at the slightest opportunity and happy to sustain indefinitely; there was a comfort-able 5,000-odd r.p.m. on the rev-meter and plenty of throttle in hand. Indeed, with the rider normally seated, the timed mean maximum speed proved to be 99 m.p.h. (a ton in normal weather for sure) with a best run of 108 m.p.h.

And to reach those speeds, even from rest, required little more than a quarter of a mile. The drill was to notch second at about 45 m.p.h., third at 70 and top as soon as the speedometer showed a ton. Those speeds correspond approximately to the peak-power engine speed of 6,800 r.p.m.; and the reason the makers stipulate that as the limit in the lower gears is that the engine can otherwise over-rev quicker than a chronometric rev-meter can keep pace. There is no performance gain in over-revving, only needless wear, tear and vibration, although two-rate valve springs and hollow, barrel-shape light-alloy push-rods help to keep valve float at bay until well beyond peak revs. (For production-machine racing the more serious contender would probably change to a magnetic rev-meter and change up at 7,000 r.p.m.)

In the context of standing starts, the figures shown in the data panel could have been bettered fractionally had it not been necessary to feed the clutch in at compara-tively low r.p.m. to avoid time-wasting wheelspin on the damp surface. Incident-ally, the Avon high-lystresis Grand Prix rear tyre provided above-average adhesion during hard acceleration or fast cornering on wet roads.

Adopted primarily for safety at sustained

There is plenty of finning and air space between the widely splayed exhaust ports

141

three-figure speeds, the tyre brought another benefit. The curved cross-section of its racing-pattern tread added a refinement to the superlative handling for which Dominators are renowned. At low and medium speeds the machine responded sensitively to the slightest banking effort and the balanced front wheel swung into the turn to exactly the right degree. However high the speed, on straight or curve, the steering never showed the least inclination to waver.

As befits a super-sports mount, springing both front and rear was firm and very effectively damped; for the cost of a fairly hard ride on low-speed bumps it ensured great stability at high speeds with no tendency to pitching on undulations.

The flat handlebar resulted in a riding posture that, after several consecutive hours in the saddle, felt slightly cramped but not stupidly so. A rubber band crisscrossed round the twistgrip by a factory tester was a tacit admission of the slipperiness of the plastic sleeve—and most effective in improving grip.

Once they had bedded down the brakes lost their initial slight sponginess and stopped the Sports Special powerfully and smoothly from any speed. Controllability was such that there was no risk of locking a wheel inadvertently, even on wet roads; and there was no loss of efficiency following prolonged riding in heavy rain.

At 20 degrees, the steep downdraught angle of the inlet tracts called for sparing use of the float tickler before starting and for a small but quick tweak of the twistgrip at the end of the kick-starter swing to "catch" the engine. Failure to observe these precautions resulted in an over-rich mixture in the cylinders so that a wide throttle opening was then needed before the engine would start.

Idling was slow but slightly uneven; riders whose everyday mileage includes much town traffic will find it well worth while precisely synchronizing the settings of both throttle cables, throttle stops and pilot air screws to get the cleanest possible tickover and small-throttle getaway.

To cope with the engine's tremendous

punch the Dominator clutch has extrastrong springs and five friction plates instead of the usual four. Clutch operation as a result is heavy, though not too heavy for the tough brand of enthusiast for whom the Sports Special is produced. And correct control adjustment is particularly important, for pressure-plate movement is only just sufficient to give complete freedom with the necessary trace of cable backlash.

All gear changes, upward or downward, were clean and positive. With the engine idling slowly, bottom-gear engagement at rest was well-nigh noiseless. And neutral could be found easily from bottom or second while the machine was rolling or immediately it had come to rest.

Lighting was average. In other words, while 80 m.p.h. cruising caused no anxiety after dark on roads with cats-eye reflectors, 60 m.p.h. was as much as felt safe on roads without these aids.

Save that the chaincase outer half must be removed to get at the clutch pressureplate adjustment, no problems are posed by maintenance. A penny serves to unfasten the dual-seat and so reveal the tool kit. If required, the rear wheel can be removed without disturbing the chain or brake. Incidentally, a change from a falling to a rising rear-brake cam lever means that the finger adjuster on the brake rod is no longer tucked awkwardly behind the left-hand silencer but is really easy to reach.

Finish? A workmanlike black and silver, with chromium plating available for the mudguards at extra cost.

That, then, is the Dominator 650 Sports Special—Norton's answer to the sportsman's prayer. It is a 49 b.h.p. roadster whose quietness, smoothness and lack of fuss makes its speed deceptive; a machine with such superb handling and braking as to make nearly two miles a minute as safe as a stroll in the garden.

SPECIFICATION

ENGINE: Norton 647 c.c. (68 x 89mm) overhead-valve vertical twin. Crankshaft supported in ball and roller bearings; plain big-end bearings. Light-alloy cylinder head; compression ratio, 8.9 to 1. Dry-sump lubrication; oil-tank capacity, 4¼ pints.

CARBURETTORS: Two Amal Monoblocs; air slides operated by handlebar lever.

IGNITION and LIGHTING: Lucas magneto with auto-advance. Lucas RM19 alternator, with rotor mounted on drive-side crankshaft, charging Lucas 6-volt, 13-amp-hour battery through rectifier. Lucas 7in-diameter headlamp with pre-focus light unit.

TRANSMISSION: A.M.C. four-speed foot-change gear box. Gear ratios: bottom, 11.6 to 1; second, 7.57 to 1; third, 5.52 to 1; top, 4.53 to 1. Multiplate clutch with bonded friction facings running in oil. Primary chain, ⅜ x 0.305in in pressed-steel oil-bath case. Rear chain, ⅝ x ⅜in with guard over top run. Engine r.p.m. at 30 m.p.h. in top gear, 1,750.

FUEL CAPACITY: 3¾ gallons.

TYRES: Avon: 3.00 x 19in Speedmaster front; 3.50 x 19in Grand Prix rear.

BRAKES: 8in diameter front, 7in diameter rear, both 1⅛in wide; finger adjusters.

SUSPENSION: Norton Roadholder telescopic front fork with hydraulic damping. Pivoted rear fork controlled by Girling spring-and-hydraulic units with three-position adjustment for load.

WHEELBASE: 55¼in unladen. Ground clearance, 5¼in unladen.

SEAT: Norton dual-seat; unladen height, 31in.

WEIGHT: 434 lb fully equipped, with full oil tank and approximately one gallon of petrol.

PRICE: £255; with purchase tax (in Great Britain only), £311 2s. Extras: Rev-meter, £5 15s (plus £1 5s 3d p.t.); chrome mudguards, £3 5s (p.t., 14s 4d).

ROAD TAX: £4 10s a year; £1 13s for four months.

MAKERS: Norton Motors, Ltd., Bracebridge Street, Aston, Birmingham, 6.

DESCRIPTION: The Motor Cycle, 21 September 1961.

To improve idling, a balance pipe joins the two parallel inlet tracts

PERFORMANCE DATA

(Obtained at the Motor Industry Research Association's proving ground at Lindley, Leicestershire.)

MEAN MAXIMUM SPEED: Bottom: *46 m.p.h.
Second: *71 m.p.h.
Third: *98 m.p.h.
Top: 111 m.p.h.
*Equivalent to peak-power engine r.p.m.

HIGHEST ONE-WAY SPEED: 118 m.p.h. (conditions: strong threequarter wind; rider wearing one-piece waterproof oversuit).

MEAN ACCELERATION:

	10-30 m.p.h.	20-40 m.p.h.	30-50 m.p.h.
Bottom	2 sec	2.2 sec	—
Second	2.8 sec	3.2 sec	3.2 sec
Third	—	4.8 sec	4.8 sec
Top	—	5.8 sec	6.1 sec

Mean speed at end of quarter-mile from rest: 95 m.p.h.
Mean time to cover standing quarter-mile: 14 sec.

PETROL CONSUMPTION: At 30 m.p.h., 81 m.p.g.; at 40 m.p.h., 72 m.p.g.; at 50 m.p.h., 64 m.p.g.; at 60 m.p.h., 56 m.p.g.

BRAKING: From 30 m.p.h. to rest, 29ft (surface, dry concrete).

TURNING CIRCLE: 15ft 6in.

MINIMUM NON-SNATCH SPEED: 20 m.p.h. in top gear.

WEIGHT PER C.C.: 0.67 lb.

AJS Model 18 Statesman

It was something of an achievement that *The Motor Cycle* was able to carry out a full road test of an AJS of any kind! Right from the close of the Second World War, the Plumstead end of the AMC combine had been antagonistic to the motor cycle press, refusing to supply any models for road-testing (although the other members of the combine—Norton, James, and Francis-Barnett—were always far more accommodating).

Such an attitude must surely have had an adverse effect on home market sales, particularly in the great outback north of Watford where the natives regarded AJS and Matchless as 'foreign', anyway. Still, Plumstead was beginning to see the light as the 1950s ended, and with the new decade came a more co-operative mood.

The Model 18 was the last survivor of the traditional British 500 cc single with separate engine and gearbox. As road-tester Peter Fraser remarks, the machine's ancestry could be traced to pre-war days. Nevertheless, there was no remaining Wolverhampton blood in the line of descent, and the true begetter was the Matchless G80 Clubman of the late 1930s, hairpin valve springs and all; even then, there had been an AJS Model 18 equivalent in the catalogue, but that one had coil valve springs.

Over the years since the return of peace, the Model 18's engine had been the subject of much redesign work, and there would be more to come before Associated Motor Cycles plunged into financial disaster in July of 1966, bringing an end to Model 18 production.

First major engine change came in September, 1957, when the substitution of a Lucas RM15 alternator for the old magneto and direct-current-dynamo electrics had meant a new crankcase assembly and, at the same time, a cast light-alloy primary chaincase in place of the pressed-steel case which (unless the owner knew the secrets of black magic) almost invariably leaked oil. There was a new timing-side cover, too, incorporating a contact-breaker assembly driven from the end of the inlet camshaft.

Oddly enough, the familiar long-stroke dimensions of 82·5 × 93 mm (498 cc) were retained, even though the competitions version of the Model 18, listed as the Model 18CS, had changed to oversquare dimensions of 86 × 85·5 mm (498 cc) as long ago as 1955. The original Burman gearbox was superseded by an AMC unit (and fitted also by Norton) from May, 1956.

In the next two years there were minor titivations, including the option of a two-tone blue and light grey finish instead of traditional black, and the fitting of chromium-plated tank side panels at extra cost.

The next substantial improvement took place in 1960 when the single-downtube cradle frame was replaced by a new duplex frame that was to last the production life of the bike.

On the 1964 Model 18 Statesman standard Girling rear dampers replace the earlier special units. By this time, too, the front forks and wheels are Norton

Mechanically, there was a redesigned cylinder head with hemispherical combustion chamber, and embodying an angled inlet tract to promote gas swirl. The piston was now flat-top, with valve-head cutaways.

As for the company itself, in September 1959 AMC bought the old Indian Sales Corporation of USA, and henceforth (for a few years, anyway) it would be a wholly-owned division of the Plumstead-based group, distributing AJS and Matchless models in America; that did not last long, and by 1962 the USA distribution was in the hands of Joe Berliner, of New Jersey. For some while there had been rumours that the old AMC factory at Plumstead was to be sold for re-development, and this was confirmed by a news item in June, 1961, that AMC were to carry out a phased move to a new single-storey works outside Sheerness. Four months later, this plan was shelved because, said the company, there was a shortage of the required type of labour in the Sheerness area.

The AJS Model 18, meantime, had acquired an improved oil-pump drive with stronger tooth form, and an external circlip at the upper end of the inlet valve guide, for a more positive location in the head.

So far, the dignified AJS appearance of old had been maintained, but 1962 brought huge die-cast-zinc chromium-plated tank badges in the worst tradition of juke-box Gothic, presumably at the behest of Joe Berliner. At the same time, the entire AJS and Matchless ranges, which had muddled along for decades using nothing but model numbers, were given names, the Model 18 becoming the Statesman, for no obvious reason. Not that anybody on this side of the Atlantic ever called it that, naturally.

More practically, the 1962 Model 18 gained a larger battery, a

Adoption of alternator electrics in 1958 brought a change from pressed-steel to a cast-light-alloy primary chaincase, so eliminating a characteristic AJS feature—the permanent oil leak

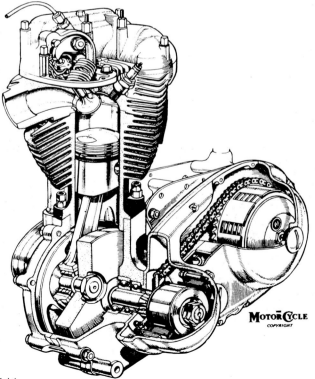

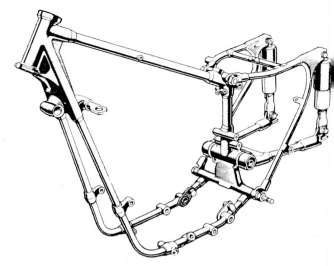

Brazed-lug frame construction, as exemplified by the 1960-onward AJS singles including the Model 18. Steering head and rear fork pivot lugs were malleable-iron castings

more comfortable dual seat, and a better and more insulated method of locating the fuel tank on the frame.

A year later, there were smaller (18-in diameter) wheels, more rounded battery box and oil tank, a fuel tank with knee recesses, and a new full-width hub containing cast light-alloy brake shoes.

The final major change in Model 18 design came in 1964 when a new engine, based on the oversquare Model 18CS unit, was put in hand. The 82·5 mm bore × 93 mm stroke and 497 cc capacity, legacy of the 1930s, was at last discarded in favour of the 86 × 85·5 mm (498 cc) dimensions of the scrambler. The main external change was that the archaic external pushrod tubes were replaced by a cylinder barrel with cast-in pushrod tunnel, the head and barrel being held to the crankcase by through-studs.

Internally, there was a new crankshaft assembly with steel instead of iron flywheels, a double-row-roller big-end bearing with duralumin cage, a roller timing-side main bearing, and totally revised oiling system employing a Norton gear pump instead of the former plunger pump. By this time, of course, AMC had closed the Norton works at Bracebridge Street, Birmingham, and had transferred Norton production to Plumstead, a fact reflected in the use of a Norton Roadholder telescopic front fork instead of the long-in-the-tooth Matchless Teledraulic design.

This should have been the finest Model 18 of all time but, alas, it had insufficient time in which to prove itself. Sinking ever deeper into the mire, AMC were now carrying out a remarkable juggling act, by which Matchless and AJS models found themselves powered by Norton engines in an attempt to find something for Joe Berliner to sell. It was all too late, a hoped-for reconstruction of the group with the aid of USA capital came to nothing and, inevitably, an official receiver was appointed.

There was a 1967 range, announced by Dennis Poore's new and unfamiliar firm of Norton-Matchless Ltd, but it was entirely twin-cylinder, and the Model 18 had gone for good. Under new management, AJS would live again but (oh, horror!) as a *two-stroke*; that rumbling sound heard up in Wolverhampton was A. J. Stevens and his brothers turning in their graves.

498 c.c. A.J.S. Model 18 Statesman

DISCRETION, dignity and an ability to cope with hard work without showing signs of stress—these are some of the essential attributes of a statesman. Thus when A.J.S. decided to give their machines names in addition to terse designations it was fitting that they should call the 498 c.c. Model 18 the Statesman.

A robust, good-looking roadster single with an ancestry reaching back to well before the last war it can claim, in the motor-cycle sense, to embody all these qualities. The main source of the Statesman's appeal is that it offers a pleasing compromise between the modern and traditional in matters of styling.

Riding the A.J.S. the first few miles reminded one, at a time when vertical twins are fashionable, of the particular charm of the lusty, tractable single. With a maximum in the eighties, the Model 18 is certainly no sluggard. In fact the machine was capable of sustaining 70-75 m.p.h. indefinitely.

In that range the engine was working well within its limit. Hills or headwinds on main roads could be tackled comfortably, the engine pulling hard in top gear. If the occasion demanded that the speed be maintained a quick change into third was the drill. This ratio (6.13 to 1) proved invaluable when a high average was required especially on hilly, winding roads. Speedy overtaking could be achieved in third—which provided good acceleration between 30 and 70 m.p.h.

At the lower end of the scale the engine would slog like a side-valve. The combination of good flywheel effect, a moderate (7.3 to 1) compression ratio and an efficient auto-advance control made a major contribution to this impression. Indeed, advocates of manual ignition control would find a very hard case to answer. There was no pinking during the test, even when deliberate attempts were made to provoke it. Premium-grade petrol was used throughout.

Possessing all the mechanical quietness which was the hallmark of its predecessors, the Statesman also has an effectively subdued exhaust. Although an air filter is not fitted to the carburettor as standard, induction roar was not obtrusive. This generally low noise level, therefore, plus the fact that there was ample power at low revolutions, enabled the machine to be ridden discreetly in the most congested of urban areas.

Carburation was clean throughout the range. The engine picked up unhesitat-ingly as soon as the throttle was opened and, once warm, would idle with a steady, reliable beat.

The speedometer read approximately 5 per cent fast, and the instrument would have been easier to read, especially in conditions of poor visibility, had the needle been backed by a black back-

The contact breaker is driven off the inlet camwheel and is readily accessible. Two screws secure the light-alloy cover

Following pages: nobody liked the massive metal tank badges of the Model 18, which is why Ray Bruner's 1965 machine has plain gold transfers (*Bob Currie*)

Robust roadster single, combining good power output and tractability: first-class handling and braking

Orthodox handlebar layout is employed. The switch on the left of the headlamp controls the lights while that on the right is for ignition

This shot emphasizes the trim, workman-like appearance of the Statesman. The duplex frame has lugs for sidecar attachment

position makes itself known. In this respect the Statesman earned high marks. If any criticism is due, it is that the footrests could with benefit be positioned an inch or so farther to the rear, to relieve the rider's arms from some strain when cruising for long periods in the seventies.

Controls fell readily to hand or foot as the case was. The dual-seat proved very comfortable and generous enough dimensionally to accommodate a passenger without cramping. Fitted as standard, the passenger's footrests had rubbers of the same size as those for the rider and resulted in greater comfort than the usual type. Plastic handlebar grips are fitted. Owing to the nature of the material, and insufficient depth of pattern, the amount of friction they offered, especially during cold or wet conditions, was considered inadequate.

Both front and rear brakes were light in action and could be delicately controlled. During performance tests successive stops from maximum speed

ground (about two-thirds of the needle rotates over a light grey surface). While the performance figures were being obtained the main mileage record jumped 1,000 miles. A trip mileage recorder is fitted, and could easily be reset by means of the knob protruding from the base of the headlamp.

Handling inspired confidence at all times. The machine could be ridden to a standstill in heavy traffic feet-up without undue effort. Steering lock was felt to be rather limited for a model of this nature. The lack of it made manhandling in and out of limited garaging space, a twice-daily task for many ride-to-work enthusiasts, more awkward than was thought desirable. Centre and prop stands are provided. Both were easily operated and gave safe support.

On the open road the Statesman could be ridden to the limit of its performance

without betraying any tendency to deviate from the chosen line. Zestful cornering was encouraged by the way in which the model could, with little effort, be banked from side to side through bends.

Both front and rear springing are hydraulically damped and possessed just that right degree of firmness—an effective compromise between the stiff action needed for stability at high speeds and a soft one for comfort at lower speeds. When the machine was ridden one-up, the three-position Girling units were used in their softest setting. By means of the C-spanner provided in the tool kit they proved quickly adjustable. The Model 18 displayed no tendency to pitching on undulating surfaces and was ridden on unmade, potholed roads without the suspension ever bottoming.

As the miles on a journey mount up so the suitability, or otherwise, of the riding

Adjustment of the clutch thrust rod is simply effected. Removal of a threaded cap exposes the adjuster in the centre of the clutch pressure plate

For 1962 a silver-coloured metal motif embellishes the fuel tank of the Statesman

were made without any loss in efficiency or of adjustment.

Starting a big single when overnight temperatures are around freezing point calls for a certain amount of technique. On the Model 18 the drill was to flood the carburettor slightly, close the handlebar-mounted air lever and, with the exhaust-valve lifter in operation, give a long, swinging kick, releasing the lifter when the kick-starter pedal was at the bottom of its travel. In practice the method advised by the makers of easing the engine over compression, releasing the valve lifter and then kicking did not spin the engine sufficiently to start it in severe conditions. It was quite effective enough,

though, as soon as the engine was warm.

Clutch operation was progressive, but on the heavy side. Hard usage during the test caused no loss of adjustment. Gear changes in both directions were both positive and silent. Bottom-gear engagement with the engine idling caused, at worst, no more than a slight click. Neutral could be selected without difficulty.

Lighting was adequate for cruising in the sixties after dark. The dipped beam could be readily selected by an easily accessible switch on the handlebar. The headlamp can be adjusted after slackening the two pivot bolts. The charging rate at 30 m.p.h. in top gear was sufficient

for the generator to balance the full lighting load.

Mounted under the seat, the horn would be more effective if it had a louder and perhaps higher-pitched note. Complete experimental discharging of the battery proved that the emergency-start system was up to its task and that the generator could restore the battery to a useable state of charge after a few miles running.

Located on the left just below the dual-seat, the roomy tool box could be opened with a coin. The tool kit provided is reasonably comprehensive and contains enough tools for most routine maintenance jobs. A most informative instruction book is also provided. Opening the tool box exposes the battery for inspection. It is held in position by a tensioned rubber strap which has the advantage that, besides being easy to undo, it will not be affected should it become exposed to electrolyte spray. The battery level can be checked with the battery in position.

Removal of two screws allows a light-alloy cover to be detached from the timing chest thus revealing the contact breaker (which is driven by the inlet camwheel).

The Statesman is finished in black relieved by touches of chromium plating. The absence of the familiar A.J.S. gold lining on the fuel tank will be regretted by many enthusiasts. But for those who prefer colour, the model is available in blue with white mudguards.

To sum up, then, the Statesman is a good-looking, well-mannered mount, equally suitable for the daily round or for long week-end runs.

Specification

ENGINE: A.J.S. 498 c.c. (82.5 x 93mm) overhead-valve single. Crankshaft supported in plain and ball bearings; roller big-end bearing. Light-alloy cylinder head; compression ratio 7.3 to 1. Dry-sump lubrication; oil-tank capacity, 4 pints.

CARBURETTOR: Amal Monobloc; air slide operated by handlebar lever.

IGNITION and LIGHTING: Lucas coil ignition with auto-advance. Lucas RM15 alternator with rotor mounted on drive-side crankshaft, charging Lucas 6-volt, 11-amp-hour battery through rectifier. Lucas 7in-diameter headlamp with pre-focus light unit.

TRANSMISSION: A.M.C. four-speed foot-change gear box. Gear ratios: bottom, 12.86 to 1; second, 8.53 to 1; third, 6.13 to 1; top, 5.02 to 1. Multi-plate clutch with bonded friction facings running in oil. Primary chain, ⅜ x 0.305in in light-alloy oil-bath case. Rear chain, ⅝ x ⅜in with guard over top run. Engine r.p.m. at 30 m.p.h. in top gear, 2,000.

FUEL CAPACITY: 4¼ gallons.

TYRES: Dunlop. 3.25 x 19in ribbed front; 3.50 x 19in Universal rear.

BRAKES: 7in-diameter front and rear; finger adjusters.

SUSPENSION: A.M.C. Teledraulic telescopic front fork with hydraulic damping. Pivoted rear fork controlled by Girling spring-and-hydraulic units with three-position adjustment for load.

WHEELBASE: 55¼in unladen. Ground clearance, 5¼in unladen.

SEAT: A.J.S. dual-seat; unladen height 31in.

WEIGHT: 403 lb fully equipped, with full oil tank and approximately one gallon of petrol.

PRICE: £208 10s; with purchase tax (in Great Britain only), £254 7s 5d Extras: Blue finish with white mudguards, £3 10s (plus 15s 5d p.t.); quickly-detachable rear wheel, £2 2s (p.t., 9s 3d).

ROAD TAX: £4 10s a year; £1 13s for four months.

MAKERS: A.J.S. Motor Cycles, Plumstead Road, London, S.E.18.

DESCRIPTION: *The Motor Cycle,* 14 September, 1961.

PERFORMANCE DATA ◀ ••••••••

(Obtained at the Motor Industry Research Association's proving ground at Lindley, Leicestershire.)

MEAN MAXIMUM SPEED: Bottom: 38 m.p.h.*
Second: 57 m.p.h.*
Third: 77 m.p.h.
Top: 82 m.p.h.
*Valve float occuring.

HIGHEST ONE-WAY SPEED: 87 m.p.h. (conditions: strong following wind; rider wearing two-piece suit and overboots).

MEAN ACCELERATION:

	10-30 m.p.h.	20-40 m.p.h.	30-50 m.p.h.
Bottom:	3.6 sec.		
Second	4.8 sec	4.4 sec	4.6 sec
Third:	—	7 sec	5.8 sec
Top:	—	9.2 sec	8.6 sec

Mean speed at end of quarter-mile from rest: 68 m.p.h.
Mean time to cover standing quarter-mile: 18.4 sec.

PETROL CONSUMPTION: At 30 m.p.h., 84 m.p.g.; at 40 m.p.h., 72 m.p.g.; at 50 m.p.h., 64 m.p.g.; at 60 m.p.h., 52 m.p.g.

BRAKING: From 30 m.p.h. to rest, 29ft 6in (surface, dry tarmac).

TURNING CIRCLE: 16ft.

MINIMUM NON-SNATCH SPEED: 20 m.p.h. in top gear.

WEIGHT PER C.C.: 0.81 lb.

Ariel Sports Arrow

Ariel general manager Ken Whistance and his happy crew at the Selly Oak works in Birmingham went right out on a limb when tooling-up for quantity production of Val Page's imaginative 249 cc two-stroke-twin Leader. The construction of the machine entailed a complete breakaway from anything ever before built at the factory, for it relied intensively on steel pressings, with the major item an immensely strong hollow beam (formed from two edge-welded pressings) from which the engine-gear unit was suspended. Dies to produce pressings that big were rather costly.

To recoup the outlay, the Leader just *had* to sell. But regrettably, although the public at large were content to admire from a distance, they were slow in coming forward to buy. However, the Leader was by no means a flop (in fact, the Selly Oak people threw a party to celebrate the 25,000th Leader to come off the assembly line) but it was no sales record-buster, either.

The Leader was conceived as a super-tourer, with built-in everything from engine enclosure, legshields and handlebar screen, to rear carrier and metal pannier boxes. This was fine, except that the specification was far too staid for ebullient youth. To cater for the young rider, something rather more sporty, perhaps, was needed, yet making use of the pressings produced from those expensive dies.

As Val Page was on the point of retiring from work, development of a derived model more acceptable to the younger element was passed to Bernard Knight. He discarded the Leader's superstructure and enclosure, and started again from the front fork, frame beam, and engine unit. A rather smaller dummy 'tank' pressing was devised (the real fuel tank, as on the Leader, was within the frame beam, with the filler cap under the termite-proof plywood base of the seat), with ears projecting forward of the steering head to carry the headlamp.

A tool box was sunk into the top face of the dummy tank, and removal of the tool box gave access to parcel space (and to the tyre pump). A neat touch was that access to the rectifier was gained by removing the left-side tank badge and so disclosing an aperture.

Careful use of two-tone paintwork produced a machine which was still unorthodox in appearance, yet looked lighter and nippier than the Leader. Nor was it just a matter of looks. It really *was* lighter, by almost 50 lb, and since the engine was the same for both models, the loss of weight resulted in a rather better performance.

This, then, was the Arrow, launched in December, 1959. It sold well in Britain, if not abroad, and it was adopted for beat patrol work by some urban police forces. What was rather less expected was that the road-racing boys should see in the Arrow a potential racer. Nevertheless, it was an Arrow tuned by

A ghosted view of the Arrow, showing the fuel tank location within the massive pressed-steel frame beam. Construction of the trailing link front fork is especially interesting

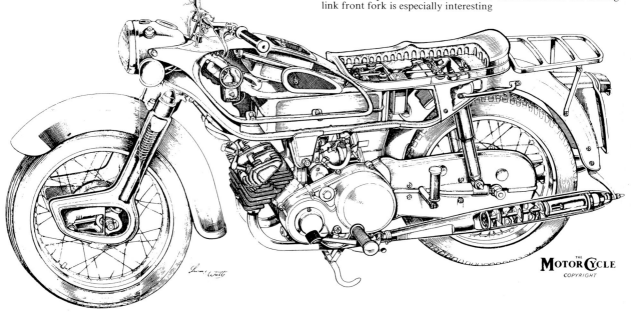

Hermann Meier and ridden by Mike O'Rourke that gave Britain its best 250 cc TT placing for many a long year, by finishing seventh (at an average speed of 80·18 mph) in the 1960 event, right astern of Taniguchi's works Honda.

In the months ahead, others (notably Peter Inchley and Maurice Spalding) followed O'Rourke's example and brought Ariel Arrows to the race-circuit starting grids.

In a very different field, trials ace Sammy Miller (accompanied by Jeff Smith on a C15T BSA) took an Arrow up Ben Nevis until deep snowdrifts barred further upward progress. For the record, Sammy had substituted a 20-in front wheel, for better ground clearance, and had lowered the gearing overall until bottom ratio was something like 30 to 1.

Aided and abetted by Ariel development engineer Clive Bennett, the old firm of Ernie Earles and Bill Boddice concocted a *four-cylinder* Ariel Arrow racing sidecar outfit, and it was intended that Ron Langston should drive it in the 1962 Sidecar TT. It got as far as the Isle of Man, but the device coupling the two Arrow engines came adrift as Ron was being pushed away for his first practice lap. After a rebuild he tried again, only to suffer a broken connecting rod.

So, the double-Arrow was a non-starter. But unknown to the public it was also a mobile test-bed for the Lucas company's experiments in electronic ignition, and if only for that reason it deserves a place in history.

The Leader had been voted Machine of the Year in 1959, and the Arrow took the same title for 1960. With the announcement in January, 1961, of yet another variant on the twin-two-stroke theme, it seemed that Ariels were bidding fair to make it three-in-a-row.

The newcomer was, of course, the Sports Arrow—quickly nicknamed the Golden Arrow because of the gilded finish of its dummy tank and rear number plate pressing. At first, the gold was combined with light battleship grey for the remaining parts of the model, but this later became a richer ivory.

To add yet more glamour, there were whitewall tyres, semi-dropped handlebars, and chromium-plated covers for the timing side and the front fork legs, while a small perspex sports handlebar screen completed the picture. To justify the 'Super Sports' tag, a $1\frac{1}{16}$-in bore Amal Monobloc carburettor was

Ariel experimental chief Clive Bennett works with Ernie Handley (*left*) and Ernie Earles on the unique four-cylinder Ariel Arrow which Ron Langston was to have raced in the 1962 Sidecar TT. The power band was too narrow

employed instead of the $\frac{7}{8}$-in Monobloc of the standard Arrow.

The model was possessed of abundant energy, and on a Golden Arrow borrowed from the Selly Oak development department for an hour or two, I was able to climb the long slope to the Wyche Cutting (the gap through the ridge of Worcestershire's Malvern Hills) in third gear and on half throttle. To anyone who knows the area, that was a pretty convincing demonstration.

The power output of the Golden Arrow was 20 bhp at 6,650 rpm, and it retained this figure throughout its production run. By the beginning of 1963, motor cycle sales as a whole were plunging, and the BSA Group's decision to close Selly Oak and transfer Leader and Arrow production to the main Small Heath works was no doubt justified.

It has been said that at the time of the closure, Ariel's order book stood at only 15 machines. One snag was that certain overseas markets, including the USA, did not like the idea of a pressed-steel frame (which was illogical, since they happily accepted Honda and Suzuki lightweights, of very similar construction). To overcome the objection, development of a tubular-framed Arrow was put in hand, and the two prototypes covered quite a respectable test mileage.

Alas, there never was a production tubular-frame Arrow, and the reason was that Burman, the gearing manufacturers who provided the internals for the Leader/Arrow box, were now so deeply involved in the production of car steering mechanisms for Austin-Morris that they wanted to take their leave of the motor cycle field. To bridge the gap, BSA explored the possibility of filling the Arrow gearbox shell with C15 internals, but it could not be done without considerable redesign of the complicated Ariel crankcase-gearbox casting. With overall sales so low, this was not possible.

To use up Ariel frame pressings, a 199 cc budget version of the Arrow was announced early in 1964 (the bait was that the purchaser paid a cheaper 'Under-200 cc' insurance rate) but by then the end was already in sight, for production of the Leader and all three versions of the Arrow stopped in 1965.

'I shot an Arrow in the air . . .' In March, 1961, trials ace Sammy Miller (Ariel Arrow) and moto-cross champion Jeff Smith (BSA) tried a motor cycle climb of Ben Nevis. Deep snow near the summit frustrated their efforts.

Above: Tools and inflator are carried in a compartment in the dummy tank. Right: Sleek and cobby—and glamorous—the Sports Arrow looks every inch a thorough-bred

Below: First steps in front-wheel removal are to take off the chromium-plated covers at the base of the fork legs and to insert the special tools through the holes provided and into the links. Bottom: Fuel filler and battery are revealed by raising the hinged dual-seat

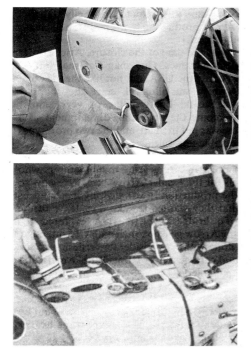

247 c.c. Ariel Sports Arrow

HIGH-PERFORMANCE TWIN WITH SUPERB HANDLING

IT is not so very long ago that Ariels, renowned for their range of four-strokes, took a bold and somewhat unexpected step. Casting their established models—including the illustrious Square Four—on the scrapheap they staked their all on the success of an unconventional two-stroke twin; it was, of course, the lavishly-equipped Leader two-fifty. The gamble paid off, and soon there was a second version of the same basic design in the lively but low-cost Arrow. And that, too, hit the jackpot.

Could Ariels do it yet again? Indeed they could, for just over a year ago a third variation of the theme was revealed. Gaily finished with gold-enamelled tank shell and rear-number-plate pressing, it was the Sports Arrow. Chromium plating brightened the front-fork cover plates, tool-box lid and right-hand engine cover. White-wall tyres were specified at front and rear. The cast, light-alloy primary chaincase was highly polished. An abbreviated flyscreen graced the rakish, low-level handlebar. Control levers were of ball-end pattern.

Nor was the beauty merely skin deep. This was a true sports mount, fitted with a larger-diameter carburettor than the road-ster model, and with corresponding modi-cations to the cylinder-wall porting whi boosted the power output to a healt 20 b.h.p. at 6,500 r.p.m. As tested in 1962 guise, the machine appears ev more glamorous, for now the gilded ta shell is allied to an ivory finish for frame, forks and mudguards, so produc almost a "Regency" effect.

And what of the overall impression the Sports Arrow? Favourable, m favourable. Speed the test machine p duced, and then some, but the charm in the manner in which the model produc its performance. Its range-mates, Leader and Arrow, had already achieve reputation for rock-steady steering and t attribute is, of course, equally applica to the sports version. Normally, a tu two-stroke can be a thirsty little beast the Ariel turned out to be surprisingly li on fuel and, in give-and-take goi throughout the test, produced an avera figure of about 70 m.p.g.

However, there were also one or points to be noted on the debit side of ledger. Starting from cold, for instan usually called for a dozen or so prods of

Specification

ENGINE: Ariel 247 c.c. (54 x 54mm) two-stroke twin. Separate iron cylinders and light-alloy heads. Roller big-end bearings. Crankshaft supported in three ball bearings. Compression ratio, 10 to 1. Petroil lubrication; mixture ratio, 20 to 1 (except Shell 2T or B.P. Zoom, 25 to 1).
CARBURETTOR: Amal Monobloc with 1 1/16in choke. Rod-operated strangler. Mesh-type air filter.
TRANSMISSION: Four-speed, foot-change gear box in unit with engine. Ratios: bottom, 19 to 1; second, 11 to 1; third, 7.8 to 1; top, 5.9 to 1. Three-plate clutch operating in oil. Primary chain 3/8 x 0.225in in oil-bath case; rear chain 1/2 x 0.305in, in pressed-steel case. Engine r.p.m. at 30 m.p.h. in top gear, 2,600.
IGNITION and LIGHTING: Lucas 50-watt RM18 alternator. Coil ignition. Lucas 13-ampere-hour battery. 6in-diameter headlamp with 30/24-watt main bulb.
FUEL CAPACITY: 3 gallons, including reserve.
TYRES: Dunlop 3.25 x 16in whitewall; studded rear, ribbed front.
BRAKES: 6in diameter x 1 1/8in wide, front and rear.
SUSPENSION: Ariel trailing-link front fork, hydraulically damped Pivoted rear fork controlled by two Armstrong spring and hydraulic units.
WHEELBASE: 51in unladen. Ground clearance, 5in, unladen. Seat height, 28 1/2in unladen.
WEIGHT: 305 lb, including approximately one gallon of petroil.
PRICE: £190 15s 7d, including British purchase tax.
ROAD TAX: £2 5s a year.
MAKERS: Ariel Motors Ltd , Grange Road, Selly Oak, Birmingham, 29.
DESCRIPTION: *The Motor Cycle, 19 January 1961.*

Performance Data

(Obtained at the Motor Industry Research Association's proving ground, Lindley, Leicestershire.)
MEAN MAXIMUM SPEED: Bottom: 30 m.p.h.
Second: 49 m.p.h.
Third: 64 m.p.h.
Top: 78 m.p.h.
HIGHEST ONE-WAY SPEED: 81 m.p.h. (conditions: light three-quarter breeze, 10-stone rider wearing helmet, riding boots and two-piece trials suit).

MEAN ACCELERATION:

	10–30 m.p.h.	20–40 m.p.h.	30–50 m.p.h.
Bottom	2.1 sec	—	—
Second	3.9 sec	4.5 sec	—
Third	—	8.0 sec	7.7 sec
Top	—	15.4 sec	13.2 sec

Mean speed at end of quarter-mile from rest: 70 m.p.h. Mean time to cover standing quarter-mile: 17.6 sec.
PETROIL CONSUMPTION: At 30 m.p.h., 108 m.p.g.; at 40 m.p.h. 82 m.p.g.; at 50 m.p.h., 74 m.p.g.; at 60 m.p.h., 56 m.p.g.
BRAKING: From 30 m.p.h. to rest, 30ft (surface, dry asphalt).
TURNING CIRCLE: 12ft 10in.
MINIMUM NON-SNATCH SPEED: 18 m.p.h. in top gear.
WEIGHT PER C.C.: 1.23 lb.

pedal with the strangler fully closed. Once the engine was warm a first-kick start could be guaranteed. Then there was the riding position. A down-turned handlebar is certainly not to everyone's taste though, admittedly, it is traditionally a part of a sports-machine specification; but here the footrests are in a normal, forward position and, if full use is to be made of the dropped bar, the resulting crouch is not the most comfortable. As for the flyscreen, while this may have its advantages when a rider is well tucked down, for normal riding it is little more than ornamental and, indeed, tends to obscure part of the speedometer dial.

The acceleration of the Ariel, as reference to the data panel will show, was pretty fantastic for a two-fifty. The standing quarter-mile in 17.6s.?. That is as good as, if not better than, the average five-hundred—nor was it a fluke reading, for the figure was the average of several runs. One conclusion which could be drawn is that the engine possesses an unusually wide power band; and that was borne out by the road performance.

With most sports two-strokes the power is concentrated at the upper end of the rev scale and, after a slow build-up, comes in almost as though the rider has been kicked in the rear. With the Sports Arrow the power build-up is more evenly spread and, as a result, there is less need to recourse to the lower gear ratios.

In illustration of this, it was quite possible to allow the machine to accelerate steadily from speeds as low as 25 m.p.h. in top though, of course, a drop into third produced a much zippier getaway. Furthermore, where time was not pressing, long, main-road hills could be climbed with top gear still engaged.

When main-road conditions allowed, many miles were covered with the speedo-meter needle varying between 60 and 65 m.p.h. (an electronic test proved the dial 6 per cent optimistic). Even at 60 there was plenty of urge still to come should the need arise.

Ariel steering is already a byword, and so utterly safe did the Sports Arrow feel that there was the greatest possible fun to be had from flinging the model through a twisty section of road. A further safety factor is the performance of the 6in-diameter brakes at front and rear, and the quoted figure of 30ft from 30 m.p.h. is

genuine enough. Nor are the stoppers in any way "sudden," for the machine comes to a halt smoothly and progressively.

The gear-change pedal has a light, if somewhat long movement, and ratios could be located readily. Noiseless changes, upward or downward, were child's play, although the change was found to be unusually sensitive to primary and rear-chain adjustment.

In town areas the large-capacity twin silencers earned high marks for the exhaust's quiet, droning song. When the taps were opened wide, or when the Ariel was accelerated hard, the song changed to a deeper, louder tune but this was always of an acceptable standard. Mechanical noise from the engine and transmission was at a commendably low level. An annoying clatter from below was traced to a bouncing centre stand; a change of stand spring brought little improvement. Another source of annoyance was the tool box, inset in the upper face of the "tank" pressing; access to the box itself was simple enough, but to extract the tyre pump the tool tray, held in place by a spring cross-bar, had first to be removed—and replacement of the bar was something of a fiddle. However, this small point was far out-weighed by the many practical features of the model.

Handling? Absolutely top-line—in fact there's many a *racing* machine which uses the standard Arrow beam and front fork. Suspension? Top-line again; one-up or two-up, the Sports Arrow floats over the bumpy surfaces. Speed? Near-80, if you want it; day-long cruising in the sixties, if you wish.

Following pages: the Sports Arrow was usually called the Golden Arrow, from its tank finish. Shown here is a 1963 version (*National Motorcycle Museum*)

153

BSA Rocket Gold Star

Even the most rabid BSA enthusiast will have to admit that at various times in the firm's history, Small Heath gave birth to thorough stinkers—the 1921 Senior TT models, the 1928 175 cc two-stroke, and so on up to and including the Ariel Three tricycle moped. Yet between times some highly covetable models trundled down Armoury Road, and one of these was the Rocket Gold Star.

In a sense, the Rocket Goldie was already obsolete when it was first announced in February, 1962. It was the last of the pre-unit twins, essentially a marriage of the well-tried A10 Super Rocket engine with a modified single-cylinder Gold Star frame, and because BSA had already begun production of their A50 and A65 unit-construction twins this was just a handy way of using up surplus stocks of parts. Once the supply of pre-unit engines had dried up, there would be no more Rocket Goldies, which explains why the model was only listed in 1962 and 1963.

Nevertheless it was a very handsome machine, and so sought-after nowadays that fake Rocket Gold Stars are making an appearance. Beware, you would-be buyers, especially at auction sales. A favourite dodge is to instal an A10 engine in a single-cylinder BSA frame, and here the immediate give-away is the bulge in the right-hand cradle tube (which, on a single, is necessary to clear the oil-pump housing). It should also be noted that in 1962, Rocket Goldie engine numbers ran from DA10R.5958 onward, and frame numbers from GA10.101 onward. The corresponding 1963 identifications are engine numbers from DA10R.8197 onward, and frame numbers from GA10.390 onward. The same engine number sequences cover Super Rocket and Spitfire models also, but *only* the Rocket Gold Star used GA10-series frames.

The only major difference from the light alloy-head Super Rocket engine was a compression ratio of 9 to 1, instead of 8·25 to 1. Ignition was by magneto with manual advance/retard

On clubman-type racing machines torque characteristics are a compromise between touring and racing requirements. Here is Maurice Spalding on a BSA Rocket Gold Star in the 1962 Thruxton 500-miler

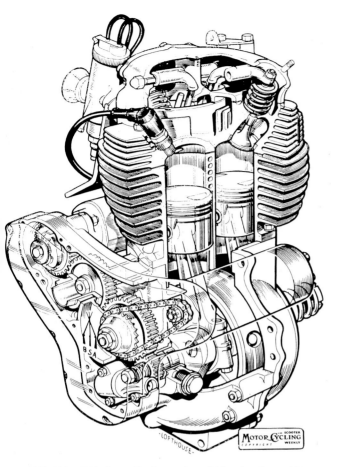

The 1960 646 cc BSA Super Rocket engine which, when housed in a basically Gold Star frame, produced the much-coveted Rocket Gold Star. It was the final development of the pre-unit BSA twin

lever, a direct-current dynamo looked after the electric supply, and the exhaust system embraced siamese pipes and a single, Gold Star-type silencer on the right.

The front fork and wheel were pure Goldie, and since the twin was intended for clubman racing it featured a quickly-detachable headlamp with plug-and-socket wiring harness connection, reversible handlebar, and an exceptionally close-ratio gearbox (overall figures were 4·52, 4·96, 5·96 and 7·92 initially, although this was perhaps a mite *too* close, and for the following year they were widened slightly, as indicated in the specification panel).

There was also a list of racing goodies available, including light-alloy wheel rims, rear-set footrests, clip-on bars and a 'track silencer'. In roadgoing trim, power output of the engine was 46 bhp at 6,250 rpm, but with modest tuning this could be pushed up to 50 bhp.

The Rocket Gold Star did not do much production-machine racing. One example, shared by David Dixon and Maurice Spalding, and prepared by Syd Lawton, failed to distinguish itself in the 1962 Silverstone 1000 and Thruxton 500; it did finish, but well down the field—at Silverstone, with a serious oil leak and a loss of power ten laps from the end, which meant very careful nursing until the chequered flag went out.

Three Rocket Gold Stars contested the 1963 Thruxton marathon, with the machine shared by Ron Langston and Dave Williams tipped to have the best chance. Unluckily, the lap-scorers credited them with a lap too few in the early stages, but once the correction was made it was seen that they were up in a creditable third place. But later in the race an oil union fractured, and much time was lost at the pits in effecting a repair. Then it was 'on with the race', and Ron and Dave did well to work their way back to sixth place in the multi-cylinder class by the end.

The model was officially out of production by the time of the 1964 Thruxton 500 (although in fact the factory records show that 12 more were built after August, 1963). Again the same three pairs of riders rode the same three Rocket Goldies, but this time there was to be no joy in the BSA camp. Ron Langston and Dave Williams were out after no more than 22 laps, as the result of a blown cylinder head joint; R. Mahan and G. Smith followed six laps later with gearbox problems, while D. Face and E. Denyer lasted for 125 laps before making their exit with faulty ignition. Ironically, it was around this time that production-machine racing began to get into its stride internationally, but effectively the Rocket Gold Star was no longer around.

Finally, here are a few notes for restorers of the model, by courtesy of Colin Wall. Correct mudguards for the Rocket Gold Star are rather difficult to find. They are identified by a beaded flare on the leading edge of the front guard, and the trailing edge of the rear guard—they are *neither* single-cylinder Gold Star type, *nor* A65 Lightning pattern. There should be six separate stays to the front guard.

The rear registration plate is of the open-sided type, not the boxed-in plate mounting of the roadster twins, and is identical to that used on the mid-1950 Bantams. The dual seat is the same as that of the A10 of the early 1960s, but the rev-meter is driven at a 3 to 1 ratio, and is of a type used exclusively on the Rocket Gold Star and Super Rocket.

It was a favourite habit of Rocket Gold Star owners of the day to replace the standard four-gallon steel tank with a glass-fibre or light-alloy unit, as fashion dictated. Nevertheless, the bike looks far better when fitted with the original tank. This should have chromium-plated side panels outlined in maroon (not red). The rest of the tank is finished in silver, and for a good match Colin recommends Volkswagen Beetle silver.

A BSA Rocket Gold Star comes in for awed scrutiny at the 1962 Earls Court Show. It was carrying about £60-worth of optional extras

Following pages: last of the BSA separate-engine vertical twins was the 650 cc Rocket Gold Star of 1962-3 (*National Motorcycle Museum*)

ROAD TESTS OF NEW MODELS

646 c.c. B.S.A. Rocket

Scintillating high-performance road burner: good brakes, excellent rider comfort and docile traffic manners

AN 85 m.p.h. top-gear spread speaks volumes for the tractability of a sporting engine. And on top of this the 646 c.c. B.S.A. Rocket Gold Star has effortless, surging acceleration through the gears and a tireless 90 m.p.h. cruising gait. The maximum of 105 m.p.h. obtained on test could certainly have been bettered had the November weather been co-operative.

The standard Super Rocket engine, with compression ratio raised from 8.25 to 9 to 1, is housed in a Gold Star frame. Narrow, chromium-plated mudguards, four-gallon petrol tank with snap filler, rubber gaiters and chromed dust covers on the front fork and matching speedometer and rev-meter are inherited from the Gold Star.

For production-machine racing, the full range of Gold Star extras and a track silencer, said to boost power output by 4 b.h.p., are available.

Although most of its contemporary rivals boast twin carburettors for maximum performance, the Rocket Gold Star has a single Amal Monobloc. This is perhaps one of the prime factors in the sweetness of carburation at the lower end of the scale.

From tickover at 800 r.p.m., the engine answered the throttle crisply and instantaneously, provided the ignition lever was used intelligently. From 1,500 r.p.m., beefy, usable power was on tap right up to the manufacturers' recommended ceiling of 6,800 r.p.m., at which 46 b.h.p. is developed.

CLOSE RATIOS

Gold Star close-ratio gears are employed; a bottom ratio of 8.39 to 1 necessitated slipping the clutch to prevent the r.p.m. dropping below 1,500. Above 15 m.p.h., the clutch could be ignored and the ignition lever gradually moved to the fully advanced position. (The 10-to-30 m.p.h. acceleration figure in the performance data was obtained with the ignition fully retarded at 10 m.p.h.)

Although 100-octane petrol was used, pinking was audible if the throttle was opened hard on full advance at any engine speed.

Moving the ignition lever to the one-third-retard position made it possible to thread dense traffic in a docile manner, but top was not engaged in 30 m.p.h.-limit areas. It was after the derestriction signs that the model really gathered itself up.

The close-ratio gears meant a drop of only 1,000 r.p.m. between first and second, 800 between second and third and 400 between third and top. As you might guess, acceleration was exceptionally rapid—guaranteed to satisfy the most hardened enthusiast.

The delightfully subdued drone from the siamesed exhaust system allowed full use of the performance without fear of causing offence. Because of the wide spread of power, upward gear changes were normally made at 5,400 r.p.m.—rather than at the ceiling of 6,800—equivalent to a corrected 50 m.p.h. in bottom, 66 in second and 80 in third. The speedometer read a constant 4 m.p.h. fast.

Tweaking the twistgrip half way continued the rush of the speedometer needle round to the 85 mark. The appallingly poor weather during the test period—continuous rain and mist—dictated cruising speeds no higher than 85 to 90 m.p.h.

A further tweak of the grip at ninety unleashed a fresh surge of power until the needle was hovering near the magic 100, but to achieve a genuine "ton" it was necessary to chin the tank top.

While not in the turbine-smooth category, the power unit was no rougher than one would expect of a vertical twin with high-kick pistons, and was commendably free of any noticeable vibration period.

COOL CLUTCH

In spite of being continually slipped in traffic, the clutch showed never the slightest sign of protest. Even after six full-throttle standing starts, when the performance figures were being obtained, only an insignificant amount of free play

Compression ratio of the engine is boosted to 9 to 1

Gold Star

Weather conditions were poor during the test

319 GOP

appeared at the clutch lever; this free movement disappeared as the plates cooled.

The gear change was light and crisp in movement and positive at all times; neutral was easily selected from bottom or second.

After the front wheel had been balanced and both wheels correctly aligned, steering and handling were of true sporting class. Straight-ahead steering was precise up to 90 m.p.h. but then became progressively lighter until at maximum speed, 105 m.p.h. on a wet road, the front wheel tended to wander slightly. Tightening down the steering damper effected a partial cure.

NO BRAKE FADE

Roadholding and stability under normal conditions allowed high average speeds to be maintained safely. Stiffening the action of the front fork would probably eliminate a tendency for slight rolling on fast corners.

As befits such a high-performance model, both brakes were light in operation and extremely powerful. Initially, dust in the drum caused loud squealing from the front brake. In spite of repeated hard application from maximum speed, neither brake showed any tendency to fade, nor were they affected by prolonged riding in heavy rain.

The sharpened Super Rocket engine is housed in a Gold Star duplex-loop frame

319 GOP

"That's the girl who packed me up because I wouldn't give up motor cycling"

The model was supplied with a down-turned touring handlebar. This brought too much weight to bear on the rider's wrists, particularly in traffic, so a more comfortable position was obtained by reversing the bar. A satisfactory compromise would be a shorter, straighter bar to provide slightly more forward lean without lowering the wrist level.

DE-LUXE SEATING

All controls were well placed for ease of operation and a reasonable range of adjustments is allowed. A more prominent dipswitch lever would have been preferred.

Well shaped and deeply upholstered, the dual-seat provided exceptional comfort no matter what mileage was being covered. It did not need a very long run in the rain, however, to prove the drawback of a narrow sports front mudguard —the amount of road filth that blows back on the machine and rider.

Lighting was adequate for mile-a-minute cruising after dark and the dipped beam was satisfactory. Loud enough for jaunts about town, the horn would have to be more penetrating to be much use during fast, open-road touring.

Accessibility for routine maintenance tasks was good, but the tool kit did not include a spanner for adjusting the rear wheel. The roll-on centre stand required only moderate effort to operate, but its feet were too sharp; parking places had to be carefully chosen, for the legs would gradually dig into tarmac. A prop stand is available at extra cost.

The Rocket Gold Star, then, is that rare bird, a high-performance motorway express which is almost equally at home in less exciting urban surroundings.

Triumph Sports Cub

It stands to reason that if you want better quality, you have to pay more for it, and likeable though Triumph's little 199 cc Tiger Cub may have been in standard form, the Sports Cub version was a more expensive but far sturdier job. And so it should have been, sharing as it did many of the attributes of the competitions Cubs.

To recap on Meriden history, a Trials Tiger Cub had been catalogued in the late 1950s, but since it sported a standard-type front fork complete with nacelle-mounted headlamp, one could hardly accuse the makers of being serious about it.

But the Tiger Cub family began the 1960s with the benefit of an entirely new crankcase assembly, in which the timing-side casing incorporated the gearbox, while the drive side embodied the primary case. Based on this engine, new and tougher trials mounts were evolved by the factory competitions department for Triumph teamsters such as Ray Sayer, Gordon Blakeway, and Roy Peplow.

But not only was there a T20T Trials Cub in the 1961 programme; there was, too, a model listed as the T20S/L Scrambles Cub. Intended mainly for export to the USA, this was really the first Sports Cub. Discarding the fork-top nacelle, it featured a separate headlamp on brackets from the fork shrouds, while downstairs a sports camshaft and a 9 to 1 (instead of 7 to 1) compression ratio helped to boost the power output from the standard Tiger Cub's 10 bhp to a much more businesslike 14·5 bhp.

The official trials team popped up in the results at regular intervals (Johnny Giles won the West of England event in 1961, in addition to doing well in the Scottish Six Days Trial), but early in 1962 the news began to spread that Triumphs were going to build for sale a batch of genuine works-replica trials models, features of which would be a front fork with two-way hydraulic damping—in fact, the same fork as used on the 350 cc 3TA twin—plus a heavier-duty oil pump, and a more robust crankshaft with a larger-diameter big-end bearing, and a ball main bearing instead of a bush at the timing side.

Trials fans banged in their orders straight away, with the result that no fewer than *thirty* Triumph Cubs appeared in the entry for the 1962 Scottish Six Days Trial! Scott Ellis put up the Best 200 cc performance, while an Army trio, all on Trials Cubs, grabbed the Services Team Award.

This was fine, but the same press release that gave news of the works-replica trials model had given news, also, of a new super roadster, to be designated the T20S/H Sports Cub—the first mention of the model by this name. It carried the same strengthened crankshaft and ball main bearing as the trials mount, but continued the 9 to 1 compression ratio of the scrambler. Other details included rectifier-and-battery lighting, a quickly-detachable headlamp, and a larger fuel tank (3 gallons, instead of the 2⅜ gallons of the standard Tiger Cub).

From that point on, the Sports Cub was on its way, from year to year taking the benefit of improvements pioneered on the models used by the works trials and moto-cross riders.

Identification point for 1963 on all Cubs was the adoption of finned, cast-light-alloy rocker box covers instead of plain, and on the Sports Cub a rev-meter could be supplied if the customer so wished. Still the developments continued (for 1964, a solid crankpin and, for longer life, an oil-pump driving worm made from aluminium bronze). For all that, the oil pump appeared to be something of an Achilles heel of Cub design, and it would be a couple of years yet before the designers got things to their liking.

The 1965 season was a further landmark in the life of the Cubs and, especially, the Sports Cub. That year, the Scrambles Cub was dropped, and the home-market 199 cc range comprised the

Feet-up over the loose boulders of Laggan Locks in the 1962 Scottish Six Days Trial goes Scott Ellis, winner of the 200 cc Cup on his 199 cc Triumph Tiger Cub

Unexpected location for a Tiger Cub Engine was in Martin Legg's 1964 drag bike, known as 'Time Traveller'

Trials Cub, standard Tiger Cub, and Sports Cub, with the addition of the Mountain Cub for export to the USA only.

New throughout was a graphite-impregnated sintered bronze big-end bearing. A folding kick-start pedal appeared on the Trials and Sports models and, for the Sports Cub, came the heftiest front fork yet—from a Bonneville, no less!

Visitors to Meriden around this time may have been puzzled to see batches of Cubs painted drab olive green and equipped with pannier frames and similar military accoutrements. The reason was that the Cub had gone into service with the Danish and French Armies (although not with the British Army,

Inside view of the 1963 199 cc Triumph Sports Cub unit. By this time there was a duplex primary chain, and the contact breaker had moved to a location in the timing case. Power output was 14·5 bhp at 6,500 rpm

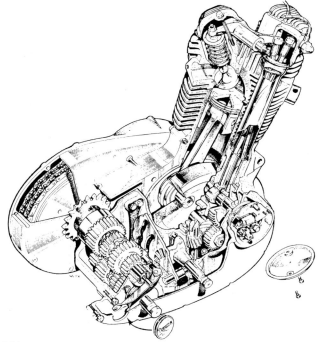

curiously enough). The Mountain Cub was a lot more colourful, painted in bright yellow and equipped with rifle clips.

In truth, the Mountain Cub was the first British-built trail bike, and was intended for the use of hunting enthusiasts in the USA. The bright yellow colouring was a safety precaution, a measure of protection against the trail-riding hunter from being shot at by other trigger-happy 'hunters'.

Through all of this, a little news item which appeared in February, 1965, could well have been overlooked. Because of the demand for Triumph twins, it said, the Cub production line was to be moved to the BSA premises at Small Heath, Birmingham. But there was more to it than that, because the BSA-Triumph group was moving towards greater integration of the two marques.

That became evident when the 1966 range was announced. At last the Cubs had a totally new oil pump—totally new for them, that is, because it was actually the slide-type pump that had been used on the vertical twins since 1937 or so. The Sports Cub and TR20 Trials Cub remained in the programme, but significantly there were two newcomers, the Tiger Cub and Super Cub, which discarded the familiar Meriden frame and, instead, made use of the frame, front fork, wheels and (on the Super Cub) fuel tank of the 175 cc two-stroke BSA Bantam.

The main differences between the standard Cub and the Super Cub were in the matter of trim, the former having a painted tank of the old Tiger Cub pattern, and the latter a chromium-plated BSA Bantam tank with Triumph badges.

The change was not necessarily for the bad, and a test of the Bantam-framed standard Cub showed that, if anything, the model felt a shade bigger than the genuine Meriden-bred article. A new Amal Monobloc 375/44 carburettor (without air slide) was specified, and this gave the machine a remarkable 96 mpg consumption figure at a steady 50 mph.

But, sad to say, BSA-Triumph were adopting a 'biggies only' policy, and 1967 brought the end of the line for both the Bantam and Cub. Uneconomical to build, said those in command, and the tooling for both models was promptly scrapped. It is too late now to argue the whys and wherefores, but in retrospect it does seem to have been a very mistaken policy. The absence of British lightweights from the shops meant that a youngster had to buy foreign for his first bike. And it was only natural that, when he wanted to advance to something bigger, he would return to the same dealer—and buy something bigger but of the same foreign make.

ROAD TESTS OF NEW MODELS

MERIDEN BABY WHICH CAN SHOW ITS HEELS TO MANY A BIG 'UN

199 c.c. Triumph Sports Cub

HEARD the lads talk of the Baby Bonnie? This is the model they mean; and just a brief run is enough to give a clue to the nickname, for crammed into a 199 c.c. pot is a helping of the same kind of boisterous energy which characterizes the 649 c.c. Bonneville twin.

Just look at the performance figures! Over 70 in top, and just 20s for the standing quarter. A showing like that would be no disgrace to a three-fifty. Certainly the Sports Cub is a little more pricey than the standard Tiger Cub roadster. But for the extra £22 the customer gets an engine which is virtually that of the scrambles model, 9 to 1 compression ratio and all, with the benefit of a beefed-up bottom-end assembly, more robust oil pump and increased oil supply.

In addition, the fork (which has two-way damping) has internals similar to those used on the Tiger 90 three-fifty; and there is a gear box with close third and top ratios, and a detachable headlamp with plug-in connection to the wiring harness.
Oddly enough, the first impression of the riding position is that the seat appears somewhat high. That's an optical illusion, for at 31in seat height both feet of an average-stature rider can be firmly planted on the roadway. It isn't that the rider is way up there: it is merely that the bike is way down here! And (again, oddly enough) the lean-forward attitude dictated by the low, flattish handlebar seems to emphasize the small size.

But there's nothing tiny about the Triumph's heart. A bit thumpy at low engine speeds, maybe, in that firing strokes could be felt as tremors through the footrests and handlebar. But open the grip and the power comes flooding in, sending the revs soaring up the scale and smoothing out the delivery.

This model is meant to buzz, and for it to produce its best the revs have to be kept up—which, of course, is where that close gap between top and third ratios pays dividends.

Change-up speeds? Say, 40 in second, 60 in third. Play tunes on the box, and the bike will sing along in the sixties with no bother at all.

Mark you, that 9 to 1 compression ratio makes itself felt when the time comes to kick-start. A really hefty jab at the pedal is called for—and two-hundred or not—an exhaust-valve lifter or compression-release valve would be a worth-while addition.

But it is all a matter of acquiring the knack. No carburettor air slide, but that doesn't matter much. A fairly liberal flooding of the carburettor, and the engine got cracking at about the third kick even on a frosty morning.

Down-for-down, up-for-up on any Triumph; and on the Sports Cub there was never any doubt about gear engagement. And it was easy enough to find neutral with just a flick of the toes.

However, before the first start of the day, it was found best to depress the starter pedal a time or two with the clutch withdrawn, just to free the plates.

Safety Plus

Heavy rain, black ice, half-gales; this test had the lot—and there was a heartfelt vote

Following pages: last of the Triumph 199 cc line, the Bantam Cub employed BSA frame and cycle parts (*Andrew Morland*)

165

SPECIFICATION

ENGINE: Triumph 199 c.c. (63 x 64mm) overhead-valve single. Steel-back, white-metal big-end bearing; crankshaft supported in two ball bearings. Light-alloy head; compression ratio, 9 to 1. Oil-tank capacity, 2¾ pints.
CARBURETTOR: Amal Monobloc with gauze-element air filter.
IGNITION and LIGHTING: Lucas RM18 alternator with coil-ignition, auto-advance and emergency-start circuit. Lucas 8 ampere-hour battery charged through silicon-crystal rectifier. Lucas detachable 6in-diameter headlamp with 30/24-watt main bulb.
TRANSMISSION: Triumph four-speed gear box in unit with engine. Gear ratios: bottom, 19.8 to 1; second, 13.4 to 1; third, 8.6 to 1; top, 7.13 to 1. Multi-plate wet clutch. Primary chain, ⅜in duplex, in oil-bath case; rear chain, ½ x 0.205in, with guard over top run. Engine r.p.m. at 30 m.p.h., 2,850.
FUEL CAPACITY: 3 gallons.
TYRES: Dunlop, 3.00 x 19in ribbed front; 3.50 x 18in studded rear.
BRAKES: 5½in-diameter front and rear.
SUSPENSION: Telescopic front fork with hydraulic damping. Pivoted rear fork controlled by Girling suspension units.
WHEELBASE: 50in unladen. Ground clearance 8½in unladen. Seat height 30in unladen.
WEIGHT: 240 lb, with approximately one gallon of petrol.
WEIGHT PER C.C.: 1.2 lb.
PRICE: £188 8s, including British purchase tax.
ANNUAL ROAD TAX: £2 5s.
MAKERS: Triumph Engineering Co Ltd., Meriden Works, Allesley, Coventry.

PERFORMANCE DATA

MEAN MAXIMUM SPEED:
Bottom: *28 m.p.h. Second: *42 m.p.h. Third: *66 m.p.h. Top: 74 m.p.h. *Valve float occurring.
HIGHEST ONE-WAY SPEED: 77 m.p.h. (conditions: moderate rain showers, strong three-quarter wind, rider wearing two-piece suit and overboots).
MEAN ACCELERATION:

		10-30 m.p.h.	20-40 m.p.h.	30-50 m.p.h.
Second	...	4.6 sec	5.4 sec	—
Third	...	—	8.6 sec	8.6 sec
Top	...	—	11.0 sec	9.2 sec

Mean speed at end of quarter-mile from rest, 63.8 m.p.h.
Mean time to cover standing quarter-mile, 20 sec.
PETROL CONSUMPTION: At 30 m.p.h., 118 m.p.g.; at 40 m.p.h., 100 m.p.g.; at 50 m.p.h., 86 m.p.g.; at 60 m.p.h., 72 m.p.g.
BRAKING: From 30 m.p.h. to rest, 32ft (surface, damp tarmac).
TURNING CIRCLE: 12ft 9in.
MINIMUM NON-SNATCH SPEED: 20 m.p.h. in top gear.

of thanks to the makers for the light, low-down weight and precise handling which eased the job of negotiating the dicey patches. Against that, the howling gusts which caught the model on passing side-street junctions could certainly be felt by the rider.

And there were one or two relatively fine days, when the Cub could be let off the leash. So full marks for the nicely tucked-in footrests, which meant that the little sportster could be heeled through a

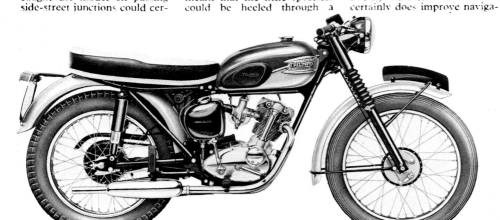

bend with no fear of anything grounding.

Suspension, particularly at the front, seemed a little too firm for orthodox tastes, but that's how sports-model fans like it; and a stiffish front fork certainly does improve naviga-

tion on a twisty section of road.

No trouble in making a getaway from a standing start on M.I.R.A.'s 1-in-4 test hill, with the clutch fully home before many feet had been covered. And here's a point: the Tiger Cub has never been noted for unobtrusiveness, but the mute fitted in the silencer tail pipe of the Sports Cub did a grand job of chopping the edge from the characteristic bark, even under hard acceleration.

Lighting was above expectations, permitting the use of relatively high cruising speeds at night, though the location of the dip-switch button on the top face of the headlamp shell was rather inconvenient.

Handsome? Hmm; let's say cobby, rather. The Sports Cub looks a goer, and in this case looks don't lie. It's a model which is enormous fun to ride—and watch out, you two-fifty merchants; this is **a** Cub with claws!

Triumph T120 Bonneville

A few readers may disagree with the choice, but if I had to pick out just one bike as *the* British motor cycle of the 1960s, I would plump unhesitatingly for the Triumph Bonneville—known affectionately by riders the world over as the 'Bonnie'. Introduced at the very last minute into the 1959 Meriden programme (it was not even listed in the early editions of the 1959 Triumph catalogue), it was still there in the 1981 equivalent, 22 years later; there have been, of course, many changes over the years. In 1959, it was a 650 cc pre-unit job with (for 1959 only) the famous Triumph nacelle headlamp. In the early 1980s, it was a unit-construction 750 cc machine with, at option, full electric starting and cast light-alloy wheels.

Between times, the Bonnie covered itself in glory in production-machine racing, all but died in the financial collapse of the BSA-Triumph group, was sentenced to death by the incoming NVT management, was absent from the market during the 18-months workers' sit-in, and came back to life under co-operative ownership.

Inevitably, it was pressure from the USA for more power that led Meriden to investigate ways of wringing still higher performance from the 649 cc Tiger 110 sports engine. But there was a limiting factor, because the crankshaft was still the old three-piece-suite (two half-shafts, bolted through flanges to a separate central flywheel) that had characterised Triumph twins—the 3T excepted—since Edward Turner's first 498 cc Speed Twin of 1937.

The design department came up with a one-piece shaft, over which a flywheel ring could be threaded, then secured to a central boss by radial studs. With this stronger crankshaft, the search for more power could continue. In the USA, Triumph-powered projectiles had been prominent since the mid-1950s in speed record attempts on the Bonneville Salt Flats of Utah, notably by Johnny Allen and Jess Thomas who each topped the flying mile at over 214 mph. The name of the new twin-carburettor sports twin, the T120 Bonneville, was a tribute to the salt-flats heroes.

The 1959 Bonneville had a deceptively sedate appearance, with fully-shrouded fork legs, touring handlebar, and the original type of single-down-tube frame. But the 1960 version was radically different. Not only was there a new duplex-tube frame and revised steering geometry, but the sporting image was

Rare version of the Triumph Bonneville was the Thruxton Bonnie production racer catalogued for 1965. With racing seat and fairing, it was a replica of the models raced by Percy Tait and Fred Swift

strengthened by the use of a quickly-detachable chrome-plated headlamp, gaitered fork legs, and twin Amal Monobloc carburettors fed from a single float chamber suspended by rod from a rubber diaphragm. An alternator was fitted for lighting purposes, but magneto ignition was retained.

Although around this time production-machine racing had not yet achieved the boom of later years, it was beginning to get a hold, with the Thruxton 500-mile marathon as the highlight of the season. In consequence, Triumph offered a list of racing goodies including a timing cover which incorporated a rev-meter-drive mounting, and a humpy racing seat.

The process was to culminate in the full-blown Thruxton Bonneville exhibited on the Triumph stand at the 1965 Blackpool Show. Complete with racing seat and fairing, and priced £30 above the roadster Bonnie, it was a replica of the model which (shared by Percy Tait and Fred Swift) had taken second place in the 1964 Thruxton 500-Mile race, and the reason for cataloguing it was that under the Thruxton regulations, no machine could qualify for entry unless at least 100 examples had been sold to the public through conventional channels.

Before then, though, the Bonneville had undergone a drastic redesign, to emerge for 1963 as a unit-construction model, fired by coil ignition and housed in yet another new frame, this time a reversion to single-down-tube style. The Bonneville's handling had not been everything it should be, but with the arrival of Doug Hele (a refugee from Norton) things improved. In particular, a more substantial tie-up between the frame loops and the ends of the rear fork pivot held frame whip effectively in check, while changes in the head angle gave precision steering.

In the USA, Gary Richards had clocked 149·51 mph on an unfaired Bonneville as early as' 1960, upping that figure to 159·54 mph the following year. British Triumph fans concentrated more on the production races which were gaining

Man on the 649 cc Triumph is none other than film star Dean Martin. He used the bike instead of a car to go to and from the studios daily

momentum, with the addition of the Hutchinson 100 to the long-established Thruxton event.

It was in 1967 that enthusiasm reached a peak, with the staging of the first Production-machine TT in the Isle of Man. Naturally, Bonnevilles dominated the 650 cc field, and to the 1967 Thruxton laurels (a win for Percy Tait and Rod Gould, with Joe Dunphy and Ray Pickrell as runners-up) could now be added the Proddy TT crown; winner John Hartle returned a commendable 97·1 mph average speed, and four more Bonnevilles—and a Tiger 110—finished in the first 11 places.

In the spring of 1969, Percy Tait brought more joy to Meriden by scoring his second Thruxton 500-Miles victory in three years, with other Bonnevilles filling second, fifth, sixth and seventh places. Better yet was to come, when Welshman Malcolm Uphill won the 1969 Production-machine TT at an average speed of 99·99 mph, having scored the first 100 mph-plus Island lap by a production machine from a standing start.

Nevertheless, 1969 was virtually the Bonneville's farewell year where production-machine racing was concerned, because by that time an even more potent model, the three-cylinder Trident, was poised ready to take over the torch.

The roadster Bonneville was still a public favourite, but the fates were poised to give it a heck of a wallop, from which it would take a long time to recover. BSA and Triumph had embarked upon a course of integration and, accordingly, had established an expensive 'think-tank' of boffins at Umberslade Hall, a country mansion beween Birmingham and Stratford-on-Avon.

One outcome was a new frame, based on a thin-wall backbone tube which would serve also as an oil reservoir, and this frame was intended to be used by both Small Heath and Meriden. However, it ran into many problems, and while these were being sorted out the Triumph production lines ground to a halt for more than three months.

When the frames did start coming through, it was found that the Bonneville engine would not fit—and the seat height was 2 in too elevated for the height of the average rider.

It did all get sorted out eventually, but what happened next is really a story of the 1970s and, thereby, beyond the scope of this particular book.

The Bonneville adopted unit construction in October, 1962, at the same time mounting the contact-breaker on the end of the exhaust camshaft. New, too, was the trapped-ball method of operating the clutch thrust rod

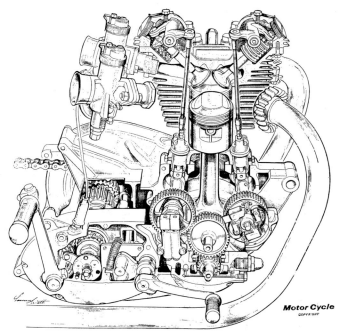

Motor Cycle
COPYRIGHT

THINK of a superlative, double it . . . but no, don't even try. Words alone cannot amply describe the Bonneville 120, cold figures can but hint at the performance. It looks immensely powerful, sturdily and solidly built, yet set off by a glamour finish of white and lacquered gold. Given its head, it will whistle up into the treble figures, smoothly and safely. But there is also a fair helping of sweetness and humility down in the lower reaches of the rev band.

Built for the chap who travels far and fast, the Bonnie has a specification which borders on the brutal, embracing twin carburettors, 8.5 to 1 compression ratio and a power curve which climbs to 46 bhp at 6,500 rpm, then stays at that right up to the 7,000-rpm mark.

Such a model could be a real handful in city streets—lumpy, erratic, straining at the leash. But not so. How it's done is a Meriden mystery (though coil ignition and auto-advance come into it), for the Bonnie emerges as a gentlemanly, unobtrusive, tractable traffic-threader, quite amenable to being trickled along at 30 mph (or slower) in top, the grip only fractionally off the stop.

For all its urban docility, though, this is a Tarzan in city suiting—remarkably patient but with an underlying longing for freedom. Leave built-up areas behind, open the grip that little bit more and you'll note with surprise (though not alarm; the model is too well-bred to cause alarm) that the needle is much farther round the dial than you had imagined it to be.

That's mainly because the power flows in as a surging tide rather than as a noticeable kick in the pants.

Brisk even in the lower

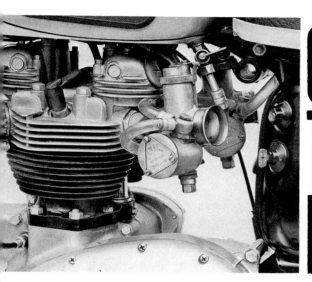

win carburettors and an 8.5 to 1 compression ratio all help to ive exciting performance. Note the lighting and ignition switches on the right

649 CC TRIUMPH BONNEVILLE

ROAD TESTS OF NEW MODELS

229KNX

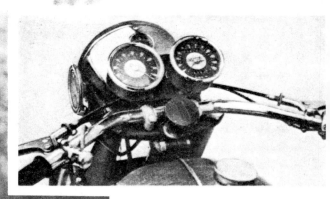

Left is the revmeter, right the speedometer. The revmeter is an extra.

reaches, acceleration becomes shattering from 65 mph onward in top gear.

Use the gear box, changing from 48 mph in bottom, 66 mph in second and about 90 mph in third—and you find the sort of acceleration which, by rights, should be kept for the sprint strip.

That 14.6s figure for the standing quarter-mile was repeated time and again.

Cruising speed is difficult to pin-point. If time was not pressing there could be quiet pleasure in a 45 mph amble, the engine spinning over lazily, the exhaust note just a gentle, low-pitched drone. Yet if 65 or even 85 mph was your aim, the Bonnie would play along with amiable nonchalance.

Naturally enough, it is only

on a motorway that the machine can break out its true colours. Less congested, far more scenic than M1, the M5 road was chosen for a mid-week run.

Heading westward into a blustery wind, 100 mph was shown on the clock with the rider sitting up and feet on the normal rests. However, an electronic check showed that the speedometer was wildly optimistic, and the true speed was more like 90 mph. Still pretty good, though.

For the return run, the pillion rests were brought into use. Chin on the tank, it was possible to hold an indicated 120 mph for a full 15 miles. All highly flattering—but 7,000 said the revmeter, and that is equivalent to a true reading of 108 mph.

Battery, tool roll, tyre pump and oil-tank filler cap are located under the dual-seat which is hinged along the left side

At that, there was no feeling of distress, either mechanical or personal.

In high-speed work, riding position is all-important. In this respect the Bonnie cannot be faulted. Maybe the seat is a little high for short-leg riders, but at least the model can be laid into a bend without anything grounding. The handlebar is nicely placed to allow a wind-cheating forward lean.

Long, sweeping curves find the big Triumph at its best, for on the latest unit-construction version there is rock-steady navigation all the way—no slow-speed roll, no over-the-ton weaving.

Suspension at front and rear is firm, yet extremely comfortable. The result is a machine which remains eminently controllable, whatever the circumstances.

No air slides are fitted to the carburettors, so for a cold-morning start there is need to flood both float chambers fully.

The engine department produces a beefy 46 bhp at 6,500 to 7,000 rpm, but in traffic it is a thorough gentleman

SPECIFICATION

ENGINE: Triumph 649 cc (71x82mm) overhead-valve twin. Plain big-end bearings; crankshaft supported in two ball bearings. Light-alloy cylinder head; compression ratio 8.5 to 1. Dry-sump lubrication; oil-tank capacity, 5 pints.

CARBURETTORS: Two Amal Monoblocs, $1\frac{1}{16}$in-diameter chokes.

IGNITION and LIGHTING: Lucas RM19 alternator, charging six-volt, 12-amp-hour battery through rectifier; coil ignition with auto-advance. Quickly detachable (multi-pin and socket connection) 7in-diameter headlamp with 30/24-watt main bulb.

TRANSMISSION: Triumph four-speed gear box in unit with engine. Ratios: bottom, 11.81 to 1; second, 8.17 to 1; third, 5.76 to 1; top, 4.84 to 1. Primary drive by $\frac{3}{8}$in duplex chain in oil-bath case; final drive by $\frac{5}{8}$x$\frac{3}{8}$in chain with guard over top run. Engine rpm at 30 mph in top gear, 1,940.

FUEL CAPACITY: 4 gallons.

TYRES: Dunlop or Avon (Avon on test machine): 3.25x18in ribbed front, 3.50x18in studded rear.

BRAKES: 8in-diameter front, 7in-diameter rear with floating shoes.

SUSPENSION: Triumph hydraulically damped telescopic front fork. Pivoted rear fork controlled by Girling dampers adjustable for load.

DIMENSIONS: Wheelbase 55in unladen. Ground clearance 5in unladen. Seat height $31\frac{1}{2}$in unladen.

WEIGHT: 399 lb, including approximately $1\frac{1}{2}$ gallons of fuel.

PRICE: £326 13s 3d, including British purchase tax. Revmeter £8 3s. 8d. extra. Pillion footrests £1 5s. 1d, extra.

ROAD TAX: £4 10s a year; £1 13s for four months.

MAKERS: Triumph Engineering Co, Ltd, Allesley, Coventry.

PERFORMANCE DATA

(Obtained at MIRA Proving Ground, Lindley, near Nuneaton.)

MEAN MAXIMUM SPEEDS: Bottom, *53 mph; second, *70 mph; third, 96 mph; top, 110 mph. *Valve float occurring.

HIGHEST ONE-WAY SPEED: 112 mph (conditions; damp track, light tail wind. Rider wearing one-piece leathers).

MEAN ACCELERATION:

	10-30 mph	20-40 mph	30-50 mph
Bottom	2 sec	1.8 sec	2.4 sec
Second	3.2 sec	3 sec	2.6 sec
Third	—	4.4 sec	4.4 sec
Top	—	5.6 sec	5.4 sec

Mean speed at end of quarter-mile from rest: 94 mph.
Mean time to cover standing quarter-mile: 14.6 sec.

PETROL CONSUMPTION: At 30 mph, 100 mpg; at 40 mph, 88 mpg; at 50 mph, 78 mpg; at 60 mph, 66 mpg; at 70 mph, 54 mpg.

BRAKING: From 30 mph to rest, 30ft 6in (surface, dry asphalt).

TURNING CIRCLE: 15ft 10in.

MINIMUM NON-SNATCH SPEED: 18 mph in top gear.

WEIGHT PER CC: 0.61 lb.

Then, too, the high compression ratio calls for a really beefy swing of the kick-starter pedal, but that is a knack which is easily acquired.

Excellent indeed is the lightness and gradual take-up of the clutch operation, provided by the new scissors-pattern thrust-rod mechanism. And there is unexpected lightness in the twistgrip movement; though the grip operates two throttle slides simultaneously, the effort required is no more than on a conventional single-carb model.

With the engine cold, gear engagement was entirely noiseless, though on this particular model it became somewhat clashy when working temperature was reached, unless care was taken to change up slowly and deliberately, and to accompany downward changes by a slight blip of the throttle.

VALVE GEAR

Again, a warm engine brought an increase in audibility of the valve gear, though no more than is acceptable for a super-sports machine.

Pleasantly subdued at moderate speeds, the exhaust note became flatter and more noticeable under hard acceleration, but it was not objectionable.

Good by normal standards, the electrics were a little disappointing in view of the Bonneville's high potential. Too, the placing of the lighting switch (on the left mid-riff panel, below the dual-seat nose) was decidedly inconvenient, making it difficult to change from pilot

to main beam when on the move, and precluding the giving of a warning flash from the headlamp when overtaking.

Just about adequate—but no more—for town work, the electric horn proved useless at higher speeds.

Not new, but a highly creditable feature for all that, is the pedal extension fitted to the Triumph centre stand. The Bonnie is admittedly bulky, yet it could be parked without the slightest effort.

A prop stand is also provided and this, too, was very simple to operate.

Braking is well in keeping with the general nature of the performance. The smooth and gentle retardation provided by the front brake, in particular, contributed greatly to the pleasure of using the machine in the manner for which it was intended.

After several hundred miles of heavy towsing there was no sign of oil leakage from the engine, but one silencer bolt had been lost, allowing some gas leakage at the joint between silencer and exhaust pipe on that side.

A few criticisms, then—but they pale into insignificance when set against the overall picture of a machine which must be not far short of the ultimate in super-sports luxury.

Made to be ridden hard, it was ridden hard; and the amount of enjoyment it provided is something which can never be listed in a mere performance summary.

The centre stand is very easy to operate—this is helped by a pedal extension on the left. Pillion footrests were fitted after pictures were taken

Following pages: Triumph's prestigious T120 Bonneville was in production throughout the 1960s. This is how it looked in 1960 (*National Motorcycle Museum*)

Norton ES400

In itself, the electric-start 384 cc Norton twin hardly qualifies as one of Britain's truly great motor cycles. But it did originate on the drawing board of one of our most illustrious designers—Bert Hopwood, no less, the man responsible for such all-time greats as the Norton Dominator, BSA Golden Flash, and Triumph Trident. Not only is it technically interesting, but it represents the small-capacity Norton vertical twins (the others were the 249 cc Jubilee and 349 cc Navigator), and on that score alone it merits attention.

Strictly speaking, the ES400—originally known as the Norton Electra—was not a Birmingham-bred model, but was brought into being at the AMC factory in Plumstead, after Bracebridge Street production had ended. Its life was a short one, spanning the period from January 1963 to the liquidation of AMC in mid-1966, but its origins went back to the 249 cc Jubilee which had been announced in November, 1958.

That model was indeed a Bracebridge Street project, and the 'Jubilee' name marked the 60 years since James Lansdowne Norton had founded the Norton Manufacturing Company in August, 1898, to produce cycle chains and fittings. All the same,

by 1958 Nortons were well and truly a part of the AMC empire, and a policy of integration demanded that the new lightweight should make as much use as possible of existing chassis parts. That is why the first Jubilees were virtually four-stroke Francis-Barnetts, using what was in essence the frame of the Francis-Barnett Light Cruiser with its part-tubular, part-pressed-steel construction. The front fork, front mudguard, headlamp and wheels were also Francis-Barnett items, while the extensive tail pressings, smaller versions of those featured on the Dominator 88 and 99 de Luxe, were produced by FB's presswork subsidiary, Clarendon Pressings.

However, the power unit was the really interesting part, and here Bert Hopwood had broken new ground in various directions. The crankshaft was a one-piece iron casting, with big-end journals the same size as those used on the Dominator

The ES400 was a descendant of the 250 cc Norton Jubilee, here seen in de Luxe form with the then-fashionable tail panelling and well anced front mudguard. Frame members and other pressings were produced by Francis-Barnett—and it looked like it!

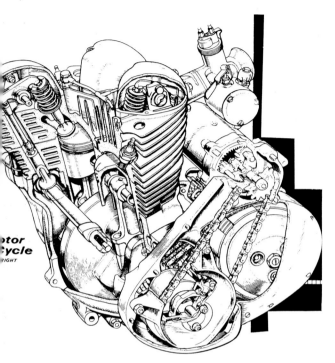

Actual capacity of the ES400 was 397 cc. Note the planetary reduction gearing at the end of the electric starter motor, and the sprag-type freewheel outboard of the crankshaft-mounted alternator. Electrics were 12-volt Wico-Pacy with relay-type automatic voltage control

otor
cycle
RIGHT

twins. Cast-iron cylinder barrels were separate, and embedded for almost half their height in the crankcase mouth. Also separate, the light-alloy cylinder heads embraced a 'back to front' rocker arrangement, with the valves inboard of the pushrods; valve clearance was adjusted by means of eccentrically-mounted rocker spindles.

The Jubilee had genuine unit-construction of engine and gearbox, although the gear assembly (except for the clutch) was that of the semi-unit 248 cc AJS/Matchless lightweights.

Demonstrably a tourer, the Jubilee did not appear to have any competitions potential, but intrepid specials-builder Bob Collier thought otherwise. Over the years he had taken (and was to take) some very odd pieces of machinery through the Scottish Six Days Trial, and for the 1960 event he proposed to take a 249 cc Jubilee—in as standard a condition as may be—hitched to a Watsonian Bambini glassfibre scooter sidecar, into what turned out to be the final year in which a sidecar class was included in the Scottish.

Even with a 70-tooth rear sprocket fitted, the outfit had to be charged at the observed hills, with Bob and crewman Gordon Wilde giving as much leg assistance as they could. The weekly Press reported that the Jubilee's climb of the Ben Nevis sections, on the Wednesday run, was 'the fastest yet'. It had to be; it was the only way the little outfit could get to the top. Not only did Bob and Gordon finish the trial, but they gained a first-class award.

Late in the 1960 season a cheaper (and more handsome) 'standard' edition of the Jubilee was announced, with conventional mudguards in place of the voluminous pressings. And something else was on the boil, because within a few weeks a 349 cc twin had joined the range. This was the Navigator, very much on Jubilee lines but with a number of essential differences.

For one thing, the very oversquare Jubilee dimensions of 60 × 44 mm bore and stroke were replaced in the Navigator by 63 × 56 mm. That meant a new crankshaft, and in view of the extra power output it was decided that this should not be cast iron, but forged steel.

For the same reason, the two cylinder barrels were cast en bloc (although separate barrels were retained for the Jubilee). A Norton Roadholder front fork was substituted for the Francis-Barnett item, and Norton hubs with Dominator-size brake drums completed the specification.

But at the end of 1961 AMC shareholders were given the shock news that the group was diving into the red. Retrenchment was necessary, and that included closing Bracebridge Street and moving Norton production in with AJS and Matchless. Very few Norton personnel were willing to transfer to the alien south, and so when the Berliner Motor Corporation, AMC's USA distributors, made tentative enquiries about a bigger, electric-starting Navigator, the challenge was taken up by the Matchless drawing office.

The first two prototypes, sent to America late in 1962, were actually 397 cc models, achieved by boring the Navigator block out to its practical limit of 66 mm bore and, at the same time, lengthening the stroke to 58 mm. The latter change, however, proved to be unnecessary, and the production Norton Electra settled down at 384 cc (66 × 56 mm), retaining the Navigator crankshaft.

Electric starting was effected by mounting a Lucas M3 starter motor (as fitted to the 1981 Triumph Bonneville, incidentally) at the rear of the cylinder block. On the end of the starter motor was carried a sun-and-planet epicyclic mechanism affording an initial 5·4 to 1 reduction, and from there a chain drove to a sprocket incorporating a sprag mechanism, on the remote end of the engine shaft, outboard of the alternator. Overall reduction worked out at 11·14 to 1. A 12-volt electric system was necessary to operate the starter motor, and this included a 12-volt Wipac alternator and 12-volt, 12-amp-hour Exide battery.

Norton silver and black was the livery adopted for the ES400, but in the few years remaining the Jubilee and Navigator appeared with various colour schemes, including a deep translucent burgundy. However, AMC's financial worries were growing ever more desperate, and the abbreviated Norton range for 1966 as published by *Motor Cycle* embraced the Jubilee and ES400, but discarded the Navigator. Curiously, though, handlebar-tip direction indicators—possibly the first to be fitted as standard to a British motor cycle—were included in the ES400's British-market price of £259 10s.

In its short time of production, the ES400 did not really have time to get established. But its little kick-starter brother, the Jubilee, became the subject of a *Motor Cycle* reader's report published in August, 1965. In general, owners liked it, but there were a number of uncomplimentary remarks, especially in respect of oil leaks, poor dealer service and dodgy Wipac electrics. As one correspondent summed up: 'The Jubilee fills a vacant spot in the current range of British bikes, that of a 250 cc four-stroke twin, for which there is an obvious demand. But unfortunately, it doesn't fill it as well as it might.' Similar comments could probably have been made of the ES400.

Following pages: the 1964 ES400, which resulted from adding electric starting and raising capacity of the Norton Navigator unit (*National Motorcycle Museum*)

ROAD TESTS OF NEW MODELS

Mudguards are chrome plated. The starter motor nestles behind the cylinder block

384cc NORTON

APART from its extra 35 cc, three up-to-the-minute features distinguish the 384 cc Norton ES 400 twin from its famous sister, the Navigator. They are 12-volt electrics, push-button starting and grip-tip winkers. Other, less obvious, differences are that the steering head on the ES 400 is gusseted while the rear brake is of 7in diameter compared with the Navigator's 6in.

With the engine not too cold, the electric starter worked a treat. But it was hard put to spin the crankshaft fast enough for reliable starting when the ES 400 had just spent a frosty night in the open. The best drill then was to use the kick-starter initially—a couple of prods sufficed—and press the button for subsequent starts.

Incidentally, it is not necessary for the gears to be in neutral when using the electric starter. If a gear is engaged you merely declutch.

Along with the headlamp dip switch and horn button, the starter button is incorporated in a Wipac Tricon ring switch just inboard of the left hand-grip. On the other side of the bar, the winker switch could not be operated without releasing the twistgrip: an improvement would be to change this switch to the left.

Grip angle proved comfortable though reach to the clutch and front-brake levers was a shade on the long side. The footrests were low enough to give a wide knee angle but the starter-drive case fouled the rider's left leg.

Burbling unobtrusively through dense traffic or swinging along the open road at 70 mph came alike to the ES 400. Though healthy, the exhaust note was not objectionable; the twistgrip could be tweaked hard without giving offence.

Bottom-end punch was good without being startling—the engine gave its best results in the middle and upper rpm range. On the open road it was usual to let speed build up to an indicated 45 mph (true 42) in second and 60 mph (true 56) in third before changing up.

The needle would climb steadily to the 70 mark and anchor itself there on half throttle. Full throttle brought a further 5 mph and under favourable conditions, with the bulkily clad rider normally seated, the needle would hover on 80 indefinitely.

Provided the engine was allowed to spin freely, hill climbing was first class; only the steepest main-road gradients pulled the speed down appreciably.

Few vertical twins are vibrationless but the ES 400 is no great sinner. A tremor was felt through the handlebar when the engine was spinning fast but was never at any time uncomfortable.

Light and smooth in operation, the clutch showed no objection to a succession of six full-throttle standing starts when the performance figures were obtained. But, before the first start of the day it was advisable to free the plates by pumping the kick-starter with the lever pulled up to the handlebar.

Well chosen, the lower three gear ratios are slightly higher than on the Navigator, though top is the same.

Movement of the gear pedal was light and short. Noiseless upward changes were easily made but downward changes required precise blipping of the throttle if slight clashing of the dogs was to be avoided.

There was not the slightest difficulty in identifying the characteristically precise Norton steering. Absence of top hamper contributes to effortless handling and the ES 400 could be placed almost to a hair and cornered with utter confidence.

With the footrest rubbers well chamfered in the 2,000 miles already logged by the ES 400, the only limits to cornering angle were the centre-stand extension on the left and footrest hanger bolt on the right. Stability on slippery surfaces was remarkable.

Firm at low speeds, the front fork cushioned road shocks well at higher speeds. In contrast the rear-suspension units were soft in action and this gave rise to slight pitching and occasional weaving on fast bumpy bends.

SPECIFICATION

ENGINE: Norton 384 cc (66x56 mm) overhead-valve parallel twin. One-piece forged-steel crankshaft supported in ball bearing on timing side and roller bearing on drive side; shell-type plain big-end bearings. Separate light-alloy cylinder heads; compression ratio 7.9 to 1. Dry-sump lubrication; oil-tank capacity 5 pints.

CARBURETTOR: Amal Monobloc; air slide operated by handlebar lever.

ELECTRICAL EQUIPMENT: Coil ignition with twin contact breakers. Wipac 85-watt alternator, with rotor mounted on left-hand end of crankshaft, charging two Exide 6-volt 12-amp-hour batteries (in series) through rectifier. Separate Lucas electric starter driving crankshaft by chain. Wipac 7in-diameter headlamp with 50/40-watt pre-focus light unit.

TRANSMISSION: Norton four-speed foot-change gearbox in unit with crankcase. Gear ratios: Bottom, 15.4 to 1; second, 9.62 to 1; third, 6.98 to 1; top, 5.72 to 1. Multi-plate clutch with bonded friction facings running in oil. Primary chain, ⅜in duplex in cast-aluminium oil-bath case. Rear chain ⅝ x 0.305in with guard over top run. Engine rpm at 30 mph in top gear, 2,400.

FUEL CAPACITY: 3 gallons.

TYRES: Avon: front 3.00 x 19in Speedmaster Mk II; rear 3.25 x 18in Safety Mileage Mk II.

BRAKES: 8in diameter front, 7in diameter rear, both with finger adjusters.

SUSPENSION: Norton telescopic front fork with hydraulic damping. Pivoted rear fork controlled by Girling spring-and-hydraulic units with three-position adjustment for load.

WHEELBASE: 50½in. Ground clearance, 6in. Seat height, 30in. (All unladen.)

WEIGHT: 354 lb. fully equipped, with full oil tank and approximately one gallon of petrol.

PRICE: £259 10s including British purchase tax.

ROAD TAX: £4 10s. a year; £1 13s. for four months.

MAKERS: Norton Motors, Ltd, Plumstead Road, Woolwich, London, SE18.

DESCRIPTION: Motor Cycle, 31 January 1963.

PERFORMANCE DATA

MEAN MAXIMUM SPEED: Bottom, 36 mph.*; second, 58 mph*; third, 75 mph; top, 78 mph. *Valve float occuring.

HIGHEST ONE-WAY SPEED: 83 mph (conditions: light tail wind; 13-stone rider wearing two-piece waxed-cotton suit and overboots).

MEAN ACCELERATION:

	10-30 mph	20-40 mph	30-50 mph
Bottom	3.4 sec	—	—
Second	5 sec	5.4 sec	5 sec
Third	—	7 sec	7.2 sec
Top	—	9 sec	9 sec

Mean speed at end of quarter-mile from rest: 73 mph.

Mean time to cover standing quarter-mile: 17.8 sec.

PETROL CONSUMPTION: At 30 mph, 81 mpg; at 40 mph, 79 mpg; at 50 mph, 64 mpg; at 60 mph, 51 mpg.

BRAKING: From 30 mph to rest, 38ft (surface, dry tarmac).

TURNING CIRCLE: 15ft.

MINIMUM NON-SNATCH SPEED: 16 mph in top gear.

WEIGHT PER CC: 0.92 lb.

ES 400

The head-on view on the left emphasizes the slimness of the ES 400 and the excellent positioning of the flashing turn indicators on the ends of the handlebar

Below: The ES 400 shares with the three-fifty Navigator its enviable reputation for unsurpassed roadholding. Stability on wet roads was outstanding

Brakes on the model tested were below Norton standard—both lacked bite and the rear was particularly spongy. However, stopping power from high speed was considerably better than is suggested by the figure in the performance panel.

Headlight intensity was markedly good, the wide beam spread allowing day-time cruising speeds to be used in absolute safety after dark, but a sharper cut-off to the dipped beam would have been appreciated by oncoming drivers.

It was a change to ride a machine with a strident horn note; that of the Norton was loud enough even for high-speed motorway riding.

Most routine maintenance tasks were easily carried out—but not so valve adjustment. This entailed removing the petrol tank; and detaching the exhaust rocker covers was a bit of a fiddle because of the proximity of the steering-head gusset plates. The adjustment itself, by means of eccentric spindles, is straightforward.

Some difficulty was experienced in replacing the tool box lid because of its distortion; it is secured by a single slotted screw.

Throughout the 700 miles of the test the power unit remained completely oiltight and oil consumption was negligible. Since the petrol tap has no reserve position a careful check had to be kept on mileage.

With hard riding, the refuelling range was about 150 miles—on the short side for a machine of this type.

Smartly finished in black and matt silver, with chromium-plated mudguards, the ES 400, provides a lot of fun and is certain of an enthusiastic following among those who want a "three-fifty" with the plus of more power and luxury.

Above can be seen the cast aluminium case enclosing the chain drive from the Lucas electric starter to the left-hand end of the crankshaft

Right: A separate set of contact points serves each cylinder. Access for adjustment merely involves removal of a cover held by two screws

Below: Matching the oil tank on the other side, the left-hand pannier compartment houses the tool roll and quickly detachable batteries

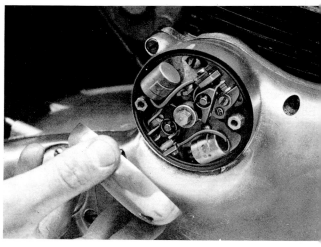

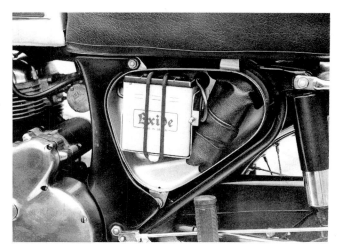

"Ah see that MacGregor has started motor cycling . . ."

USED ENGINE OIL 2ᵈ PINT

Royal Enfield Continental GT

When a young rider gets a bike, his first move is very often to strip it of this and that, and substitute whatever the current fashion in bolt-on goodies may be, so that the model looks as unlike the catalogue job as possible. Twenty-odd years later, a vintage nut may come along, to rescue the delapidated heap from the dusty corner of a garage, and spend untold wealth on seeking the very bits necessary to restore it to original showroom order.

Customising takes many forms, and back in the mid-1960s the lads of the village usually wanted to pretend they were racers; so the vogue was for clip-on handlebars, glassfibre fuel tanks, humpy-back seats, swept-back exhausts, rear-set footrests and reversed gear pedals. There was no real harm in that, of course, save that a novice rider is not the best engineer in the world, and the quality of some of the cheap fittings made by back-street workshops was dubious in the extreme. More than one accident was caused by the dodgy welding of cheap clip-on bars giving way at the time of stress.

So, reckoned Leo Davenport, the former TT winner who was in charge of Royal Enfield in its latter years, if a lad was going to customise his machine into a pseudo-racer anyway, why not offer him a bike on which the customising has already been carried out—professionally, and therefore more safely, at the works? Leo passed the word to Reg Thomas, in the Royal Enfield drawing office, and the result was the cheerful little Continental GT.

In essence it was just a dressed-up Crusader Sports, but most competently done, and really eye-catching with a bright red tank (glassfibre had not yet been outlawed) carrying flamboyant Royal Enfield lettering in white, twin 'brake cooling' discs on the front wheel, chromium-plated exposed rear damper springs, and all the other trimmings to gladden the heart of an apprentice coffee-bar cowboy.

The beauty was more than skin-deep, too, because compression ratio had been raised to 9·5 to 1, the inlet port in the head was opened out and a 1⅛-in choke Amal Monobloc carburettor fitted—incidentally, with a bell-mouth intake instead of an air filter; but real racers didn't use air filters, anyway. Moreover, crankcase breathing had been entirely revised, the waste gases now making their way to atmosphere by way of a big-bore plastic pipe draped along the underside of the seat on the left-hand side and so to the tail of the rear mudguard; that, too, was the way the real racers did it.

In truth, the better crankcase breathing was long overdue, because the Crusader family of engines had for years suffered from high blood pressure. There is no denying that they went like stink, but the crankcase joints were anything but oiltight, nor did it help matters that many riders tended to overfill the gearbox. So take note, any reader thinking of restoring a little Enfield, that there is indeed a gearbox oil-level plug. It's the middle screw of the right-hand engine cover.

The Redditch people had certainly extracted good mileage from their 248 cc unit-construction power plant, which was first announced (as the Crusader) late in 1956 (work on it had begun in 1954). The inspiration had come from managing director Major Frank Smith, but the design work was the

The sheer cheek of it! Australia's Gordon Keith takes his 250 cc Royal Enfield Continental round the outside of Alastair Copland (650 cc Triumph Bonnevile) at Castle Combe. The machine was fourth in its class

department of Reg Thomas, and it was the first engine for which he had been given full responsibility. The company did not award Reg the title of 'designer', and his official status was Chief Draughtsman, with Chief Engineer Tony Wilson-Jones taking over the development of the engine to production form.

Very unusually for a small four-stroke single, the Crusader unit disposed its camshaft and pushrods on the *left*, in the same casing as the primary drive. Unusually, too, the Lucas alternator was on the right of the engine, in its own compartment where it would not become contaminated with primary-drive oil and sludge. More novelty was in the use of a one-piece cast-iron crankshaft, RR56 light-alloy connecting rod, and steel shell big-end bearing. Bore and stroke dimensions were well oversquare at $70 \times 64 \cdot 5$ mm, and a generous overlapping of the main and crankpin journals provided a stiff and sturdy shaft assembly.

From the original Crusader, the family of unit two-fifties seemed to spread out in all directions, to encompass the Crusader Airflow (with voluminous dolphin-type touring fairing), a trials version campaigned with considerable success by Johnny Brittain, the Super-5 which introduced a five-speed gear cluster and a good but unpopular trailing-link front fork, the Crusader Sports, the Olympic Sports and, especially for the great Australian outback, a sheep-herding variant listed as the Wallaby.

The Crusader Sports had come on the scene in October, 1958, bringing a sportier camshaft with quicker-lift cams and more overlap. The public liked it on the whole, and one contributor to a *Motor Cycle* readers' survey declared it to be 'The most underrated bike on the market'. They liked the traditional rear hub cush-drive. They gave the brakes a resounding 90 per cent mark of approval. They declared it to be easy to work on, simple and reliable. But they also criticised the valve gear as noisy, slated the engine oil-tightness, and noted a lack of precision in the gear change, sometimes resulting in a box full of neutrals.

From experience, the imprecise gear change was especially noticeable on the Super-5, but to give credit to the Royal Enfield people, they did work at it, and the five-speed cluster of the Continental GT was a considerable improvement.

Uncharacteristically, and way outside their country-cousin image, the Royal Enfield people introduced the Continental GT in November, 1964, with real flair and showmanship and, of course, it paid off handsomely in the amount of publicity gained. The plot was that a model should be ridden from John O'Groats

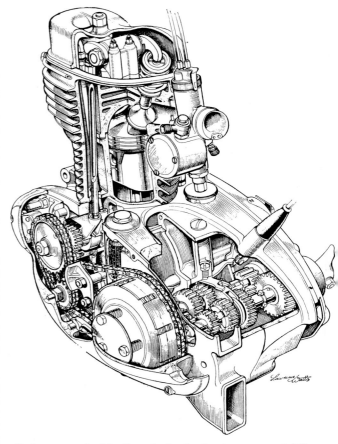

Basic power unit of the Crusader family, the clean, compact, 248 cc ohv four-speeder. One unusual feature is the timing sprockets on the same side as the primary chain. Note the duplex camshaft chain with slipper tensioner. The unit-construction power house has a common oil supply for engine and gearbox

to Land's End, with riders from the major motor cycle journals each taking a stint (*Motor Cycle* took over for the final stretch, David Dixon riding the Taunton to Land's End leg). The trip was completed in 24 hours but—and this was the imaginative bit—at Oulton Park and at Silverstone, well-known road racers took over for a quick blast. At Oulton, Geoff Duke ripped off five rapid laps, while at Silverstone, John Cooper took it round for eight laps (he lapped at over 70 mph, by the way).

It was perhaps a cafe-racer model. But it could give a good account of itself, for all that, and one or two found their way into club racing. A couple of the more enterprising Royal Enfield dealers (Gander and Grey, and Deeprose Brothers) went so far as to produce even sportier versions, and the Gander and Grey Gannet with its worked-on engine (10 to 1 compression ratio, bigger inlet port, lead-bronze big-end shells, race fairing and light-alloy wheel rims) was quite a serious racing tool.

There was no change in Continental GT specification for 1967—except for the USA, where they wanted a braced moto-cross handlebar to be fitted, heaven knows why—but that was its final year. On the stocks was a new unit-construction 175 cc overhead-camshaft model but, unfortunately, the monetary value of the Enfield Cycle Company Ltd was less than the site value of the Redditch works. Financiers moved in, closed down operations (although the Interceptor continued for a short while longer, built at Bradford-on-Avon by Enfield Precision Ltd) and sold the Redditch plant as an industrial estate. Asset-stripping, it's called.

As part of the publicity concerning the Continental's debut, John Cooper hammers the model around Silverstone for eight laps, averaging over 70 mph

248 cc ROYAL ENFIELD Continental GT

ROAD TESTS OF NEW MODELS

Above: The swept-back exhaust pipe accentuates the sporty lines of the neat power unit. Top: Handling is well up to par and the engine will push the model along at nearly 80 mph

"JOINED the coffee-bar crowd, then?" The questioner was Jeff Smith, leaning from his scrambles pick-up as the little red bike came alongside in heavy traffic. One couldn't help but grin. Clip-ons and rear-set footrests are not everyone's cup of Maxwell House.

Still, give a chap a hot two-fifty and it's a certainty that he will want to drape it about with bolted-on goodies. So (reasoned Royal Enfields), let's fit the doodahs and whatsits —revmeter and all—from the word go. Besides, a bike properly sports-tailored at the factory can be a better proposition than one to which clip-ons have been added by unskilled hands.

What emerges is just about the snazziest-looking sportster ever. There's a sleek, glass-fibre tank in fire-engine red, adorned by the Royal Enfield name in bold, white lettering; a huge breather pipe, in clear plastic, led to the tail of the machine; two big dummy brake-cooling discs on the front hub; a racing-style dualseat with a fashionable humped rear pad.

Real pay-off, though, is that the Continental GT goes every bit as well as it looks.

Anyway, not to worry about the riding position, which is more comfortable than it looks once you get used to it. This bike was never intended as a town runabout and inching forward in slow-moving traffic at rush hours does induce wrist-ache—

Following pages: made for the young-in-heart, the 1966 Continental GT was a best-seller of the Royal Enfield range (*National Motorcycle Museum*)

but show it an open road, let it get into its stride, and it becomes a different bike altogether.

The low bars allow you to tuck your elbows in neatly; get down to it properly and watch the needle go soaring round the dial—past the 90 mph mark in favourable circumstances (this was on MIRA's outer circuit, be it added).

To produce the very best in performance, you keep an eye on the revmeter rather than the speedometer and change up at the peak bhp point (7,500 rpm) in each cog.

As on the majority of

is all one hundred per cent motor cycle, a complete machine rather than a collection of bits and pieces in a frame.

Nothing flaps, vibrates or rattles, while the celebrated vane-type shock absorber in the rear hub plays its part in keeping the power supply smooth all the way.

Nothing rattles? Well, maybe the valve gear does (clearances are bigger than is usual on a roadster) but even that is a solidly soothing sort of rattle, somehow quite appropriate.

example of friendly persuasion.

With both brakes used together, a stopping distance of 28ft 6in from 30 mph was recorded, a performance far above average. Nor did heavy braking at the end of a series of flat-out runs produce any sign of fade.

For an out-and-out sports model, the GT proved to be remarkably economical, returning a consumption figure of 115 mpg at a steady 30 mph. Understandably enough, the tank level sinks a bit more rapidly when the grip is held open, but not so rapidly as all that.

Nobody is going to grumble at 64 to the gallon at a maintained 70-per.

One of the most noticeable features of the Continental GT is the big-bore breather pipe. All very sporty-looking, but it isn't just for show.

On this model the designer has completely revised the breathing arrangements of the basic Crusader design, with the aim of overcoming past criticisms of external oiliness.

In that he has succeeded entirely. Through miles of hard riding the engine unit remained completely oil-free.

It *is* possible to ride a GT quite quietly through built-up

The sleek little Royal Enfield in its red-and-chromium-plate overcoat

machines, the speedometer was inclined to flatter; it read about 6 mph fast in the higher reaches.

Much of the credit for the high-average potential should go to the springing—a little on the soft side, but with impeccable damping which allowed the machine to float over the ripples as though it were a hovercraft.

Maybe it is sticking one's neck out to describe the navigation as faultless, but any doubters should try a GT for themselves.

Except for having somewhere to hang the twistgrip and control levers, a handlebar of any kind is well-nigh superfluous, for this is a machine which flows through the bends without a waver.

Most satisfying of all is the conviction you feel that this

Brake and gear-change pedals marry in nicely with the rear-mounted footrests and can be operated from the crouch without any awkward wiggling of the ankles.

Gear-pedal travel is extremely short and the cogs mesh cleanly, without clash or any effort.

Neutral is a shade tricky to find, particularly with the model at a standstill. It helps to permit the clutch just to bite while the pedal is eased upward from the second-gear position.

Both handlebar levers are long, ball-ended and light in operation.

Royal Enfield machines have a reputation for good braking, but the front stopper of the GT is surely the best that Redditch has yet produced. Not vicious, rather a prime

Paired speedometer and revmeter in the fork-top panel together with the lighting switch

areas, by judicious use of the throttle, but when the throttle is used joyously the exhaust is apt to be raucous. Therein lies the only black against the model.

Lighting is well up to the mark, with a main beam amply bright for main-road cruising in the sixties at night. However, the ammeter can't be seen unless you sit up and peer over the flyscreen.

This is undoubtedly the finest two-fifty Royal Enfields have ever made, one which can be enjoyed every mile of the way.

It is sweet-natured and accommodating—built to go and built to stop. The factory are entitled to be proud of it.

Left : Impressive-looking front wheel with its bolted-on light-alloy discs and brake air scoop.   Right : Electrical equipment under the seat enclosed by a neat, glass-fibre shield

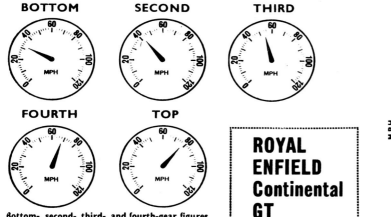

Bottom-, second-, third-, and fourth-gear figures represent maximum-power revs, 7,500

ROYAL ENFIELD Continental GT

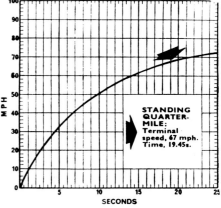

ACCELERATION

STANDING QUARTER-MILE: Terminal speed, 67 mph. Time, 19.45s.

MOTOR CYCLE Road Test

ENGINE
Capacity and Type: 248 cc (70 × 64.5mm) ohv single.
Bearings: Ball and roller mains; plain big-end.
Lubrication: Wet sump; capacity 3 pints.
Compression Ratio: 9.5 to 1.
Carburettor: Amal Monobloc, 1⅛in-diameter choke. Air slide operated by handlebar lever.
Claimed Output: 21 bhp at 7,500 rpm.

TRANSMISSION
Primary: ⅜ × 0.225in chain in oilbath case.
Secondary: ½ × 0.305in chain.
Clutch: Multi-plate running in oil.
Gear Ratios: 17.4, 12.82, 9.57, 7.52 and 6.02 to 1.
Engine rpm at 30 mph in top gear: 2,600.

ELECTRICAL EQUIPMENT
Ignition: Battery and coil.
Charging: Lucas 60-watt alternator to six-volt, 13-amp-hour battery through rectifier.
Headlamp: 6in-diameter with 30/24-watt main bulb.

FUEL CAPACITY: 3¼ gallons.

TYRES: Dunlop Gold Seal: 3.00 × 18in ribbed front; 3.25 × 17in studded rear.

BRAKES: 7in diameter front; 6in diameter rear.
SUSPENSION: Telescopic front fork with two-way hydraulic damping; pivoted rear fork with Girling spring-damper units.
DIMENSIONS: Wheelbase, 52in; ground clearance, 5½in; seat height, 29½in. All unladen.
WEIGHT: 306 lb including half a gallon of petrol.
PRICE: £275 including British purchase tax.
ROAD TAX: £4 a year.
MAKERS: Enfield Cycle Co, Ltd, Hewell Road, Redditch, Worcs.

PERFORMANCE

(Obtained at the Motor Industry Research Association's proving ground, Lindley, Leicestershire.)
HIGHEST ONE-WAY SPEED: 85 mph (10½-stone rider wearing two-piece suit and boots; strong following wind).
BRAKING: From 30 mph to rest on dry tarmac, 28ft 6in.
TURNING CIRCLE: 18ft 6in.
MINIMUM NON-SNATCH SPEED: 17 mph in top gear.
WEIGHT PER CC: 1.23 lb.

FUEL CONSUMPTION

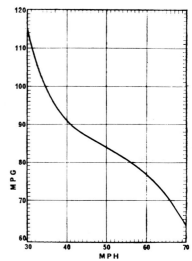

AJS Sapphire Ninety

Just why the design staff (or maybe the directive came from Higher Up) at the Woolwich plant of Associated Motor Cycles should have been so ornery, must remain one of life's little mysteries; but it was indeed so. For example, the very trim and pretty little two-fifty introduced in March, 1958, as the Model 14 AJS—or, if you didn't like the colour or the tank badge, the Model G2 Matchless—looked for all the world as though it were a unit-construction job in the modern idiom.

By that time, of course, virtually every new bike incorporated unit construction of engine and gearbox, for sound technological reasons. Indeed, AMC themselves used it in their new range of single-cylinder two-strokes. Yet here was their new four-stroke, still with the old-fashioned construction of separate engine and gearbox. This was not because this was a convenient short cut to make use of an existing gearbox design, either. This was the first quarter-litre model to emerge from Woolwich since pre-war times, so the box was quite new. The method of construction was cunningly disguised by extending the right-hand engine cover rearward, and by making the gearbox circular and locating it in circular openings in the rear engine plates. It was held secure by two metal straps.

Novel thought, maybe? Not a bit of it, because it was simply a reversion to the identical arrangement used on Model J and Model H Matchless twins as long ago as 1918!

Certainly there were some advantages, as designer Phil Walker explained. Primary chain adjustment was simply a matter of slackening off the gearbox clamp straps and rotating the entire box as necessary, thus doing away with the need to incorporate some form of jockey pulley or chain tensioner in the primary drive. Also, it made engine or gearbox overhaul or replacement much simpler.

In other respects, quite a lot of ingenuity had gone into the design, notably in the angled cylinder head (a light-alloy casting) adopted to give incoming gas a swirl effect. In typical Matchless style, hairpin valve springs were employed right up to almost the final season of production. A neat touch was the incorporation of a small ($2\frac{1}{2}$ pt) cast-light-alloy oil tank within the fore part of the right-hand engine cover.

At $69 \cdot 85 \times 64 \cdot 85$ mm bore and stroke, the engine was oversquare, and to minimise side thrust or piston slap the crankshaft was offset from the cylinder centre line by $\frac{1}{4}$ in (the désaxé effect). Compression ratio was $7 \cdot 8$ to 1, and an Amal carburettor with $1\frac{1}{16}$-in choke (unusually big for a two-fifty) was employed. The piston was wire-wound in its lower groove.

Frame design was relatively straightforward except that the

The AJS Sapphire 90 was not the first Woolwich product to use a cylindrical gearbox. The same principle was employed on this 1918 Model J Matchless twin!

engine cradle was a steel pressing, and the front fork was a lightweight telescopic component, similar to that of a James.

At first, only a roadster was available, but by September, 1958, a scrambler had joined the range. This was the AJS 14CS, and because it did have a bearing on the later two-fifties, it is worth looking at in detail. Chassis changes included a heavier-gauge frame front down tube, and the familiar Teledraulic front fork from the three-fifties. Internally there were lightened flywheels, a 10·5 to 1 compression ratio, and gear pinions made from 'a superior grade of steel' (which did not say much for the standard components!)

For 1961, the scrambler was further improved by the adoption of a new crankshaft assembly with larger crankpin and a heavier-duty connecting rod. Crankcase breathing was now by a direct vent instead of through a hollow bolt, and carburettor size had been upped to 1⅛-in choke. That season, too, the AMC models were all given names, and under AJS badges there were the 14 Sapphire, 14CS Scorpion Scrambler and (a newcomer) 14S Sapphire Sports. The Matchless equivalents were named G2 Monitor, G2CS Messenger, and G2CS Monitor Sports.

First mention of a still sportier two-fifty came in May 1962. This was the 14CSR Sapphire Super Sports, graced with the Teledraulic front fork and engine internals of the Scrambler, plus a larger inlet valve and lengthened induction tract. The wheels had full-width hubs, and the engine appeared to be all-alloy, but in fact the cast-iron cylinder barrel had a coat of aluminium enamel.

By this time the range of two-fifties was at its peak, with the choice of four models under each marque name, but now the tide was on the ebb. For 1963 the 14S Sapphire Sports, and 14CS Scorpion Scrambler were discontinued. In Britain, one never saw a Matchless or AJS 248 cc scrambler anyway, although it may have been different in the USA.

On to 1964, and out went the standard model, leaving only the 14CSR Sapphire Super Sports (and its Matchless buddy) to carry the flag. But in June of that year the machine was given a great boost when Peter Williams and Tony Wood, co-riders of a 14CSR prepared and entered by Tom Arter, pulled off a resounding victory in the 250 cc class of the important Thruxton 500-Miles.

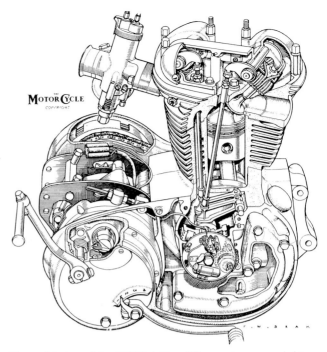

Unusual feature of the AJS/Matchless 250 cc engine was angled positioning of the cylinder head which, in turn, meant an unorthodox pushrod layout. The cylindrical gearbox was rotated to adjust the primary chain

During the early stages the little Ajay had held a consistent third spot behind the more flamboyant Honda and Montesa of the initial leaders. But after 3½ hours the pacemakers were out, and the steadily circulating AJS was into the lead. And there it stayed to the very end, winning at an average speed of 61·6 mph.

The last major changes in the design were made for the 1965 season, when the traditional hairpin valve springs gave way to coil, a new high-crown piston gave 9·5 to 1 compression ratio, and there was a closer-ratio gear cluster. For some unaccountable reason, too, the machine underwent another name change. The Model 14CSR bit remained (most youngsters translated the initials as 'Coffee Shop Racer', by the way—and handled the machine accordingly) but now it was the Sapphire Ninety; although if the 'ninety' was supposed to indicate its performance potential, it was very wide of the mark.

It was to survive for just one more season, 1966, when the machine was still catalogued by the financially-ailing AMC group amid a welter of Norton-engined Matchless and Matchless-engined Nortons. Final modifications were a swept-back exhaust pipe in the BSA Gold Star style, and light-alloy instead of chromium-plated mudguards.

So died what was a happy little machine that, on the whole, was well-liked by the younger set. Usually, it could be counted on for a top whack of 80 to 85 mph (although, to give of its best, good use had to be made of the gear pedal). Usually, too, it would cover 78 or so miles to the gallon if handled enthusiastically, or up to 100 mph if the rider was more prudent.

Certainly it had its faults, but these were mainly minor. The centre stand was too weak and sometimes allowed a bike to fall over when parked. A fractured gear selector spring was a regular occurence. Electrics (by Wipac) were not the most reliable that ever were. Spares from the factory and retailers were not always readily obtainable. And the small (2½ pt) oil tank capacity made it essential to carry out relatively frequent oil changes.

But it was a very forgiving little bike, for all that, and a particularly comfortable one to ride.

Tony Woods heads his Sapphire 90 into a corner during the 1964 Thruxton 500-Miles. He shared the bike with Peter Williams and they won the 250 cc class at an average speed of 61·6 mph

ROAD TESTS OF NEW MODELS
248 CC AJS SAPPHIRE NINETY

LAST SUMMER saw this sports model really hit the limelight with a clear-cut class win in the Thruxton 500-Mile Race. Its success, which remained a talking point long after the meeting, was a reminder that the quarter-litre market is not the exclusive preserve of non-British manufacturers. Following this, in the autumn when the AJS 1965 range was announced, there was news of modifications to give more go to the Sapphire Ninety, as this 248 cc model is now named.

Coil valve springs replace the hairpin variety. Compression ratio is stepped up from 8 to 1 to 9.5 to 1 and gear ratios are closer than before. A larger-capacity silencer is fitted. It is tucked in and raised slightly to keep it out of the way when cornering.

First impressions mean a lot. When you straddle the Sapphire Ninety you are assured that AJS don't regard riders of two-fifties as necessarily on the small side.

Dimensions of the handlebar-seat-footrest set-up are such that whether your pals call you Lofty or Titch you should feel at home.

The handlebar is almost flat with slightly downswept grips and induces a forward lean rather than a crick-in-the-neck crouch. The riding position allows you to tuck in and adopt a relaxed, comfortable stance when hustling.

A criticism of the Matchless equivalent model tested in 1962 was that, on full lock,

Smooth contours give the power unit an attractive appearance and make cleaning easy

---

Specification and Performance Data

ENGINE: AMC 248 cc (70 × 65mm) overhead-valve single-cylinder. Double-row roller big-end bearing; crankshaft supported in a ball and a roller bearing on the drive side and a plain bearing on the timing side. Light-alloy cylinder head, cast-iron cylinder barrel. Compression ratio 9.5 to 1. Dry-sump lubrication; oil capacity, 2½ pints.

CARBURETTOR: Amal Monobloc 1⅛in choke; air slide operated by handlebar lever.

ELECTRICAL EQUIPMENT: Coil ignition. Wipac 54-watt, alternating-current generator mounted on drive-side crankshaft charging Exide 11-amp-hour battery through rectifier. Wipac 6in-diameter headlamp with pre-focus light unit and 30/24-watt main bulb.

TRANSMISSION: AMC four-speed gear box clamped to rear of engine. Gear ratios: bottom, 17.97; second, 11.68; third, 8.05; top, 6.51 to 1. Multi-plate clutch with bonded friction facings. Primary chain ⅜in duplex in cast-aluminium case. Rear chain ½ × 0.305in

with metal guide over top run. Engine rpm at 30 mph in top gear, 2,800.

FUEL CAPACITY: 3¼ gallons.

TYRES: Dunlop: front 3.25 × 17in ribbed; rear, 3.25 × 17in studded.

BRAKES: 6in-diameter, front and rear; finger adjusters.

SUSPENSION: AMC telescopic front fork with hydraulic damping. Pivoted rear fork controlled by Girling three-position, spring-and-hydraulic units.

DIMENSIONS: Wheelbase, 53in. Ground clearance, 5½in. Seat height, 30in. All unladen.

WEIGHT: 330 lb, fully equipped, including approximately one gallon of fuel.

PRICE: £224 18s 5d, including British purchase tax.

ROAD TAX: £2 5s a year.

MAKERS: Matchless Motor Cycles, Ltd, Plumstead Road, London, SE18.

DESCRIPTION: "Motor Cycle," 22 October 1964.

MEAN MAXIMUM SPEEDS: Bottom*, 31 mph; second*, 48 mph; third*, 70 mph; top, 82 mph. *Valve float occurring.

HIGHEST ONE-WAY SPEED: 83 mph (conditions: still air, rider wearing two-piece suit).

MEAN ACCELERATION:

	10-30mph	20-40 mph	30-50 mph
Bottom	3.8 sec	—	—
Second	4.6 sec	4.8 sec	—
Third	—	7.8 sec	6.8 sec
Top	—	11.2 sec	9.8 sec

Mean speed at end of quarter-mile from rest: 70 mph.

Mean time to cover standing quarter-mile: 19.4 sec.

PETROL CONSUMPTION: At 30 mph, 112 mpg; at 40 mph, 84 mpg; at 50 mph, 66 mpg; at 60 mph, 58 mpg.

BRAKING: From 30 mph to rest, 30ft (surface, dry tarmac).

TURNING CIRCLE: 14ft.

MINIMUM NON-SNATCH SPEED: 19 mph in top gear.

WEIGHT PER CC: 1.32 lb.

In any case, one soon became accustomed to the heaviness and then it passed unnoticed.

Suspension at both ends was firm and well damped and contributed to predictable handling when flicking the machine quickly through a right-left-right series of bends. Rippled surfaces on metalled roads or pot holes on unmade tracks failed to catch the suspension off guard.

The power bonus makes itself felt in the middle and upper part of the range. There is an overall impression of increased liveliness, and the unit is remarkably free from vibration. **Bull point is that the added power has not been obtained at the expense of tractability.**

The Sapphire would woofle along at 30 mph in top gear on a trace of throttle and without any fuss. At this pace in built-up areas there was just a subdued burble from the exhaust.

Mechanical noise was at a commendably low level, but the exhaust note became obtrusive at wide throttle openings.

The Smiths speedometer is easily read and was no more than 2 mph optimistic throughout the range. There is no trip mileage recorder, but the total mileage is shown to the nearest tenth.

For high-speed, open-road cruising, suitable gear-change speeds were 28, 40 and 60

one's thumbs could be trapped against the petrol tank. This does not occur on the Sapphire Ninety.

Almost smooth, plastic handlebar grips are fitted. They do not provide enough friction, especially when they are wet.

Control layout is good. Levers and pedals are correctly positioned for easy use.

During the test the AJS was ridden in a variety of weather conditions and over a variety of surfaces, some of them exceedingly slippery.

No praise is too high for the handling; the rider felt confident of staying in control at all times.

A trace of heaviness could be detected in the steering when traffic threading at walking pace, but this was more than offset by rock-steady adhesion to line at the other end of the scale.

Top: Handling is exemplary and inspires confidence at all times. Note the new silencer. Above: The Sapphire Ninety contrives to look up-to-date without recourse to unnecessary gimmicks

Following pages: no concours d'elegance winner, Mark Tudor's 1965 Sapphire 90 is a workaday machine which has given its owner long and faithful service (Bob Currie)

193

mph. The 1965, closer spacing of the ratios enhances the appeal of the machine. Happy cruising speed was 60 to 65 mph.

Restarting from a standstill on a 1 in 6 hill was accomplished without difficulty. The clutch could be fully engaged after covering the first yard or so.

Using third gear, main-road gradients were dismissed with nonchalance. This ratio (8·05 to 1) provided brisk acceleration for overtaking whether solo or two-up.

ZIPPY

In fact, acceleration in general, producing as it does a standing-start quarter-mile in under 20 seconds, is decidedly brisk and is more than adequate to hoist the model into the zippy class.

Gear selection is so smooth and easy that it immediately calls to mind the knife-through-butter cliché, although

Removal of the left side cover gives access to the ignition coil and rectifier. The battery is located under the seat

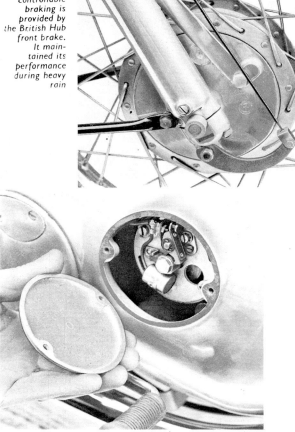

Excellent controllable braking is provided by the British Hub front brake. It maintained its performance during heavy rain

Two screws secure the contact breaker cover on the right of the power unit. Points adjustment is easy

a shade less pedal travel would be preferred.

Ratios should be swapped as fast as the pedal could be operated.

The clutch engaged smoothly in normal usage, but full-power take offs when the standing-start quarter-mile figure was being obtained produced some snatching. There were never any signs of clutch drag. No adjustment was required throughout the period of the test.

Starting proved simple. It was advisable to leave the carburettor tickler alone and use the handlebar-mounted air-slide lever. The engine was sensitive to the air setting until the proper operating temperature had been reached.

NO PINKING

Fuel consumption was light, especially in view of the performance available. The engine performed quite happily on premium-grade petrol and showed no tendency to pink under heavy load.

Oil is contained in a separate sump on the right of the crankcase. Consumption was negligible even during sustained hard riding. Oil tightness was marred by a slight weep from the gear-box end cover.

Performance and handling can be exploited to the full only if matched by the brak-

ing. In this respect the AJS earned full marks. Both brakes were light in operation and efficient at all speeds.

Ventilation scoops are provided on the front brake but, on the test model, the slots had not been properly cleared of metal. However, no fading was experienced.

Lighting was adequate for 60-mph cruising after dark. The dipswitch has a wipe action; this is excellent as it ensures that there is no possibility of lag during the change from main to dipped beam or vice-versa.

Action of the lighting and ignition switches was spongy. A firm action with a positive click when the movement is complete would be more acceptable.

Accessibility for routine maintenance of rocker settings, contact-breaker, battery and other items is good. The tool kit supplied with the machine is adequate.

Thanks to the smooth contours of the power unit and liberal use of chromium-plating cleaning is a straightforward task.

The Sapphire's attractive finish is given the final touch by its blue and chrome and gold-lined petrol tank. Here is a bike which is easy on the eye: easy on the pocket for tax, insurance and fuel; and with its peppy performance, easy to have fun on.

DMW Sports Twin

In the matter of motor cycle design ingenuity, the big battalions certainly had no monopoly on talent, and at least two of Britain's smaller manufacturers could produce machines packed with features that were truly brilliant. One such was Greeves, famous for its pioneer work with cast-light-alloy frame members and rubber-in-torsion front suspension. Another was DMW—and perhaps 'was' is the wrong term to use, because the company still exists, and although motor cycle production is currently rather low key, sophisticated telescopic front forks are currently marketed under the alternative Metal Profiles trade mark. Twice running, in the late 1970s, a 250 cc DMW with an engine of the firm's own make won the ACU Midland Centre trials championship.

By one line of descent, ancestry of the DMW can be traced back to the Wolverhampton-built Diamond of vintage years, touching HRD and taking in Calthorpe along the way, but the initials were originally those of Dawson's Motors, Wolverhampton, and the DMW name first appeared on the tank of some grass-track specials raced by W. L. ('Smokey') Dawson in 1938-9. Smokey was interested in suspension systems, too, and from 1940 onwards DMW—then in a very small way of business—began converting customers' bikes to swinging-arm rear suspension. They were among the first British makers to offer a telescopic fork (the DMW Telematic of 1944), and a full-width front hub with dual drum brakes, in 1945.

Production of complete motor cycles, powered by a 125 cc Villiers engine unit, began in 1947, and in those early years the make gained a high reputation in the competitions field, especially in the International Six Days Trial. But it was for the excellence of their roadsters that they were to become still better known, and the credit for this must go to pre-war BSA trials ace, Mike Riley, the company's designer and engineer.

Particularly noteworthy was the use made of square-section frame tubing (which permitted easy adaption to engines of various sizes and capacities) allied in some instances to pressed-steel and fabricated frame centre sections. The rear fork was a masterpiece, embodying snail-cam adjustment of the whole assembly just astern of the pivot point; the rear wheel spindle was a simple pull-out affair, and there was no way that the quickly-detachable rear wheel could get out of alignment.

Hubs and brakes were DMW's own, and they incorporated adjustment at the brake shoe fulcrum end, and a method of shoe expansion adapted from a Girling patent. A totally-enclosed rear transmission was an unexpected luxury on a Villiers-powered two-stroke. Some models even featured an automatic rear stop light, actuated on braking by a blob of mercury trapped in a tube, which surged forward under deceleration to make an electrical contact.

DMW were into road racing, too, initially with an overhead-camshaft 125 cc model known as the Hornet (although they supplied frames also for several of the home-built machines—DMW-Anelay, DMW-Enfield, etc—contesting the first post-war 125 cc TT races). The original Hornet employed a French AMC power unit, but with the arrival of the Villiers Starmaker the Hornet name was revived. Managing director Harold Nock assembled two Starmaker engines side-by-side, driving through a patented coupling system to a separate gearbox, but regrettably the twin (known as the DMW Typhoon) failed to live up to its early promise.

Most unusual DMW design of all was the 249 cc Deemster of the 1960s. In appearance it was a scooter, with small wheels and typically 'scooter' features such as legshields, footboards, and rear enclosure panels. Yet a closer look would reveal the twin-cylinder Villiers Mk. 2T engine housed in a normal 'motor cycle' position in the frame. Even more telling was the use of a conventional between-the-knees fuel tank.

In fact the Deemster was an all-weather, small-wheeled motor cycle, and though very few were sold to the general public, it was adopted in quite large numbers by the police of the West Midlands and rural Wales for beat patrol work. It was

The DMW was a bike with a sporting heritage. In this shot John Morris, of Bromsgrove, takes a 197 cc DMW single through a mountain village in the 1951 International Six Days Trial in Italy

Following pages: the DMW Sports Twin was an outstanding machine of its type. Shown is a 1962 model, at that time named the Dolomite II (*National Motorcycle Museum*)

197

A totally different type of 249 cc Villiers-twin-powered DMW was the Deemster—part scooter, part motor cycle. It was used by police in the West Midlands and Mid-Wales for rural patrol duties

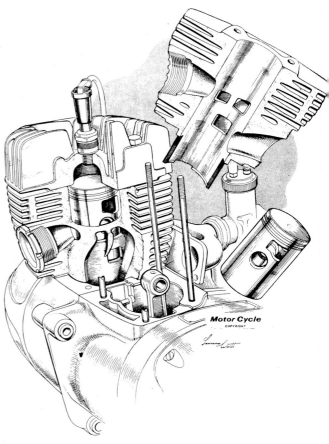

To provide increased air space between the cylinders, the Villiers Mk. 4T twin had shallower, but more numerous, transfer ports than the original Mk. 2T engine

particularly suitable for this kind of work, because the use of a small rear wheel allowed ample carrying capacity in the pressed-steel bodywork rear of the single seat for a first-aid kit, leggings, fluorescent jacket, rolled-up 'Accident' warning banner, clip-board, and other constabulary necessities. It had a radio handset on the tank top, too.

First appearance of the 249 cc Villiers 2T engine unit had been in 1956, and DMW (who are just along the road from the Villiers works) were first to incorporate the new engine in an extremely handsome roadster finished in maroon and brown. The model was really a development of the existing 224 cc DMW Cortina single, and was accordingly given the name Dolomite—Cortina being the name of an Italian resort in the Dolomite Mountains where Harold Nock had spent a winter holiday. (DMW had thought of Cortina as a model name long before Ford stole it, while at this stage British Leyland's Triumph Dolomite car was still some years off!)

In the years that followed, the DMW Dolomite twin was a permanent fixture in the company's programme. To choice it could be fitted with MP-Earles pivoted front fork instead of the telescopic type, and with electric starting on the Siba Dynastart system.

Around the middle of 1963, Villiers were faced with the problem of adapting their 249 cc twin for installation under the

A courageous DMW race design which did not live up to early pro-mise was the 500 cc two-stroke-twin Typhoon, using Villiers Starmaker cylinders and gearbox on DMW's own crankcase assembly

bonnet of the Bond three-wheeler, and to allow for a greater passage of cooling air between the cylinders and over the heads the upper works were redesigned, with shallower transfer ports, and more of them, ported pistons, and angled head finning. The modified engine was named the Mark 4T.

For Bond installation, power output remained at 14·5 bhp, as with the Mk. 2T twin. However, the 1964 programme found the Mk. 4T superseding the Mk. 2T for motor cycle use also. By this time, power had been boosted to 17 bhp at 6,000 rpm, mainly through the fitting of an exhaust system with tuned resonances.

Not that the Mk. 4T was all sweetness and light, for it had a 'top-endiness' more characteristic of Japanese buzz-boxes than of the more sedate Mk. 2T, a point brought out in the road test which follows. Gone was the Mk. 2T's torquey bottom-of-the-rev-scale punchiness, and this was a particularly sad loss in so far as DMW's police Deemster was concerned. The Mk. 4T did not suit this 'plod around the parish' model at all, and after experimenting with a Deemster powered by a 197 cc Villiers Mk. 9E single, DMW redesigned the machine around the flat-twin two-stroke 250 cc Velocette Viceroy scooter running gear. It was not very successful.

But the Mk. 4T-powered DMW Sports Twin (successor to the Dolomite) was a totally different animal. It you can find one second-hand, grab it quick because the bike was a minor classic in its own little way. True, it tended to be ignored by the general public, and in consequence not many were built before Villiers ended proprietary engine production. But that was the public's loss.

Road Tests of New Models

249 cc DMW SPORTS TWIN

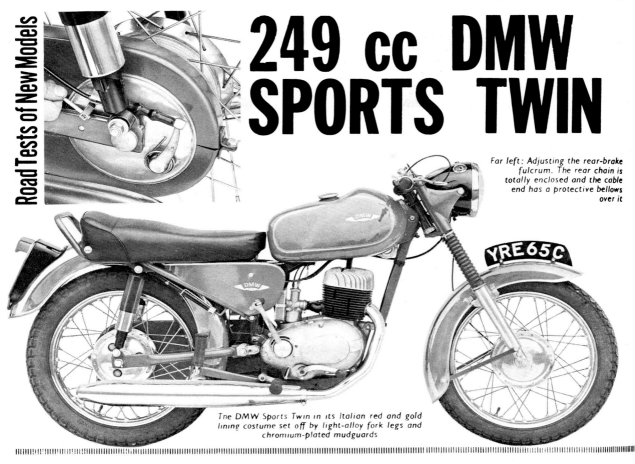

Far left: Adjusting the rear-brake fulcrum. The rear chain is totally enclosed and the cable end has a protective bellows over it

The DMW Sports Twin in its Italian red and gold lining costume set off by light-alloy fork legs and chromium-plated mudguards

PARADE this little red beauty before a crowd of typical young riders and, following the Oohs and Ahs of admiration, someone will surely ask: " What's a DMW, then? " Not surprising, that, for the make is relatively uncommon outside its native west midlands. Certainly the DMW is British; it hails, in fact, from Dudley— where it has been built for 20 years or so. The engine is the familiar Villiers (in this instance, the Mark 4T twin) but it is the ingenuity of the cycle parts and the host of individual touches which sets the Dee-Em apart from the general run.

Thus the specification embraces polished, cast-light-alloy wheel hubs (the rear wheel quickly detachable) in which are remarkably powerful, tappet-action DMW-Girling brakes. Rear dampers are three-position Girlings and you don't often see those on a lightweight. Adjustment of the totally enclosed rear chain is achieved by moving the entire fork rearward, so ensuring that the wheel cannot get out of line.

Detail work extends to little plastic bellows protecting what would normally be the exposed ends of the brake cables and to aircraft-type locknuts on the engine, damper and mudguard-mountings.

It all adds up to a top-quality machine, a shade more expensive than the rest but worthy of the closest examination.

With a label such as Sports Twin, a sporty riding position is only to be expected. Nevertheless, it is not taken to extremes. What you get here is a short, flat handlebar, and seat and footrests an inch or so more rearward than on a touring job.

The result is a lean-forward, cheat-the-wind position which can be maintained for hours without strain on your wrists or back muscles. The welded-on handlebar lever pivots are rather more inboard than usual, though the levers themselves remain within easy reach and are pleasantly light in operation.

As a matter of personal preference, the dipswitch and horn button could have been nearer the left grip, but that's something an owner can decide for himself.

One further comment about the controls. The gear pedal could be reached readily with the tester's size nines, but folk with smaller feet might prefer a pedal fractionally shorter than the one supplied.

Surprisingly, this particular Mark 4T engine required only the merest tickle of the float chamber plunger when starting, with the air lever left severely alone and the twist-grip about one-eighth open.

This might seem to point to an over-rich mixture, yet the engine two-stroked quite happily and richness was certainly not reflected in the fuel-consumption figures.

This Villiers twin is a thorough-going smoothie, utterly devoid of vibration anywhere in its make-up and able to pour out power like cream from a jug.

Not that there is too much urge downstairs, for in the lower reaches of the rev band you have to sit tight and wait for the kettle to boil.

Still, the model is a sportster and demands to be treated as such. That means winding it up in each cog before selecting the next. If such a scheme is adopted, the DMW responds brilliantly.

In top gear, for example, the bike can plod along smoothly and sedately at around 25 to 30 mph, but the acceleration from that level is all but non-existent. For a real getaway,

Left: Bob Currie gives the model an airing in the country. Below: Adjusting one of the three-way rear dampers. Note the qd rear wheel

SPECIFICATION AND PERFORMANCE

ENGINE: Villiers 249 cc (50 x 63.5mm) two-stroke twin. Cast-iron cylinder barrels, light-alloy heads. Crankshaft supported in one ball and two roller bearings; roller big-end bearings. Compression ratio, 8.75 to 1. Petroil lubrication, ratio 20 to 1.

CARBURETTOR: Villiers S25 with mesh-type air filter. Air slide controlled by handlebar lever.

ELECTRICAL EQUIPMENT: Villiers six-volt flywheel generator with remote ignition coils. Exide type 3EV11, 12-amp-hour battery. Lucas 7in-diameter headlamp with 30/24-watt main bulb; type 8H horn; stop lamp.

TRANSMISSION: Villiers four-speed gear box in unit with engine. Gear ratios: bottom, 19.3; second, 12; third, 8.3; top, 6.3 to 1. Multi-plate clutch running in oil. Primary chain ⅜ x 0.225in in oil-bath case; rear chain ½ x 0.305in, totally enclosed. Engine rpm at 30 mph in top gear, 2,600.

FUEL CAPACITY: 3¼ gallons; reserve-type fuel tap.

TYRES: Dunlop K70. 3.00 x 18in front, 3.25 x 18in rear. Quickly detachable rear wheel.

BRAKES: 6in-diameter DMW-Girling front and rear.

SUSPENSION: Metal Profiles telescopic front and pivoted rear forks. Girling spring-and-hydraulic rear suspension units, adjustable for load.

DIMENSIONS: Wheelbase, 52in. Ground clearance, 5¼in. Seat height, 30in. All unladen.

WEIGHT: 307 lb with approximately half a gallon of fuel.

PRICE: £222 15s, including British purchase tax.

ROAD TAX: £4 a year.

MAKERS: DMW Motor Cycles (Wolverhampton), Ltd, Valley Road, Sedgley, Dudley, Worcs.

iiiiiiiiiiiiiiiiiiiiiiiiiiiiiiiiiiiiiiiiiiiiiiiiiiiiiiiiiiiiiiiiiiiiiiiiiiii

MEAN MAXIMUM SPEEDS: Bottom, 31 mph; second, 43 mph; third, 56 mph; top, 69 mph.

HIGHEST ONE-WAY SPEED: 69 mph (conditions: negligible side wind; 14½-stone rider wearing two-piece suit and overboots).

MEAN ACCELERATION:

	10-30 mph	20-40 mph	30-50 mph
Bottom	4s	—	—
Second	6.4s	5.2s	—
Third	—	8.4s	8.2s
Top	—	21.4s	13.4s

Mean speed at end of quarter-mile from rest, 60 mph. Mean time to cover standing quarter-mile, 20.8s.

PETROIL CONSUMPTION: At 30 mph, 102 mpg; at 40 mph, 94 mpg; at 50 mph, 78 mpg; at 60 mph, 55 mpg.

BRAKING: From 30 mph to rest, 28ft 6in (surface, dry asphalt).

TURNING CIRCLE: 12ft.

MINIMUM NON-SNATCH SPEED: 18 mph in top gear.

WEIGHT PER CC: 1.23 lb.

it is necessary to drop down a couple of notches and take it from there; with 40 showing in third, snick into top and the model gets going like the favourite out of Trap One.

Any speed from 40 to an indicated 60-plus will serve as a comfortable cruising speed, with plenty more to come if needed. On two or three occasions, indeed, the 75 came up in favourable circumstances but that was not the strict truth, for an electronic check proved the dial to be reading around 5 mph high at its upper end.

Incidentally, the big-dial speedometer has a trip recording drum, another unexpected feature.

On gradients, speed does tend to drop away; it is necessary to slip into third fairly early so that a high average can be held.

Exhaust silence is well above average. The twin Villiers silencers are so mute that the note is almost entirely inaudible from the saddle at normal traffic speeds. Even when the machine is accelerated hard,

there is little more than a low-pitched drone.

Steering is noticeably light at low speeds, but once the Sports Twin hits its stride the handling is everything that could be expected from a factory with road-race experience.

For one-up riding, the rear dampers were set in the middle position, giving a firmish ride in keeping with the model's aim.

Ground clearance is excellent and the DMW can be heeled over extremely smartly

without any part scraping the deck.

A stopping distance of 28ft 6in from 30 mph tells only part of the story, for the brakes, though extremely effective, are far from harsh in operation. In particular, lightly stroking the front-brake lever brings an immediate check to forward progress, firm yet gentle.

On the electrics side, the Sports Twin scored further high marks. A night-time run showed that the 7in-diameter

headlamp offers near-daytime cruising potential with a beam both broad and bright; the dip-switch provided a good action.

One last surprise was that here, for once, was a two-stroke with a loud and effective electric horn.

Smartly finished in Italian red, with gold-lined fuel tank, polished light-alloy fork legs and chromium-plated mudguards, the DMW Sports Twin is a machine to which the makers, obviously, have given a great deal of thought.

BSA Bantam D14/4

'Who's to say that there won't be a Bantam with us another 20 years from now?'—I wrote that concluding sentence of the 1968 Bantam road test which follows. The answer, alas, was not all that long in coming, for although few people realised it at the time, the BSA Group's financial problems were such that the poor little Bantam was to have its neck wrung late in 1971; it was, said BSA, no longer economic to produce. There *should* have been an updated Bantam, and the back-room staff at Umberslade Hall (the BSA Group's country-hideaway think tank) produced drawings showing a very smart little job with square-edged crankcase castings not unlike those of a Sachs. Sadly, there was no longer the money available to finance the necessary tooling-up.

The earlier history of the Bantam was chronicled in *Great British Motor Cycles of the Fifties*, but to briefly recall this, the model started life in 1948 as a mirror-image replica of the pre-war DKW RT125, plans of which had been passed to BSA as war reparations. From the original rigid-frame 125 cc Bantam, a steady progress through the 150 cc Bantam Major had led to the 173 cc (61·5 × 58 mm bore and stroke) D7 Bantam Super as introduced for the 1960 programme; details included an unusual lubrication system whereby oil from the gearbox looked after the crankshaft main bearing on the ignition side, while a bleed from the primary chaincase oiled the drive-side main.

In plunger-sprung form, the basic 125 cc D1 was continued

(mainly for Post Office use) right through to 1963, selling at under £120 all-in. Most of the development was concentrated on the 173 cc version, which gained a Torrington needle-roller (instead of plain bush) little-end bearing for 1961, while in the same year a chromium-plated fuel tank and plastic name badges became available at around £4 extra.

However, the first really significant change came in July, 1966, when the D7 models (standard, and de luxe) were replaced by the new D10, featuring a 40 per cent increase in power output. Achieved by modified porting, discs attached to the flywheels to increase primary compression, a domed instead of flat-top piston, oval connecting-rod shank, and an increase in compression ratio from 7·4 to 8·65:1, the D10 now produced 10 bhp at 6,000 rpm and, on test, reached 64 mph yet without sacrificing bottom-end punch.

But that wasn't all, because by the end of the year there were no fewer than *four* D10 models, comprising the bargain-basement three-speed D10 Silver Bantam, four-speed D10 Bantam Supreme, D10S Bantam Sports, and D10B Bushman.

The Sports justified its name by featuring a humpy-backed

The D14/4 Bantam could have been a best-selling trials model, if only BSA had given proper backing to their own competitions department. Dave Rowland—here climbing Grey Mare's Ridge—finished second to the illustrious Sammy Miller (Bultaco) in the 1967 Scottish Six Days Trial, and two other Bantams won Special First Class awards

'racing' seat, handlebar flyscreen, chromium-plated mudguards and headlamp, full-width wheel hubs, a high-level exhaust system—and, believe it or not, a strip of stick-on chequered plastic tape down the centre of the tank top.

And the Bushman? That one was a workhorse, primarily for sheep-herding on Australian farms or for riding the mountain trails of the USA. Coloured a distinctive tangerine and white so that it could be spotted from afar, the Bushman used 19-in diameter wheels, and featured a high-level exhaust and sump protector plate.

The Bushman obviously had the makings of a useful little trials bike, and BSA competitions manager Brian Martin now proceeded to investigate its possibilities by building himself a Bushman with C15-type front fork, Victor Enduro air cleaner, and other bits and pieces selected from bikes in the existing Triumph and BSA ranges.

Brian collected first-class awards in the 1966 Colmore and St. David's national trials and, encouraged by this success, Mick Bowers built a similar model for his own use. Even more adventurously, Brian Martin entered a works team for the Scottish Six Days Trial, comprising Dave Rowland (riding Brian's experimental bike), Bowers (on his own privately-built model), and Dave Langston (on a special 148cc machine constructed in the competitions department at Small Heath).

The results far exceeded the hopes of the little knot of dedicated Bantam fans working at BSA, virtually in defiance of management policy. Dave Rowland finished runner-up, and both Langston and Bowers collected special first-class awards.

This was the time when BSA should have exploited such a success by marketing a small batch of trials Bantams. No special parts were required, and even though such competition models would have to be specially built, rather than left to the tender mercies of the production-line assemblers, the extra cost would have been more than outweighed by the advertising benefits of seeing the BSA name once more in the results lists, week after week.

But by this time the men at the top were well out of touch. The market for trials machines, as they saw it, was too small to bother about.

The D10 Bantams were to remain in production for little more than a single season, being replaced by the new D14/4 series from September, 1967. Power output had been raised still more and now stood at 13 bhp at 5,750 rpm, the gain resulting from fatter flywheel pads (so increasing primary compression still more), wider transfer and deeper inlet ports, and a redesigned head. Also, the exhaust pipe diameter had gone up substantially, from $1\frac{1}{4}$ to $1\frac{5}{8}$ in and there was a long, tapering exhaust.

Even this was not the final flowering of the Bantam, because there was yet another revamp early in 1969, with a diecast cylinder head, revised crankshaft, and modified crankcase castings. The Sports and Silver Bantam versions had been discarded, and now there were just the standard D175 Bantam, and D175B Bushman. Yet for all the improvements, the Bantam was under sentence of death, the last batch being built in late 1971 and offered, at bargain prices, by Cope's of Birmingham at the 1972 Midland Motor Cycle Show.

There were still those who believed passionately in the Bantam, and they included Brian and Michael Martin, and Mick Bowers. Desperately, they pleaded with the BSA management to be allowed to form a consortium, to take over the Bantam tooling and continue on a smaller scale within the group. 'There was still a potentially lucrative Post Office contract to be gained,' explains Mick Bowers, 'and the trials market would have been sufficient to keep a small unit employed. But nobody wanted to know.'

The 175 cc Bantam Super D7. In its later D14/4 form, the unit had a four-speed gear cluster, and the flywheel cheeks were fitted with steel side plates to boost crankcase compression

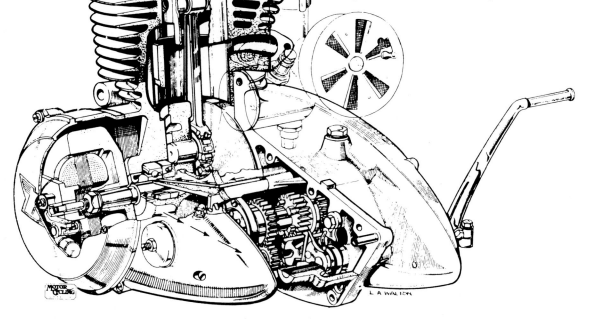

173cc BSA BANTAM D14/4

There can't be so very much wrong with a model which has held a solid place in the affections of the public for 20 years or more—and which is still a best-seller. Of course, the Bantam has changed a bit in that length of time; from a solid frame, through plunger rear springing to the current, orthodox pivoted rear fork, and from the initial 123 cc, through 148 cc to a healthy 173 cc.

Motor Cycle road test

And that is by no means the whole story. While growing up in size, it has acquired sophistication and a surprisingly big increase in power output. The long-lived three-speed gearbox has been replaced by a very welcome four-speed assembly, and instead of the former flywheel magneto and direct lighting there is a full alternator-rectifier-battery electrical system.

Minor improvements include a battery which can be kept in good order without the necessity for first detaching the dual-seat, chromium-plated fuel-tank side panels, and two handlebar mirrors fitted as standard. Yet with all this the Bantam continues to be one of the best bargains on the British market, at just over £130. Quite an achievement.

Certainly it's a lightweight—it can be lifted about without trouble when, say, a narrow garden path has to be negotiated—but there is nothing tiddler-like about the frame dimensions. The

Removal of the nearside panel reveals the battery and tool roll

SPECIFICATION

ENGINE: Capacity and type: 173 cc (61.5 x 58mm) two-stroke single. Bearings: Three ball mains, roller big-end. Lubrication: Petroil, 32 to 1 ratio. Mains lubricated from gear box and primary chaincase. Compression ratio: 10 to 1. Carburettor: Amal Concentric R626 (26mm choke). Air slide operated by handlebar lever. Mesh-and-felt air filter. Claimed output: 13 bhp at 5,750 rpm.

TRANSMISSION: Primary by ¾ x 0.250in chain in oilbath case; secondary by ½in x 0.205in chain. Clutch: Multiplate. Overall gear ratios: 18.68, 12.04, 8.55 and 6.58 to 1. Engine rpm at 30 mph in top gear: 2,800.

ELECTRICAL EQUIPMENT: Ignition by 6-volt battery and coil, with emergency-start circuit. Charging: Wipac 60-watt alternator to 6-volt, 10-amp-hour battery through rectifier. Headlamp: Wipac 5in-diameter with 30/24-watt main bulb.

FUEL CAPACITY: 1⅞ gallons.

TYRES: Dunlop Lightweight studded, 3.00 x 18in front and rear.

BRAKES: 5½in diameter front and rear, with finger adjusters.

SUSPENSION: Hydraulically damped telescopic front fork. Pivoted rear fork controlled by Girling spring-and-hydraulic units.

DIMENSIONS: Wheelbase, 50in; ground clearance, 6¾in; seat height, 31in. All unladen.

WEIGHT: 215 lb dry.

PRICE: £130 16s 6d, including British purchase tax.

ROAD TAX: £5 a year.

MAKERS: BSA Motor Cycles Ltd, Armoury Road, Small Heath, Birmingham, 11.

PERFORMANCE

(Obtained by "Motor Cycle" staff at MIRA Proving Ground, Lindley, Leicestershire.)

MEAN MAXIMUM SPEED: 64 mph (11½-stone rider wearing two-piece trials suit and boots).

HIGHEST ONE-WAY SPEED: 66 mph (light, following three-quarter wind).

BRAKING: From 30 mph to rest on dry tarmac, 29ft 6in.

TURNING CIRCLE: 12ft 6in.

MINIMUM NON-SNATCH SPEED: 20 mph in top gear.

WEIGHT PER CC: 1.23 lb.

Following pages: the BSA Bantam was developed steadily over the years. The D14/4 led finally to the 1971 Bantam 175 pictured here (*National Motorcycle Museum*)

noticeable surge of energy as the revs start to climb from the lower end of the range, and this results in some very respectable acceleration figures—up to 50 mph, that is, for though there is plenty yet to come, it does mean squeezing the bottle to get it.

Keep the motor buzzing (and that's where the four-speed gearbox helps) and the Bantam will soar up a hill with complete contempt for the gradient. Of course, ye olde-tyme Bantam would get to the top, too, in its own sweet time—either by clinging doggedly to top cog until it was almost possible to count each rev, or by screaming along in second. The advantage of the new job lies not only in that well-chosen third gear, but also in the throaty, middle-of-the-range supply of urge.

A comfortable cruising speed turned out to be an indicated 60 mph (an actual 57 mph, allowing for speedometer error) but there was more to come, given only moderate encouragement. Running before the wind, it was possible to show slightly better than 70 mph on the dial at times.

Some slight roughness was evident at very low speeds in top gear. But this smoothed out from 30 mph, and in the middle reaches the power flow was as sweet as one could wish for.

Not thirsty

It is a recognised fact that the price of pepping-up a two-stroke is increased fuel consumption. Yet the Bantam is not especially thirsty. Keep it at 30 to 40 mph, and a return of 100 mpg is guaranteed—comforting news for those in search of a light, utterly reliable workhorse for city streets. Only if the throttle is held wide open does the fuel graph take a nose-dive.

The combination of light overall weight, nice balance, a nippy engine and precise steering showed up to the full when a particularly twisty length of B-class road was tackled. Cornering was limited only by the rather low (and non-adjustable) footrests. These are conditions a Bantam rider can enjoy. For although such roads have something less than billiard-table surfaces, the jolts and jars are not passed on to the man in the saddle, thanks to efficient fore and aft suspension.

The electrical system is 6-volt, yet this is quite adequate for the nature of the model, and a particularly good word should be given to the solid and handily-placed dipswitch toggle, easily operated by a gloved hand. As mentioned earlier, the battery has been made more accessible on the D14/4. It is secured by a spring toggle clamp, and may be extracted for in-

riding position is comfortable for both lankies and shorties, and though the 31 in seat height sounds a lot, the model's slimness allows the feet to be put down very confidently at halts.

An air lever is fitted to the handlebar, and for the first start of the morning best results were obtained when this was closed for a few seconds. At other times, it

was quite sufficient just to tickle the carburettor.

Lower end

In gaining extra power output, the D14 Bantam has changed its characteristics in some degree, and it is no longer quite the low-speed slogger it used to be. There is a

Very much a two-up machine—a comfortable dualseat, pillion foot-rests and power aplenty

spection and topping-up through an opening in the tool-box backplate, on the left. In theory, this is fine; in practice, extraction is hampered by the nearness of several loose cables draped across the opening.

Fasteners

One good point is the use of two half-turn Dzus fasteners to retain the tool-box lid, instead of the captive nuts which have exasperated a whole decade of Bantam owners. Another is the effective silencer with baffles which can be extracted for cleaning.

Finished in serviceable black (or blue)

with white lining on mudguards and tank and bright plated tank side-panels, the D14/4 Bantam is a smart little model which does credit to the long-honoured name. In terms of performance, it is far removed from the original D1 Bantam of 1948, but the family resemblance is unmistakable. And who's to say that there won't be a Bantam with us another 20 years from now?

The large-bore exhaust system just clears the frame's front down tube and protects the contact breaker low-tension lead from stone damage

Bottom-, second- and third-gear figures represent maximum-power revs, 8,000

Large enough for a 500 cc machine! The air-filter element is located behind a panel on the offside

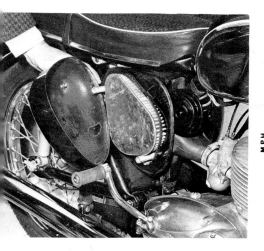

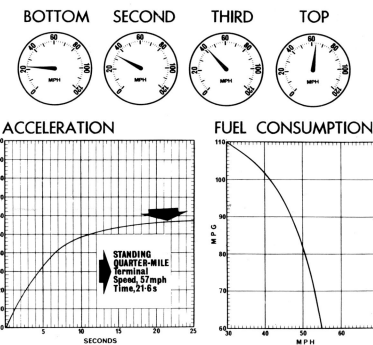

BOTTOM   **SECOND**   **THIRD**   **TOP**

ACCELERATION

STANDING
QUARTER-MILE
Terminal
Speed, 57mph
Time, 21·6 s

FUEL CONSUMPTION

BSA Victor Roadster

For a nippy little five-hundred roadster (a four-four-one initially, but it did grow into a full-blown five-hundred later) to be developed from a world championship-winning moto-cross model is a rare occurrence indeed. And where the Victor Roadster is concerned, that was only part of the story, for the tale began with a very humdrum little utility mount, the 249 cc C15.

In one sense, that first unit-construction BSA could be said to have been derived from the Edward Turner-designed 199 cc Triumph Tiger Cub (except that the cylinder was upright instead of inclined) and certainly there were strong family likenesses between the Cub and the C15 Star. As originally produced in 1959, the C15 produced a very modest 15 bhp at 7,000 rpm, but the initial roadster version was quickly followed by the C15S and C15T scrambles and trials models, and it was from these competitions variants that subsequent development took off.

Around 1960, Jeff Smith, Arthur Lampkin and one or two other riders were bounding about on C15s in the moto-cross field with considerable success, but it has to be said that by that time the bigger moto-cross BSA—the long-worshipped 500 cc Gold Star—was becoming outclassed in international competition. It was potent, but too heavy.

But could anything be done to upgrade the C15, ready to take over from the Goldie? The power was well down, of course, but on the other hand lightness and manoeuvrability would make up for that in part. BSA competitions manager Brian Martin began to experiment, and by taking a C15 barrel to the maximum bore it would stand (while keeping the stroke unchanged) he evolved a 343 cc model with which he had a blast at the 1961 Red Marley freak hill-climb.

Running on dope, the little bike zoomed up the slope to take both the 350 cc and unlimited capacity classes—an encouraging start, at the very least. The next step was to fit larger valves and carburettor, gorblimey cams and a high-compression piston. Jeff Smith took that one to Shrubland Park and ran rings round the opposition. And so was born the 343 cc B40, from which were derived a civilian roadster and a military model which was taken up by Britain and other NATO powers.

Now the B40 scrambler was fine for wiping up the 350 cc class, and also for adding 500 cc laurels if the opposition was not too strong. But even the great J. V. Smith found he was pushing his luck running it in international events. So by a little more juggling with bores and strokes an experimental 420 cc model was evolved, with which Smith gained first-time-out victory in the 1962 Hampshire Grand National.

So far, so good, but Jeff Smith was an exceptional character with a fine feeling for things mechanical, and in lesser hands the 420 cc tended to break up. The main trouble was that a lot more power was being pushed through what was still the soft-touring C15 gearbox. Designers Ernie Webster and Bert Curry got busy, and during the winter of 1963-4 devised a new version of the 420 cc moto-cross bike. The main changes included stronger, stub-toothed gear pinions in the gearbox, a more robust crankcase with ball and roller main bearings, a light-alloy cylinder barrel with chromium-plated bore—and an entirely new and lighter frame in which the main tube served as the oil reservoir.

Again Jeff gave it its first taste of battle in the Hants Grand National (this time the 1964 event), so collecting his fifth success in a row in that meeting. It soon became clear that BSA had a very tough little cookie indeed on their hands, and when the World Championship moto-cross rounds began Jeff packed the four-twenty into the back of his pick-up truck and headed for foreign parts. That summer, doing his own maintenance out in the field, he was to finish first in seven of the 14 races counting for Moto-Cross World Championship points, second in six more, and third in the remaining one—and even then the relatively lowly placing was due to a flat tyre.

As we have seen, a new and heftier crankcase had been evolved for Smith's model, and this encouraged the BSA design staff to go for still bigger things. The new casings allowed the bore and stroke to be pushed up to 79 × 90 mm, so producing a capacity of 441 cc. Again a model was made ready for Jeff Smith's sorties into the Moto-Cross World Championships. And again Jeff brought home the crown.

Translated into production terms, the machine became the

The Victor Roadster in an unusual setting. This one was being whanged around Brands Hatch by Alan Peck, prior to taking part in the Barcelona 24-Hour race

Ears muffled against the din, John Thickens puts a Grand Prix Victor engine through its paces on the test bench while Bob Currie looks on

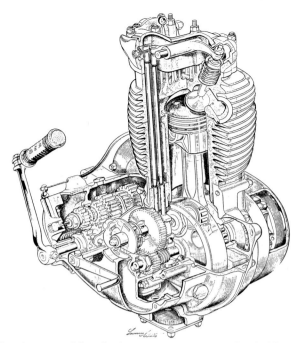

Very far removed from its C15 remote ancestor was the 1966 B44 Victor unit, forged in the heat of world championship moto-cross. The light-alloy cylinder barrel had a chromium-plated bore. Present-day descendant is the Bolton-built CCM single

B44 Victor MX, and a batch of Jeff Smith Replicas was prepared; here, the author can claim to have had a personal, if very modest, hand in things, for it was at his suggestion that the fuel tanks were painted in an eye-catching yellow—a distinct contrast with the nondescript finish of previous BSA scramblers.

The B44 Victor Roadster tested here was a surprise addition to the BSA parade at the 1966 Earls Court Show, with a 29 bhp power output which was almost double that of the modest little C15 from which it sprang.

Here, American readers may be slightly puzzled by reference to a Victor Roadster, because in the States the model was known from the outset as the B44SS Shooting Star (a name previously borne by a rather nice semi-sports A10 twin, in two-tone green). After only one year the Victor Roadster became the Shooting Star in Britain, too.

For 1969 the glass-fibre fuel tank was exchanged for a steel one with the same contours, on safety grounds, and a twin-leading-shoe front brake was employed. For 1970, there was a heavier-duty oil pump—a direct legacy of works participation in moto-cross.

But in the meantime, things had been happening on the moto-

On the titanium-frame BSA Victor MX, Jeff Smith forges ahead to win the Finnish Moto-Cross Grand Prix of 1966, near Helsinki. But the titanium frame had its drawbacks

cross scene. In an expensive bid to hold the Moto-Cross World Championship title for a third year, BSA invested in a couple of all-titanium frames, but the effort was unsuccessful because these could not be repaired on site if fractures developed. A better proposition was the still further enlargement of the Victor engine, at first to 494 cc and finally to a full 499 cc. Headed by Jeff Smith and John Banks, the moto-cross team had a victorious televised winter series on the prototype B50 models, then launched into the summer events on the Continent with new frames built from Reynolds 531 tubing.

Nor was it only the off-road stuff. For several seasons, as part of the development programme, Tony Smith had been road-racing a BSA powered initially by a 343 cc, and later a 499 cc moto-cross engine, on the home circuits. Now came international glory, when a 499 cc B50 Shooting Star shared by Nigel Rollason and Clive Brown won, outright, the 1971 Spanish and Dutch 24-hour endurance marathons, and followed up with a sterling performance in the Bol d'Or.

Strictly speaking, the early 1970s are beyond the brief of this particular book, but to round off the story of the Victor family, the B44SS Shooting Star was eventually to give way to the B50SS Gold Star; the name was an unpardonable clanger by an unfeeling BSA publicity department, for of course the machine had no connection whatever with the immortal Goldies of the past. Styling went berserk, and the alleged Gold Star sported an indescribably ugly exhaust system with a black-painted almost-vertical lozenge silencer, a headlamp hung on bent wire, and short mudguards that might have been fine in Southern California but were ludicrous anywhere else.

But by mid-1972 BSA were in deep trouble, the run-down was well under way, and the company had only months to live. Right at the very end came one further, and unexpected development, when Cyril Halliburn put together a few experimental B50 speedway engines—BSA's first foray into this branch of the sport since 1930. The speedway BSA showed distinct promise, despite its shoestring-budget development, but closure of the factory brought it to an end before it had achieved full flowering.

ROAD TESTS OF NEW MODELS

441 cc BSA B44 Victor Roadster

WHEN the curtain rose on the 1966 BSA programme, there in the limelight stood something rather unexpected—a 441 cc roadster single. "But," spluttered the know-alls, "big singles went out years ago. These days it's got to be a twin, at least." Has it, now? They're not so daft at Small Heath and the Victor Roadster, taken all round, is a very logical machine. Logical as the ideal follow-on for the man graduating from a BSA two-fifty. Logical in giving the customer the benefit of all that Victor scrambler development.

Besides, the Victor represents a new conception in relatively big-capacity singles and is totally different from the heavyweights of the past. Note the 0.76 lb figure for weight per cc in the specification panel? That's the clue.

With its short wheelbase and high ground clearance, the frame has an obvious competition ancestry; the engine-gear lower-half assembly, too, is a direct result of moto-cross participation.

However, the 29 bhp of the engine is considerably less than the output of the grand-prix job. That means that the internals, built to take a bashing on the championship circuits, should be all but unburstable in everyday road use.

Where the Victor Roadster does differ most noticeably from the scrambles version is in the use of a square-finned, light-alloy cylinder barrel which gives it the appearance of a baby Gold Star.

With a hefty 7in ground clearance and a seat height of 31in, a rider does tend to be tall in the saddle and putting a foot down at traffic halts could mean something of a stretch for the short legged.

Above: The smart, cleanly styled Victor with square-finned barrel, high ground clearance and competition-proved bottom half. Right: Heart of the Victor, the power unit, developed for the tough world of scrambles, should prove unburstable in normal, everyday use

Left: Bob Currie samples the charms of the Victor. Above: Tool roll and battery are concealed behind the left-side faired panel. The key-operated ignition switch is to the left side of the car-burettor

Normally the model has an orthodox handlebar but it happens that the test machine was one diverted from an export batch, which explains the high-rising Western bar. Tastes vary, of course, but we found the high bend, in conjunction with the high seat, gave a remarkably comfortable and controllable ride of sit-up-and-beg style.

TECHNIQUE

Starting-up may mean, for some, the recall of an almost forgotten technique; for others, new to a largish-capacity single, it is something to be learned. First thing to remember is that this is a high-compression engine and the ex-haust-valve lifter, on the left side of the bar, is no mere ornament.

Best plot was to switch on and watch the ammeter needle. With the exhaust-lift trigger pulled up, the starter pedal was pushed down gently until the piston was eased over

compression and the needle started to swing away from zero. At that, the trigger was released and one long swing of the pedal was enough to bring the engine to life.

Immediate realization is that useful power extends right down to the bottom of the rev range and that low-down punch is one of the Victor's greatest charms.

It permits the machine to get off the mark with all the urgency of an England forward streaking for a try; indeed, a little ham-fistedness in using the throttle and clutch could result in the front wheel pawing the air.

Shear heart, that's the phrase. Heart enough (as was proved while JON 119E was on duty at the Welsh Three-Day Trial) to tow a stranded competitor for 12 miles through the hills of mid-Wales. Heart enough to gallop gaily, two-up, over the switchback Tregaron pass.

Light as a model of only half its engine size, beautifully damped at front and rear and with brakes which would stop it on a sixpence, the Victor acts like a mechanized polo pony.

Lay it down, pick it up, spurt off again in a new direction . . . It could almost have been built with the cork-screws of the Tregaron in mind!

So it isn't a super-sportster? No, though an 87 mph maximum certainly doesn't indicate a slowcoach. Point is, a glamorous top speed isn't everything. The Victor's

Following pages: the 1967 BSA Victor Roadster which Peter Booth has made a fine job of restoring to catalogue condition (*Lawrie Watts*)

handleability through corners and rapid acceleration out of them will get it places quicker than some of the hotted-up glamour irons.

The turning circle is unusually small and with that amount of bottom-end poke you can have fun chuntering around in ever-decreasing circles doing a fair impression of Sammy Miller. On the road it is a shade light at the front end but that is a BSA characteristic which soon becomes accepted.

Clutch operation was sweet and gave no cause for complaint even after a series of violent acceleration tests. Put that together with a delightfully smooth and utterly clash-free gear change and you have a model which is a joy to ride.

At the current speed limit of 70 mph the engine is running particularly smoothly and happily; though some vibration can be felt through the tank on the way up there, it is never enough to be uncomfortable.

Talking of the fuel tank, this is in glass-fibre and very pleasantly styled but its capacity of a bare two gallons is on the meagre side—all right for the Americans, perhaps, using the bike for a spot of weekend enjoyment but for Britain something larger would be appreciated.

That goes for the rear chain, too: ⅝ × ⅜in is hardly man enough for a 441 cc model and it had to be adjusted several times during the test.

To get all the moans over at once (and none of them is very serious), the glass-fibre tool-box cover comes off readily enough, the space provided for the tool roll is barely adequate.

The electrics earned high marks. Even the horn note was amply penetrating, while the beam of the 12-volt, 50-watt headlamp made night riding a real pleasure.

The dipped beam was flat-topped and didn't appear to offend oncoming drivers but the dipswitch was sluggish in action and on several occasions caused both main-bulb filaments to light at once.

Accentuated by the light-alloy cylinder, piston slap was evident when the engine was cold but dwindled to an acceptable level as the Victor warmed to its work.

The same could not be said of the exhaust, however; that was definitely crisp at the best

Above: Diverted from the export line, this model is fitted with a high-style handlebar. Our tester found it comfortable. Left: That bar from a different angle. And this view emphasizes the neat lines of the glass-fibre tank with its quick-action filler cap

of times and rose to a bark when the throttle was opened hard.

Finally, some little points worth mentioning. The quickly detachable rear wheel really is good and comes out without trouble in less than a minute. Sensibly placed under the steering head, the Zener diode is on a finned, light-alloy mounting which receives a healthy cooling blast.

The oil tank cap has an attached dipstick—but don't fill the tank to the top mark, or oil will spill out of the froth-tower breather. (A revised marking will be used on later models.)

Overall impressions? A zippy, handy model which bids fair to give the big single a new lease of life. Those who have never tried the type before are in for a very pleasant surprise.

Far left: Cornering at low speed. The bottom-end punch and generous steering lock allow tight turns without resort to the clutch

Left: No more frying for the Zener diode. This one is mounted on a massive finned heat sink

SPECIFICATION

ENGINE
Capacity and type: 441 cc (79 x 90 mm) overhead-valve single.
Bearings: Roller drive-side and ball timing-side mains; double-row roller big-end.
Lubrication: Dry sump; tank capacity, 4 pints.
Compression ratio: 9.4 to 1.
Carburettor: Amal Concentric, type 930/1 30mm choke. No air slide.
Gauze and wire-mesh air filter.
Claimed output: 29 bhp at 5,750 rpm.

TRANSMISSION
Primary: $\frac{3}{8}$in duplex chain.
Secondary: $\frac{5}{8} \times \frac{1}{4}$ in chain.
Clutch: Multi-plate.
Gear ratios: 13.38, 8.33, 6.32 and 5.05 to 1.
Engine rpm at 30 mph in top gear, 2,000.

ELECTRICAL EQUIPMENT
Ignition: Battery and coil.
Charging: Lucas 100-watt alternator to 12-volt, ten-amp-hour battery through rectifier.
Headlamp: $6\frac{1}{2}$in-diameter with 50/40-watt main bulb.

FUEL CAPACITY: 2 gallons.
TYRES: Dunlop K70 3.25 × 18 ribbed front, 3.50 × 18in studded rear.
BRAKES: 7in diameter front and rear; finger adjusters.
SUSPENSION: BSA telescopic front fork with hydraulic damping. Pivoted rear fork controlled by Girling spring-and-hydraulic units; three-position adjustment for load.
DIMENSIONS: Wheelbase, 52in; ground clearance, 7in; seat height, 31in. All unladen.
WEIGHT: 336 lb, including one gallon of petrol.
PRICE: £281 14s, including British purchase tax.
ROAD TAX: £8 a year. £2 19s for four months.
MAKERS: BSA Motor Cycles, Ltd, Armoury Road, Small Heath, Birmingham, 11.

PERFORMANCE

(Obtained by " Motor Cycle " staff at the Motor Industry Research Association's proving ground, Lindley, Leicestershire)
MEAN MAXIMUM SPEED: 87 mph (11-stone rider wearing two-piece suit).
HIGHEST ONE-WAY SPEED: 90 mph (light following wind).
BRAKING: From 30 mph to rest on dry tarmac, 30 ft.
TURNING CIRCLE: 13ft 9in.
MINIMUM NON-SNATCH SPEED: 18 mph in top gear.
WEIGHT PER CC: 0.76 lb.

Motor Cycle ROAD TEST

441 cc BSA B44 VICTOR ROADSTER

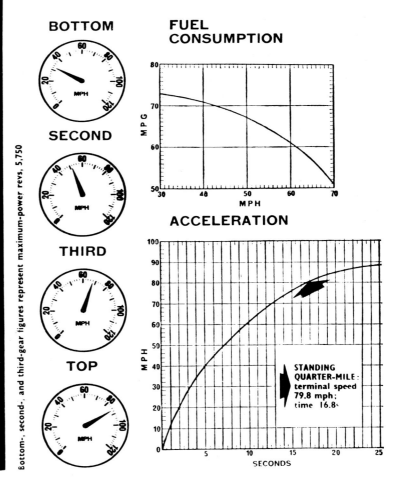

BOTTOM

SECOND

THIRD

TOP

Bottom-, second-, and third-gear figures represent maximum-power revs, 5,750

FUEL CONSUMPTION

ACCELERATION

STANDING QUARTER-MILE: terminal speed 79.8 mph; time 16.8s

Triumph TR25W Trophy

As the opening sentence of the road test makes clear, there was very little about the TR25W Triumph Trophy that was 'Triumph'—except the familiar die-cast 'eyebrow'-type tank badges and the Tiger 90 front fork. In other respects the machine was pure-bred Small Heath, and its ancestry can be traced to the first unit-construction C15 BSA of 1959. So before we get too deep into the tale, let us settle the matter of the actual capacity of the engine. Bore and stroke dimensions were 67 × 70 mm, which gives a capacity of 247 cc, but almost throughout the life of the C15 and its progeny the BSA Group advertised it as being 249 cc. Not until right at the end, with the 1971 BSA B25SS Gold Star, Triumph Trail Blazer, and others, did the literature admit to 247 cc.

So why the deception? BSA once told me that it was because their first-ever two-fifty, the 1924 'Round Tank', was 249 cc and they wanted to preserve continuity. Well, perhaps; but there was also the fact that the purchaser of a 249 cc would feel he was getting 2 cc more for his money!

Anyway, development of the original C15 began almost immediately, with much help from the competitions department and their ace moto-cross men of the day, Jeff Smith and Arthur Lampkin. Two moto-cross C15s were prepared, for Jeff and Arthur to ride in the 1960 European Championships series, and from experience gained in this way the roadster C15 was given steel instead of cast-iron flywheels for 1961.

In time, it inherited ball and roller main bearings (instead of plain and ball), needle-roller gearbox layshaft bearings, and various other goodies. The cooking C15 acquired, too, a more sporty companion in the C15 Sport Star SS80—a cheeky piece of naming which must have caused many an old Brough

The TR25W Trophy was essentially the BSA B25 in slightly different dress, and with lower overall gearing. Here is the 1967 BSA Barracuda, later renamed Starfire, and finally Gold Star 250

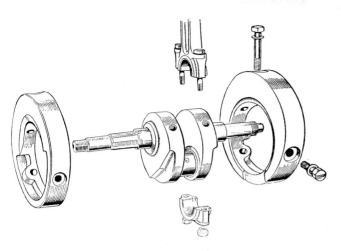

Unusual crankshaft assembly of the Triumph TR25W. The shaft was a one-piece forging, the separate flywheels being secured by radial bolts. The method of construction dictated the use of a steel-backed shell big-end bearing

Superior fancier to choke over his bread-and-milk.

But the big revamp was yet to come. While the C15 title pointed to what was originally a 15 bhp engine, the introduction in November, 1966, of the B25 Barracuda was rather more than a big jump in power output to 25 bhp at 8,000 rpm. While the general configuration appeared much as before, there were totally new crankcases, housing for the first time a one-piece forged crankshaft to the webs of which were fixed (by radial bolts in twin-cylinder style) a pair of separate flywheel rings. An added bonus of this arrangement, incidentally, was that if heavier flywheels were required for a trials version, or skimpier wheels for a grasser, the conversion was quite simple.

Other details included a duralumin connecting rod, and a steel-backed shell big-end bearing replaced the former caged-roller fitment. There was a revised lubrication system, and a new square-looking light-alloy cylinder barrel. The sculptured fuel tank was in glassfibre (at this stage, nobody had yet raised doubts about the safety of such a tank) and, all in all, the Barracuda was claimed to be 'Britain's fastest production 250'—although Royal Enfield, whose Continental GT was a usefully nippy device, would no doubt query the statement. Certainly the Barracuda did not feature very strongly in 250 cc

End of the line for the BSA/Triumph 250 cc unit was the Gold Star 250 SS of 1971. Triumph equivalent was the Trail Blazer, styling being almost identical. Sump undershield, and fork-pivot chain adjustment were inherited from moto-cross

production-machine racing, although the engine did make a considerable impact in grass-tracking, when installed in suitable frames by Hagon, Elstar, or Antig.

The BSA Barracuda sounded a nicely alliterative name, but it would appear that Small Heath had not done its homework properly, because there was already a Barracuda of somebody else's make (Bridgestone, was it?) on the USA market. After a rethink, BSA announced that from April, 1968 the B25 would be known as the Starfire. And just to make it a little bit different, it would have a full-width front hub.

A little later a Fleetstar version (in black and white) was added, for institutional purposes—police, gas board, courier agencies, etc. And the glassfibre tank gave way to one of identical outward appearance, but made in steel, with anodised-light-alloy badges.

First news of the Triumph TR25W came from the USA, where the model was launched in January, 1968, basically as a trail bike and therefore featuring lower overall gear ratios than its BSA counterpart, in addition to a high-level exhaust pipe on the right. Its European debut was to have been at the Amsterdam Show, a month later, but due to a mix-up it was held up by Dutch customs officials, and never reached the exhibition.

On the British market, the TR25W Trophy (rather an unfortunate choice of name as there was already a 650 cc Trophy in the Triumph programme) had its official launch in October, 1968, replacing the long-lived and much-loved Tiger Cub in the Meriden line up. But in fact supplies had been sneaking into the showrooms for a month or so before that, as witness the 4 September test of the model.

Incidentally, whatever happened to the 'TOP 20' registration when the BSA-Triumph Group went to the wall? Any aspiring disc jockey would have given his eye teeth to acquire it.

The next change in the little Triumph was in April, 1970, when the high-level exhaust was switched to the left side of the bike for no good reason. Indeed, it was now far less tucked-in than before, in consequence of which it had to be provided with a glassfibre heat shield, and that cannot have done much to improve riding comfort.

For 1971 came another major revamp, although this time the power unit was largely untouched. Instead, it was dropped into what was really a production edition of the works moto-cross frame, complete with oil-carrying top and front-down frame tubes. Also inherited from the moto-cross mounts was a pivoted rear fork with eccentric pivot mounting, so that the entire fork moved rearward to adjust the chain, thereby keeping the wheel in line. A rather doubtful change was an ugly-looking lozenge silencer, rising at the rear of the seat sub-frame tube to discharge at high level. The silencer itself was dull black, albeit decorated with a polished and perforated cover plate. For the rest, all the usual Umberslade Hall excesses were evident—vestigial mud-guards, bare fork stanchions, headlamp carried on bent wire brackets. Even they might have been forgiven by loyal BSA fans, in time. But nobody could possibly forgive the change of name from Starfire to 'Gold Star', so sullying the memory of a machine which had *earned* such a title.

By now, any differences that had existed between the Triumph and BSA two-fifties had been abandoned, and only the tank badges offered any distinction. BSA had the B25T Victor Trail at £337; Triumph countered with the TR25W Trail Blazer at the same price. Equivalent roadsters were the BSA B25R Gold Star, and Triumph TR25 Blazer SS, each at £312. But neither would survive for much longer, in the economic blizzard sweeping down on Small Heath.

249cc TRIUMPH TROPHY

Nobody's trying to kid anybody, so to get the record straight from the start let's confirm that—apart from the Triumph name on the rocker-box cover and the primary-chaincase motif—the engine-gear unit of the 249 cc Triumph Trophy is identical in every way with the equivalent model, the Starfire, in the BSA range.

Motor Cycle road test

Strictly speaking, the new Triumph is a USA-style trail bike, intended for pottering about in the mountains. That accounts for the big tyres (3·25 × 19 in front, 4·00 × 18 in rear), crankcase undershield, high-level exhaust and small trials silencer, ISDT-pattern headlamp and generally up-in-the-air build.

It accounts, too, for the lowish overall gearing. Similarity with the Starfire ends at the gearbox, and from there on the Triumph wears 15-tooth gearbox and 52-tooth rear-wheel sprockets, as against the BSA's 16-tooth and 49-tooth arrangement. As a quick check, that gives a bottom ratio of 20·79 to 1 (Starfire, 18·3 to 1) and top gear of 7·84 to 1 (Starfire, 6·91 to 1).

Apart from the mechanical differences, there is the matter of styling which, in some subtle way, really does give the newcomer a Meriden air. The fuel tank is steel (and holds a useful 3¼ gallons), the dualseat has the now-familiar Triumph cross-ribbed top; and there are typically Triumph sports mudguards, plus attractive—if somewhat angular—glassfibre covers to the tool box and oil tank.

Though versions of the TR25W being sent to the USA have Dunlop Trials Universal tyres fore and aft, models now reaching the British market have—in deference to British tastes—road-going Dunlop K70s instead.

But before going on—how about that registration number TOP 20? It's a publicity gimmick, of course, and a good one at that.

The story behind it is that the Lord Mayor of Birmingham, on a recent tour of the factory, happened to remark that his son owned a clapped-out 1965 Tiger Cub bearing that number. Not slow on the uptake, Triumph bought the old Cub, scrapped it and, for £5, had TOP 20 transferred to the new bike.

Now for the test. Get astride the model and you certainly feel a long way off the deck; touching the ground is a tip-toe

affair for anyone of average leg length. It's understandable, for to get the 8-in ground clearance required for mountain trail work, the seat height has been pushed up to 32 in.

For that reason, the high-rise handle-bar is something of a necessity if a comfortable riding stance is adopted.

With you up there and the bike some-where down below, there is the feeling that you can swing the little Triumph about between your knees. You can. There's nothing which can ground, not even a centre stand.

Some may look askance at the fat and studded front Dunlop, much preferring a ribbed job for tarmac. Nevertheless, the steering seemed perfectly acceptable.

Since we road-tested the Starfire (or Barracuda, as it was then), the Amal Monobloc is out, and the Concentric is in, even on Triumphs. No air slide is fitted to the little Trophy, and the odd thing is that it doesn't appear to appreciate a cold-start carb flood.

Turn on the juice, just a light touch of the float tickler, no more; and the engine fires, first kick, as like as not. With the engine hot, omit the tickle and it is still a first-time starter.

Spot on

Carburation was spot on with the revs climbing cleanly up the scale as the throttle was opened. and the fuel-consumption graph was impressive; over 100 miles to the gallon at a steady 30 mph is a creditable effort.

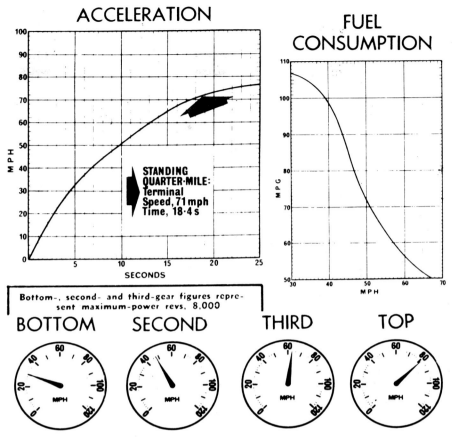

ACCELERATION

STANDING QUARTER-MILE:
Terminal Speed, 71 mph
Time, 18·4 s

FUEL CONSUMPTION

Bottom-, second- and third-gear figures represent maximum-power revs, 8,000

BOTTOM   **SECOND**   **THIRD**   **TOP**

Following pages: Dave Griffith's Triumph TR25W Trophy, which has non-standard Metal Profiles front fork and Royal Enfield front wheel (*Bob Currie*)

221

The all-round lowering of the gear ratios is noticeable straight away, and the net effect is to produce an immensely likeable model for town and around. No need to wring its neck before getting into the next notch up; the revs come freely and the acceleration is slick.

At least, it would be, if it wasn't for the piffling little silencer. Sure enough, there is a mute in the end of the tail pipe, but it still emits an embarrassingly loud bark; and that rather takes the edge off the fun of giving the bike full rein.

How does the low top gear affect the flat-out performance? Not so much as might be expected. Triumph don't put the Trophy 250 forward as a speedster (if you must have that little bit extra of top

Only the name on the rocker box identifies the timing side of the power unit from that of the 250 cc BSA engine

whack, there's always the BSA Starfire) and they were most surprised when David Dixon—in racing leathers admittedly—whammed through the MIRA speed trap at 81 mph mean. They'd geared it to do only 78!

To answer the unspoken question, bulkier Bob Currie clocked a two-way 75 mph; which probably proves something or other. Dixon's comment? 'Smashing little bike!'

If you think you've spotted a Tiger 90 front fork on the machine, you're dead right. There is a beautiful action to the front end, smooth and controlled in both directions, with hardly ever a clash; but softer rear springing would have been an improvement. Even with $14\frac{1}{2}$ stones aboard, and the dampers in the softest of the three settings, the Triumph tended to hop about on roughish going.

A $5\frac{1}{2}$-in diameter headlamp doesn't seem adequate but at least there is full 12-

volt lighting (with the diode nicely out in the cooling air, underneath the lamp) and the main beam turned out to be a surprisingly good one, ample for a night-time 60 mph gallop.

It is the type of headlamp evolved for ISDT machines, and has a push-and-push-again dip button in the top of the shell; not the ideal arrangement for a quick dip at dead of night, but effective, none the less.

There is no denying the TR25W Trophy is a smart little job in its flamboyant red finish and it is likely to create a lot of interest as news of it starts to spread around.

During the time it was in *Motor Cycle*'s hands it was used for weekend reporting of various meetings and, invariably, spectators flocked round wherever it was parked.

Their verdict was an echo of David Dixon's. A smashing little bike. It is, too!

SPECIFICATION ••

ENGINE: Capacity and type 249 cc (67 x 70mm) overhead-valve single Bearings: two ball journal mains; plain big end. Lubrication: dry sump; capacity, 6 pints. Compression ratio: 10 to 1. Carburettor: Amal Concentric 928, with gauze-and-mesh air filter. No air slide. Claimed output: 25 bhp at 8,000 rpm.
TRANSMISSION: Primary: $\frac{3}{8}$in duplex chain in oilbath case. Secondary: $\frac{5}{8}$ x $\frac{1}{4}$in chain. Clutch: multi-plate. Gear ratios: 7.94, 9.75, 12.9 and

20.79 to 1. Engine rpm at 30 mph in top gear, 3,100.
ELECTRICAL EQUIPMENT: Ignition battery and coil. Charging: Lucas 110-watt alternator through rectifier and Zener diode to 12-volt. 10-amp-hour battery. Headlamp: Lucas $5\frac{1}{2}$in-diameter with 50/40-watt main bulb.
FUEL CAPACITY: $3\frac{1}{4}$ gallons.
TYRES: Dunlop K70 studded; 3.25 x 19in front, 4.00 x 18in rear.
BRAKES: 7in-diameter front and rear, with finger adjusters.

SUSPENSION: Hydraulically damped telescopic front fork; pivoted rear fork controlled by Girling spring-and-hydraulic units with three-position load adjustment.
DIMENSIONS: Wheelbase 53in, ground clearance, 8in; seat height, 32in. All unladen.
WEIGHT: 320 lb dry.
PRICE: £269 19s 10d including British purchase tax.
ROAD TAX: £5 a year.
MAKERS: Triumph Engineering Co Ltd, Meriden Works, Allesley, Coventry.

PERFORMANCE

(Obtained by "Motor Cycle" staff at the Motor Industry Research Association's proving ground, Lindley, Leicestershire.)
MEAN MAXIMUM SPEED: 81 mph ($11\frac{1}{2}$-stone rider wearing racing leathers).
HIGHEST ONE-WAY SPEED: 84 mph (fresh three-quarter wind).
BRAKING: From 30 mph to rest on dry tarmac, 30ft.
TURNING CIRCLE: 13ft 6in.
MINIMUM NON-SNATCH SPEED: 16 mph in top gear.
WEIGHT PER CC: 1.29 lb